Studies in Modern History

General Editor: **J. C. D. Clark**, Joyce and Elizabeth Hall Distinguished Professor of British History, University of Kansas

Titles include:

Jonathan Clark and Howard Erskine Hill (*editors*)
SAMUEL JOHNSON IN HISTORICAL CONTEXT

Bernard Cottret (*editor*)
BOLINGBROKE'S POLITICAL WRITINGS
The Conservative Enlightenment

Richard R. Follett
EVANGELICALISM, PENAL THEORY AND THE POLITICS OF CRIMINAL LAW REFORM IN ENGLAND, 1808–30

Andrew Godley
JEWISH IMMIGRANT ENTREPRENEURSHIP IN NEW YORK AND LONDON 1880–1914

Philip Hicks
NEOCLASSICAL HISTORY AND ENGLISH CULTURE
From Clarendon to Hume

Mark Keay
WILLIAM WORDSWORTH'S GOLDEN AGE THEORIES DURING THE INDUSTRIAL REVOLUTION IN ENGLAND, 1750–1850

William M. Kuhns
DEMOCRATIC ROYALISM
The Transformation of the British Monarchy, 1861–1914

Kim Lawes
PATERNALISM AND POLITICS
The Revival of Paternalism in Early Nineteenth-Century Britain

Marisa Linton
THE POLITICS OF VIRTUE IN ENLIGHTENMENT FRANCE

Nancy D. LoPatin
POLITICAL UNIONS, POPULAR POLITICS AND THE GREAT REFORM ACT OF 1832

Marjorie Morgan
NATIONAL IDENTITIES AND TRAVEL IN VICTORIAN BRITAIN

James Muldoon
EMPIRE AND ORDER
The Concept of Empire, 800–1800

W. D. Rubinstein and Hilary Rubinstein
PHILOSEMITISM
Admiration and Support for Jews in the English-Speaking World, 1840–1939

Julia Rudolph
REVOLUTION BY DEGREES
James Tyrrell and Whig Political Thought in the Late Seventeenth Century

Lisa Steffen
TREASON AND NATIONAL IDENTITY
Defining a British State, 1608–1820

Lynne Taylor
BETWEEN RESISTANCE AND COLLABORATION
Popular Protest in Northern France, 1940–45

Studies in Modern History
Series Standing Order ISBN 0-333-79328-5
(outside North America only)

You can receive future titles in this series as they are published by placing a standing order. Please contact your bookseller or, in case of difficulty, write to us at the address below with your name and address, the title of the series and the ISBN quoted above.

Customer Services Department, Macmillan Distribution Ltd, Houndmills, Basingstoke, Hampshire RG21 6XS, England

Revolution by Degrees
James Tyrrell and Whig Political Thought in the Late Seventeenth Century

Julia Rudolph

Assistant Professor of History
Bucknell University
Lewisburg
Pennsylvania
USA

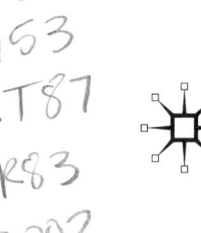

© Julia Rudolph 2002

All rights reserved. No reproduction, copy or transmission of this publication may be made without written permission.

No paragraph of this publication may be reproduced, copied or transmitted save with written permission or in accordance with the provisions of the Copyright, Designs and Patents Act 1988, or under the terms of any licence permitting limited copying issued by the Copyright Licensing Agency, 90 Tottenham Court Road, London W1T 4LP.

Any person who does any unauthorised act in relation to this publication may be liable to criminal prosecution and civil claims for damages.

The author has asserted her right to be identified as the author of this work in accordance with the Copyright, Designs and Patents Act 1988.

First published 2002 by
PALGRAVE MACMILLAN
Houndmills, Basingstoke, Hampshire RG21 6XS and
175 Fifth Avenue, New York, N.Y. 10010
Companies and representatives throughout the world

PALGRAVE MACMILLAN is the global academic imprint of the Palgrave Macmillan division of St. Martin's Press, LLC and of Palgrave Macmillan Ltd. Macmillan® is a registered trademark in the United States, United Kingdom and other countries. Palgrave is a registered trademark in the European Union and other countries.

ISBN 0–333–73659–1

This book is printed on paper suitable for recycling and made from fully managed and sustained forest sources.

A catalogue record for this book is available from the British Library.

Library of Congress Cataloging-in-Publication Data
Rudolph, Julia, 1962–
  Revolution by degrees: James Tyrrell and Whig political thought in the late seventeenth century / Julia Rudolph.
    p. cm. — (Studies in modern history)
  Includes bibliographical references and index.
  ISBN 0–333–73659–1 (cloth)
  1. Tyrrell, James, 1642–1718—Contributions in political sicence. 2. Political science—Great Britain—History—17th century. 3. Great Britain—History—Revolution of 1688. I. Title. II. Studies in modern history (Palgrave (Firm))

JC153.T87 R83 2002
320.5—dc21

2001058225

10 9 8 7 6 5 4 3 2 1
11 10 09 08 07 06 05 04 03 02

Printed and bound in Great Britain by
Antony Rowe Ltd, Chippenham and Eastbourne

To the memory of my mother, Sonia Rudolph

Contents

Acknowledgments		viii
1	Introduction: The Question of Whig Resistance Theory	1
2	Exclusion and the Evolution of Contract Theory in James Tyrrell's *Patriarcha non Monarcha*	19
3	'To preserve the Original Constitution of Parliaments': Revolution and Preservation in James Tyrrell's Whig History	62
4	Whig Theories and Theorists after 1688: the Case for Resistance	93
5	Resistance in Tyrrell's *Bibliotheca Politica*: the People and the Convention	124
6	John Locke and Whig Theory	148
Notes		168
Select Bibliography		209
Index		226

Acknowledgments

First thanks go to David Armitage, without whom this book would not have been published. He has been a great friend and mentor, and a constant source of insight and encouragement. I am also enormously grateful to Julian Franklin who helped me to formulate the doctoral dissertation upon which this book is based, and who provided thoughtful guidance while challenging me to strike out on my own.

I was also helped in the initial stages of conceiving this project by discussions with John Pocock, Steven Zwicker, Derek Hirst, Quentin Skinner and Mark Goldie. David Cannadine, Gene Rice, Rachel Weil, Peter Lake and Alison Frazier offered helpful comments on earlier drafts of the manuscript. My work also benefited from discussion with members of the New York University Legal History Seminar, especially Bill Nelson, Sally Gordon, John Baker, Paul Brand and Liam O'Melinn. Jonathan Clark helped me to envision the final version of this book, and I am grateful to him for including it in this series. My editors at Palgrave, and my copy editor Anne Rafique, have been most responsive and thorough. Robert A. Naborn contributed expert insight into the jacket image and its accompanying Dutch text. My colleagues in the History Department at Bucknell have been supportive and interested in my work. I'd also like to thank Will George, of the Department of Information Services and Resources at Bucknell, for providing much-needed computer advice.

Finally, it is with both joy and sadness that I thank my family and friends. I am thrilled, at last, to be at that point in my acknowledgements to thank my husband, Matthew Adler, who has provided me with so much emotional, intellectual and economic support. He knows this book well, but I wish he could know how much I've appreciated his help. My sons, Jonathan and Spencer, have unknowingly given me real motivation to finish this project and to produce something that, one day, they might be proud of. Diane and Barbara Rudolph, the extended Adler family, Brooke Bedrick and Anne Stetson all contributed to this work in different ways. But it was, most of all, my mother, Sonia Rudolph, who encouraged me to reach for my 'dancing star', who nurtured my desire to reflect and to write, and who led the way by the example of her own curiosity and creativity. How I wish that she could be here today to see the completion of this book.

1
Introduction: The Question of Whig Resistance Theory

One important outcome of the Revolution of 1688 in England was the public expression of a justification of resistance to government. In November 1688, and for years thereafter, a theory of resistance was articulated, mainly by politicians and authors identified with what was known as the Whig cause. This Whig theory, like so many other aspects of English liberal political thought, involved paradox, conflation and ambiguity. Seventeenth and eighteenth-century Whigs characterized the Revolution of 1688 as an extraordinary but not extra-constitutional event, as an act of resistance in extreme necessity which did not involve civil war or the entire dissolution of the government. The explanation they offered – that James II had effectively abdicated the government, and simply left a vacancy in the throne – was meant to clarify and contain these troubling, unpredictable and unprecedented events. The 'abdication and vacancy' resolution, passed by a Convention meeting in that winter of 1689, was aimed to encompass both a right of resistance to tyranny and the preservation of England's ancient constitution of king-in-parliament. This Whig theory of the Revolution gained acceptance precisely because of this duality, and because it founded a theory of resistance upon the history, laws, traditions and myths of English society.

Whig Revolution principles endured, and were transmitted with their ambiguities intact. Men such as Bishop Gilbert Burnet, spokesman for William and key defender of the legitimacy of the Revolution, confronted the implications of justifiable resistance that conflicted with the image of lawful, constitutional change.[1] In 1687 Burnet had argued that the king's violation of law and usurpation of the legislative power constituted a subversion of the very foundation of government, which would result in the dissolution of government.[2] Two years (and one revolution) later he offered a more moderate defense of resistance, asserting that submission to James II had ended when that king became tyrant rather than protector. Moreover, Burnet insisted that according to Magna Carta and England's ancient constitution, no king is irresistible.[3] In his *History of his Own Time*, Burnet adhered to the official thesis of abdication and vacancy but recognized the more radical inferences of dissolution or even popular power that might be drawn from a justification of resistance to James's tyranny and the Convention resolution.[4]

This was the same ideology of revolution endorsed by Edmund Burke in 1790. In his *Reflections on the Revolution in France*, Burke depicted England's Revolution as a moment of extremity, and an instance of just war, which did not result in dissolution and which did not deviate from the ancient constitution. He insisted that resistance was justifiable and that the Revolution was constitutional since there occurred no dissolution of government, nor any change to an elective monarchy. Yet Burke also admitted that it was an unconstitutional event, since there was no lawful method by which to dispose of one king and engage another.[5] 'Even in that extremity (if we take the measure of our rights by our exercise of them at the Revolution),' Burke explained, 'the change is to be confined to the peccant part only, to the part which produced the necessary deviation; and even then it is to be effected without a decomposition of the whole civil and political mass for the purpose of originating a new civil order out of the first elements of society.'[6] This adherence to a justification of events which at once relied upon notions of extremity, tyranny and resistance – that the extraordinary had occurred but had stopped short of 'decomposition', the truly extraordinary – was also perpetuated by William Blackstone in his *Commentaries on the Laws of England*.[7]

The apparently simultaneous assertion and denial of the dissolution of government was at the core of Whig resistance theory. The question, however, is not how confused or misguided were the Whigs, but rather how did they succeed in piecing together the Revolution Settlement, and how and why did it last? The problem for Whig politicians and theorists was how to limit their revolutionary claims: how to assert that James II's tyranny had dissolved the bonds of allegiance to him without dissolving the bonds of government and society, that the people of England had been thrust into a stance of justifiable resistance by the actions of their king but that the consequences of this conflict were not the dissolution of government, popular power and an appeal to heaven. The question was not whether, but how much revolution had occurred. The paradox lies in whether revolution admits of degrees.

Revolution, Settlement and Whig theory

The circumstances leading up to and surrounding the Revolution and Settlement of 1688–9 have been often narrated and much analyzed, but it is useful to recapitulate some of the essential aspects of the story in order to understand the old questions and new realities before the architects of the Settlement in January 1689.[8] The 'unexpected' and uncertain nature of these events has been amply demonstrated. Rather than viewing the accession of William and Mary as the inevitable postscript to the events of the 1640s and 1650s, the culmination of progress made towards constitutional monarchy and parliamentary supremacy, historians have concentrated attention upon the context of Restoration politics and the drift toward absolutism that characterized the second half of the seventeenth century.[9] There are truths, however, in both the whig and revisionist versions of the origins of the Revolution of 1688. This was an era of divine-right philosophy and a consolidation of monarchical power; of Anglican dominance; and of a consensus on the need for stability, a strong sovereign and abhorrence of the questions and struggle that lead to civil war. But it was also a time in which contract theory and notions about the popular origins of government developed and gained a wider currency, and a time of contest and challenge to the Stuart monarchs. An understanding of Whig and Tory, King and Parliament, High Church and Dissenter, illuminates the elements of dramatic change and continuity that composed the Revolution Settlement.

Appreciation of the unexpected nature of the Revolution affords some understanding of the confusions and ambiguities that were inherent to a resolution of these affairs. During the years immediately preceding the Revolution, with the defeat of Exclusion in 1681 and certainly with the failure of the Duke of Monmouth's Rebellion in 1685, the movement of England towards absolute monarchy, like that of her continental neighbors, seemed assured.[10] A period of Stuart or Tory reaction ensued after 1681, a period in which opposition to the Crown was effectively silenced. First, Charles II revoked and then reissued borough charters in such a way as to remodel their membership in the Crown's interest; in this way he sought to pack Parliament with Tory supporters. Charles also effectively controlled the courts, purging judges and packing the bench. Upon his accession, James II stepped up this process, expanding those policies pursued by his brother Charles in packing Parliament and the courts. In remodeling corporations not only did James II attack borough charters, but many company charters were also revoked and reissued and, as Mark Knights has shown, these political and religious purges had important economic consequences.[11] James also went further than his brother in his policies favoring Catholic Englishmen. James ordered the release of imprisoned Catholic recusants and had the government repay their fines; he issued dispensations from the Test Act of 1673; and he placed Catholic officers into the army, appointed them to civilian office, and placed them in the universities. James also established a Court of Ecclesiastical Commission to oversee the Church of England.[12] Finally, James used Monmouth's Rebellion as an opportunity to increase the size of his standing army.

As James began to face opposition from his own Tory-Anglican supporters, particularly to his pro-Catholic policies, he decided to try to forge another base of support in a Catholic–Dissenter alliance. This monarch's steady progress towards absolute power first truly faltered with this change of policy, signaled by the Declaration of Indulgence of 1687. This experiment in political realignment, from reliance upon Anglican loyalism to an appeal to Catholic and Dissenter support, was James II's greatest mistake. The use of toleration in aid of the goal of absolutism is generally regarded as having been doomed to failure, and James's late reversal and return to the Church party merely sealed his fate.[13] Such policies contributed a great deal to Tory acceptance and participation in the Revolution; indeed, what Mark Goldie has termed an 'Anglican Revolution' developed between 1686 and 1688 which sought to overturn the monarch's ministers and policies. This 'Anglican Revolution' culminated with the trial of the Seven Bishops, when James was faced with a policy of deliberate obstruction from the Archbishop of Canterbury and six other

Anglican bishops. Upon the reissue of the Declaration of Indulgence in April 1688 these men challenged the authority of James's declaration and refused to read it from their pulpits. Although not directed toward the goal of a Williamite revolution in 1688, this Anglican and Tory experiment in resistance to James II surely had some bearing on the success of the Revolution and the avoidance of civil war in that year.[14]

The goals of the House of Orange, and the demands of the balance of powers in Europe also played a part in the circumstances surrounding 1688. William of Orange's descent upon England has been characterized by some historians as the first and only decisive phase of the Nine Years War, a successful move in the struggle with France.[15] In seeking to stop French expansionism and aggression, William had long been concerned that England should be on the Protestant side of the European balance of power, that English strength and wealth should contribute to the containment of France. At first, then, the Dutch invasion seemed aimed at bringing James II into the anti-French camp. William did not invade simply with the intention of seizing the English crown for himself.[16]

And yet William's foreign policy goals were intertwined with his dynastic interests in the English succession. The birth of James II and Mary of Modena's son in June 1688 was a decisive factor in bringing William to England. Much as he sought marriage to Mary in 1677 as part of his Dutch-centered designs, in 1688 William was acting to ensure that this Protestant daughter, and not James's Catholic (and potentially pro-French) son, would come to power. 1688 has, then, also been termed a 'dynastic revolution' since William was concerned to protect Mary's interest in the succession to the throne.[17] The birth of James II's son was depicted as an evil Catholic conspiracy designed to divert the true Stuart succession. Many English Protestants, including the King's daughters Mary and Anne, believed that James Francis Edward was a 'supposititious' baby: they were convinced that the Queen's pregnancy had been faked, and that this baby had been smuggled into her bedchamber at the very moment of his 'supposed' birth in order to perpetuate a Catholic succession to the English throne.[18] The question of succession, of Stuart dynasty, was clearly central. The actions of the dynasts – the intractability and final desperation of James and the caution, luck and determination of William – played a defining role in the outcome of events.

The preparations of William's Dutch troops at the end of June signal the beginning of the Revolution that took place in November and December of 1688. On 30 June 1688 the trial of the Seven Bishops ended in acquittal. That same day another group of seven – the so-called 'Immortal Seven' influential Tories and Whigs – sent the invitation to the Prince of Orange.[19] This was the written summons William insisted upon so that his planned intervention would not be construed as an invasion and attempted conquest. The Prince of Orange also publicly justified his plans in his *Declaration of Reasons* published at The Hague on 30 September. This widely disseminated document claimed that William's only goal was to oversee the election of a free parliament in England. The *Declaration of Reasons* attacked James II's ministers, and promised to liberate Englishmen from these evil counselors who were threatening to replace Protestantism and law with popery and absolutism.[20]

By October, James was scrambling to recapture and consolidate support as he moved towards a retraction of his controversial, pro-Catholic, domestic and foreign policies; his actions from this point on were hasty and ill-conceived.[21] The Prince of Orange now acted upon that invitation to 'rescue the nation', and landed in the southwest of England on 5 November. King James's response was to advance troops in order to contain William's forces. On 17 November the King set out from London towards Salisbury to meet those troops. But by 23 November James had clearly failed to rally his own forces, and to provide decisive leadership to his troops at Salisbury Plain, and his military campaign ended with a retreat to London and a flood of deserters from the King's cause. Army officers and local gentry were among the defectors, but most significant were the desertions within James's family. These included his nephew, the Duke of Grafton, his son-in-law, Prince George of Denmark and his daughter, Princess Anne.[22]

Increasingly fearful for the security of his wife and son, and fearing for his own life, James prepared to leave England. The Queen and infant Prince were first sent ahead to France. King James escaped from London on 11 December, famously sinking the Great Seal of England as he crossed the Thames,[23] but he was intercepted in Kent and returned to the city on 16 December. From 11 December to 16 December a provisional government of peers had assumed governmental authority and preserved the peace. James was soon placed under Dutch guard, and now his second attempt to 'escape' was successful: the King was escorted to Rochester on 19 December and departed for France on 23 December.

Among the most exceptional and decisive aspects of the Revolution of 1688 were James II's failure to engage at Salisbury Plain and his flight to France. This withdrawal and flight of the King affected the course of the Revolution and Settlement in a number of ways. First, the establishment of a provisional government upon the first absence of the King on 11 December set an important precedent for the preservation of order, continuity, the status quo.[24] Moreover the return of the King to Whitehall on the 16th – this clear evidence that England still had a king on the throne – underscored the appearance of continuity as opposed to any conception of the dissolution of English government. The return of the King also served to clarify the differences between those groups that would forge a settlement in January and February 1689 as there was an increasing polarization of Whig, Williamite and Tory-Anglican positions. The second flight of King James, his escape to France a week later, could now be open to various interpretations. The King's removal might once again be construed as an absence but not an abdication, so that James remained a king who would again return to his throne. James's escape might also be seen as a forced flight imposed by William, now depicted as conqueror, or imposed by the Whigs, now depicted as commonwealth radicals intent upon deposing a king. From the Whigs' point of view, James's flight could be seen as an admission of guilt, as an abdication which left a vacant throne. James's capitulation and reversal of policy two months earlier, in October, helped to legitimize this interpretation and the intended resistance to the tyrannical king. Finally, James's first and second removal from England certainly were important in terms of defining William's goals. By December, William was determined to seek the throne, and the difference between his intentions as stated in the *Declaration of Reasons*, and his actions now appeared.[25]

But perhaps the most important result of James II's retreat from battle and flight to France was that an extended contest for power and a forced choice between rulers was avoided. James's withdrawal, together with the politics and prudence of the Prince of Orange and the determination and ambition of the Whigs, ensured that change was effected without a full recourse to arms.[26] The potential for a civil war like that of 1642 was, however, very real, since in a sense William's invasion had been an appeal to arms and to heaven. These novel circumstances would shape the theory and justification of the Revolution.[27] 'The flight of James,' J. G. A. Pocock explains, 'had irretrievably constitutionalized the English perception of revolution itself; the deposition of a king and the substitution of his successors, the dissolution of a regime if not of a constituted form of government, could now be seen as taking place bloodlessly, within the fabric of an ancient constitution, and without imposing on the people the savage choices about allegiance and sovereignty, violence and submission, under which they had suffered in 1642 and 1649.'[28] The Whig theory of resistance would, in time, explain the meaning of this 'constitutional revolution', this 'dissolution' 'within the fabric of an ancient constitution'. Yet when a Convention was called to settle the affairs of government in January 1689 the prospect of civil war was still present and the security of the nation was by no means clear. Members of the Convention, and indeed of the greater political nation, still had to deal with these 'savage choices about allegiance and sovereignty'.[29]

Sir Richard Temple, Whig member from Buckinghamshire, summarized the problem he saw confronting them: '[James] has quitted the government without assurance of anything; he has suppressed the parliament writs; he has taken away the great seal; and here is an apparent end of the government.'[30] The question of sovereignty, the constitutional consequences of the Revolution of 1688 and of this theoretical end of government, were hotly debated. The problem of a constitutional explanation was made acute, in part, because of the ongoing propaganda efforts of William and his supporters. One of the contexts within which the Convention met was an enduring public debate over William's *Declaration of Reasons* and the new interpretive problems engendered by William's claim to the throne. Since this *Declaration of Reasons* had been so widely received the change in William's intentions from intervention to accession was more pronounced. And since the *Declaration of Reasons* had stressed constitutional form, and parliamentary action, the absence of an obvious constitutional justification for William's move towards the throne was more problematic. It was now left to the Whigs in Convention debate to begin to advance constitutional arguments justifying this revolution and the legitimacy of William's accession to the throne.[31]

The ways in which the Convention sought to resolve these constitutional problems were as instrumental in shaping the Revolution Settlement as James's failure and flight. Robert Beddard particularly underscores the significance of that 'extraordinary resurgence' of the Whigs as 'a major political force in London and the nation at large' in the success of the Revolution Settlement.[32] These politicians and theorists took on the task of depicting the events of 1688–89, the flight of James II and the accession of William and Mary, as a constitutional occurrence sanctioned by law and history. Whigs became entangled in theoretical and historical arguments as they endeavored to defend both the right of resistance to James II's tyranny, and the *de jure* right of William and Mary to the throne. The force of opinion, tradition and history meant that an admission of the end or dissolution of government because of James's tyranny could not easily be squared with an argument for its reconstitution under William and Mary. An extra-constitutional resolution of the political crisis was anathema, while the political and legal consequences of the Restoration established the constitutional parameters within which Whig theory could operate. In contrast to Whig arguments for an accountable and limited monarchy, Restoration legislation had reinforced the independence of the king, and public sentiment continued to reject the idea of parliamentary supremacy.[33] How then could the Whigs reconcile an admission of the king's independence, and the denial of the sovereignty of Parliament, with a justification of resistance to the tyrannical James?

The Whig theory of resistance rested upon various notions of contract, fundamental law, and trust, and is most often compared to the theory set forth in John Locke's *Second Treatise of Government*. Whig theorists argued that violations of fundamental law, the subversion of the very foundation of government, constituted acts of tyranny which signaled the end of kingship and which could justifiably be resisted. At this difficult point, however, Whig and Lockean theory diverged. The difficulty for the Whigs lay in determining the consequences of this tyranny and the end of obligation and obedience. If the agreement between ruler and people is broken does the entire government dissolve, as Locke suggests, and does power return to the people to establish a new ruler or even a new form of government? Or could the rest of government remain intact and only the kingship be dissolved? This could mean that Parliament had a right to judge when a king became a tyrant, and to declare when he might justifiably be resisted and a new king installed. But that would amount to parliamentary sovereignty, and there was little desire to claim that power for Parliament. The image of a sovereign Parliament brought back fearful memories of Civil War and Commonwealth.

This problem of constitutional theory confronting the revolutionaries of 1689 has been described by Julian Franklin as the problem of resistance in a mixed government. Franklin demonstrates the way in which John Locke resolved this problem by appealing to an authority outside the constitution, and locating the final authoritative judge in the general community.[34] When government is dissolved, Locke concludes, the community regains its constituent power – the power to create government anew. The importance of this conceptualization of a constituent power for the development of a theory of sovereignty is underscored by Julian Franklin. Further, Franklin illuminates the ways in which Locke's understanding was influenced by earlier German debates on sovereignty, and their adaptation by the mid-century English theorist, George Lawson.[35]

Whig thinkers, too, took part in this tradition of theorizing about sovereignty and they were, quite often, familiar with Lawson and his German sources. Yet the Whigs deliberately rejected Lockean and Lawsonian ideas about constituent authority, or what was called the 'real majesty', of the people.[36] That explication of the consequences of resistance in a mixed government was impossible for Whig theorists who not only sought to appease fears of parliamentary supremacy, but also had to avoid ideas that smacked of popular sovereignty. Instead, Whig politicians and theorists concluded that James II's tyranny resulted in his surrender of position and power, his abdication of the throne of England; in this way resistance to the tyrant remained consistent with the doctrine of the independence of the king. Whigs and Tories were particularly anxious to maintain the idea of the independence of the king in order to preserve intact the system of property and inheritance upon which their own power was based. The consequences of admitting resistance to tyranny were dangerous because challenges to the power of the monarch easily led to challenges to established hierarchy and property rights. This was not only the substance of Tory attacks on Whig theory but also the basis of some Whig fears and criticism of Locke's theory. Men such as William Atwood and, later, Edmund Burke envisioned that dissolution would entail the destruction of the civil as well as the political order. It was, then, also posited by the Whigs that James's violent tyranny and abdication did not entail dissolution, Temple's 'apparent end of the government'. Rather, this abdication was said to lead simply to the end of this kingship which resulted in a vacancy in the throne that could be 'found' and supplied by the Convention.[37]

This notion of vacancy was designed to prove that the ancient constitution would remain undisturbed, and that the Convention was merely required to exercise its traditional, historical right. Questions about the legal powers of King, Lords and Commons, and about the locus of authority after the tyrant's abdication, were deliberately left unresolved. The abdication and vacancy thesis, Julian Franklin argues, was juridically unstable:

> To speak of 'finding vacancies' is to admit in evasive and passive language, a power in the two houses not only to depose a king but to alter the constitution of the kingship. If this were so, they were supreme within the constitution – which the Whigs would not admit. But if, on the other hand, they had no power to depose, there was no remedy within the constitution, and the consequence of James' conduct was entire dissolution of the government. This too the Whigs would not admit. But their dilemma was disguised from them by verbal subterfuges.[38]

The Whig resolution did indeed vacillate between the twin evils of dissolution to 'the people' and final sovereignty in the Parliament. Yet Franklin is mistaken in arguing that this dilemma was 'disguised' from the Whigs. In fact, the Whigs left some theoretical uncertainty in their Revolution principles in the interest of politics and peace, and their ideas survived because of this ambiguity and flexibility.

Here I seek to change the emphasis that Franklin, and others, have placed on Whig 'failure'. The received opinion of the Revolution Settlement has taken it to be confused, and has viewed Whig theory as merely mistaken and unsophisticated. Yet Whig resistance theory has been studied only very briefly, and usually in unflattering comparison with other theories of the Revolution deemed to be more 'coherent' or more 'truthful'. In John Kenyon's revisionist account, for example, various Whig attempts to provide a coherent and persuasive argument for resistance and contract were overcome by piercing Tory criticism. Moreover, in Kenyon's opinion, any resistance theory could not be squared with what he saw as the plain fact that force was not used against James II.[39] In his eagerness to show that Lockean, contractarian principles were not used to justify the Revolution, Kenyon downplayed resistance ideas and reduced Revolution theory to a narrowly conservative interpretation of abdication and vacancy.[40] And while Kenyon blamed Whig theorists for not being conservative enough, a scholar like Julian Franklin has chastised them for being insufficiently radical. Franklin usefully explores some of the differences between Whig and Lockean principles, yet he criticizes Whig authors for ignoring the implications of their defense of contract and resistance, and denying Lawsonian insights into dissolution and the role of a constituent people in a mixed constitution. For Franklin, too, Whig authors are either disingenuous or victims of self-deception. Finally, Conal Condren has done much to penetrate the conflations and distortions at work in seventeenth-century English resistance rhetoric, yet his arguments are also aimed to deny the significance, or even existence, of a Whig theory of resistance.[41]

By contrast, the argument presented here will be that Whig theory was important, influential and even successful. This success was largely based upon its duality or ambiguity – its reliance on both contract and ancient constitution.[42] Whig theory found acceptance through a deliberate reliance upon traditional beliefs about Convention and Parliament from England's past, and upon contemporary fictions about representation and the role of the people. Lockean and Lawsonian solutions are not the key to evaluating Whig principles nor, I will argue, are they the only concepts central to an understanding of the transmission of ideas about consent, freedom, resistance and popular sovereignty. Versions of popular sovereignty, dissolution and justifiable resistance were also given credence and transmitted to posterity as part of the Revolution Settlement. These more progressive or 'liberal' elements of the Whig legacy existed and survived in a partial and modified form. In providing a safe version of resistance and popular sovereignty Whig ideology met certain political and intellectual needs, and could more easily gain acceptance. Whig resistance theory, then, incorporated another version of these principles and is an important part of the history of ideas about consent, rights and resistance.

The transmission of Whig ideology

For some time now, it has been unfashionable and indeed untenable to depict 1688 as a progressive 'Glorious' revolution. Revisionist historians have made an invaluable contribution to our understanding of seventeenth-century England. The element of contingency, the role and import of the Tory majority, the conservatism of the Whigs themselves and the real persistence of the old regime, of patriarchalism in society and politics, have been justly emphasized in order to counter the old view of the inexorable flow of Whig progress. Indeed this richer understanding of English society better enables us to understand Whig ideology, and both the traditional beliefs and political circumstances that made it possible to accept the thesis of abdication and vacancy. At the same time however, in the zeal to dismantle the old Whig and new Marxist orthodoxies, historians have too often dismissed Whig ideas and reduced them to the simple 'error' of abdication and vacancy.

It seems increasingly possible to come to a more moderate and nuanced understanding of the meaning of the Revolution of 1688 now that the extremes of historiography, depicting bourgeois revolution or divine-right stability, have been assayed. It is, perhaps, now time for a history newly attuned to seventeenth-century Whig perspectives: a history with a focus on change, but with change seen as partial, modified, the slow evolution of ideology incorporating movement both 'backward' and 'forward'; and a history that follows those first attempts made by Whig historians and theorists to explain the complicated interplay of these ideas and events, to hold and examine the contradictions of non-revolutionary revolution.

The new history proposed here is also aimed to contribute to the contemporary study of the development of ideology. It builds upon the work of those intellectual historians who, in seeking to understand the life of political ideas, have worked with the insights of anthropologists and social historians into the recovery of 'mentalité'. Understanding ideology now means, in part, understanding the cultural values and common frameworks of meaning operating in past societies.[43] This approach to ideology also involves the study of what scholars, most notably those of the Cambridge School, have posited as 'intellectual context': an examination of past political and social 'languages', of the general framework of inherited assumptions and available, normative vocabularies. A major contribution of this approach has been the insistence upon the inclusion of a broad variety of contributions to social and political thought. The study of English ideology must now include Whig authors like Gilbert Burnet, James Tyrrell and the anonymous authors of polemical and political tracts, as well as John Locke. In this way the more intellectual aspects of ideology have also been elucidated. Although ideology has been seen to rely upon implicit cultural values, it has also been regarded as a conscious intellectual process which involves an exploration and affirmation or refutation of cultural values and meaning.[44] Thus an analysis of Whig ideology should entail the recognition of both conscious thought and unconscious mentality at work in seventeenth-century England.

Another way to pose this study of ideology and of context is to ask whether Whig theory was able to meet the needs of the society that accepted it. In order to understand the meaning and legacy of Whig Revolution principles it is vital to explore this social explanation of political beliefs. Investigating the history of Whig Revolution principles differs, I am arguing, from simply asking whether Whig theorists were 'right'. From the perspective of contract theory alone Whig thought was not 'right', and along these lines it has been criticized for being inconsistent and illogical by seventeenth-century Tory opponents as well as modern historians and political scientists. However, if we look outside of the lens of contract theory, the Whig theory of the Revolution clearly appears to be composed so that contemporaries might adopt their notion of revolution through accepted modes of argument. Most Whig authors were aware of the tensions in the Whig thesis of abdication and vacancy, and they were concerned to explain their beliefs. Here we must be sensitive to the kinds of explanations they offered and the bases for the acceptability of their beliefs. We must be concerned, following Quentin Skinner's advice, not only to understand the practical reasons for Whig arguments but also to see them as 'consistent with their sense of epistemic rationality'. Toward this end is directed that sensitivity to explanation and belief, in order 'to recover a particular context of presuppositions and other beliefs, a context that serves to exhibit the utterance in which we are interested as one that it was rational for that particular agent, in those particular circumstances, to have held to be true'.[45]

The Whig theorist and historian James Tyrrell was, above all, concerned with these questions about truth, acceptability and rationality. Tyrrell fits the definition offered by Quentin Skinner of a rational agent as one who is 'interested in the justification of [his] beliefs'. Skinner continues,

> [Rational agents] must be concerned with the kinds of coherence, and where appropriate the kinds of evidence, that give them grounds for concluding that their affirmations of belief can in fact be justified. They will thus be concerned, at least to some degree, to view their own beliefs critically, to consider whether they really can be justified by considering the degree to which they may be said to fit in with each other and with their perceptual experiences.[46]

James Tyrrell's *Bibliotheca Politica: Or an Enquiry into the Ancient Constitution of the English Government; Both in Respect to the Just Extent of Regal Power, and the Rights and Liberties of the Subject*, a series of fourteen dialogues between Whig and Tory, is just such a critical examination of Whig beliefs. Tyrrell, having embraced the Whig account of the 'late wonderful Happy Revolution', here carefully explored the reasoning behind his acceptance, studying the arguments on both sides 'for the satisfaction of [his] own conscience'.[47] It is this method that he recommends to others, and hopes to facilitate through his dialogues for his readers: 'looking upon it as the best and most ingenious way of Conviction to propose the Arguments fairly on both sides, without interposing my own Judgment, but to leave it to the intelligent, and impartial Reader to embrace that side on which he found the most rational and convincing Arguments.'[48] Tyrrell's remarkable attention to the whole range of arguments for and against Whig revolution affords us some insight into the presuppositions and beliefs that informed his search for 'an impartial discovery of the Truth', the rational acceptance of Whig Revolution principles.

Tyrrell's method in itself, the presentation of opposing sides towards the goal of discovering the truth, is an important indication of one of the contexts or presuppositions behind Whig theory. Whig theory is here depicted as undergoing a trial at English common law. The readers, like ordinary jurors, are assumed to have the ability to hear the evidence presented, to evaluate the credibility of the witnesses and their testimony, and to arrive at a truthful verdict.[49] This context of common law and ancient constitution was, indeed, vital to the acceptance of Whig resistance theory. Moreover, it was also a central context for the contemporary understanding of rationality and truth. The very conception of truthfulness or fact was legally constructed, and essential to this conception of a fact was the confidence in a credible process of ascertaining what was true. This method and this confidence, Barbara Shapiro argues, was taken up by practitioners of other social and intellectual endeavors – evident in John Selden's or Robert Brady's English history, in the natural history of eminent members of the Royal Society like Robert Boyle or Robert Hooke, and in John Locke's empirical philosophy. By the seventeenth and early eighteenth centuries, confidence in 'fact-finding' and the belief in men's ability to ascertain 'knowledge' was, Shapiro concludes, the consequence of a widespread familiarity with and confidence in the jury trial. The powerful concept of a fact was a vital characteristic of English culture, and is evident in Tyrrell's methods and his conclusions.[50]

Attention to James Tyrrell's work, and to his sensitivity to the many arguments and contexts within which Whig theory evolved, will make possible an understanding of Whig thought. Following Tyrrell, this historical understanding of the legacy of England's Revolution will also be a self-conscious one, written with an appreciation of the complex and contradictory ways in which ideas and ideology evolve. An intricate and rich intellectual history of Whig theory must examine the many layers, ambiguities and ironies of the Whig ideological legacy. Whig theory is significant because it incorporates a version of popular sovereignty, and thus illuminates the process of ideological change and the slow and modified transmission of concepts such as consent, rights and resistance. A study of this Whig theory enables us not only to speak past 'political languages', to understand ideas in their contexts, but also to understand why and in what ways ideas survive, what ensures that they will be transmitted and translated.

James Tyrrell and John Locke

The importance of adopting this different approach to Whig theory is evident in that it allows us to avoid common pitfalls in the interpretation of Whig thought. Most prevalent is the tendency to set up an opposition between the political theories of John Locke and the Whigs, and in this contest to dismiss Whig resistance theory as fundamentally flawed and incoherent. Moreover, controversies surrounding the political and social meaning of Locke's *Two Treatises of Government* have tended to shape, and obscure, the analysis of Whig theory. Historiographical, philosophical and political debates about Locke have set the agenda for the study of Whig thought. Finally, the evolution of the Whig historiography of the Revolution, and revisions and reactions to it, have also legitimized this focus upon defining radical and conservative, good and bad. Not only does this type of analysis fail to address the success and acceptance of Whig theory, but it also makes any real historical and contextual interpretation of Locke's work impossible.

Since Peter Laslett's foregrounding of their Exclusion context, we no longer read the *Two Treatises of Government* as if they were written in 1688 as a response to and justification of Whig Revolution. It is time to change our perspective on Whig theory as well – to look at it first and then, perhaps, to begin to read Locke in light of this Whig theory. One way in which to shift the focus from Locke to the Whigs is provided by attention to the writings of James Tyrrell. Tyrrell is Whig theory's counterpart to Locke: his essay on Filmer, *Patriarcha non Monarcha. The Patriarch Unmonarch'd*, was written at the same time that Locke was working on the *Two Treatises*.[51] *Bibliotheca Politica*, Tyrrell's exhaustive work on the Revolution, appeared in the years when Locke, if fulfilling the role of Whig spokesman, would have written a justification of 1688. Locke and Tyrrell were friends and correspondents who often engaged together in intellectual debate.[52] The story of their relationship from Exclusion to Revolution illuminates the various philosophical, political and rhetorical choices that were to be made. If we attempt to view Locke as a friend of James Tyrrell, we might perceive Locke's political theory from a new vantage point.

The works of James Tyrrell offer a paradigmatic expression of Whig historiography and constitutional theory. A real understanding of the Whig principles of abdication and vacancy emerges in the course of his exploration of contract, natural law, resistance, succession, English history and ancient constitution. Tyrrell's appreciation of the juridical and political problems facing the Whigs, and the nation, deepened during the 1680s. There is a marked change in his treatment of the problem of resistance from *Patriarcha non Monarcha* to *Bibliotheca Politica*. In the fourteen dialogues which compose his *Bibliotheca Politica*, Tyrrell's Whig spokesman explores a defense of the Revolution and confronts the possibility that dissolution of government, devolution of power to the people, and constitutional change will result from arguments based on contract, tyranny and abdication. Tyrrell's argument for revolution consistent with ancient constitution offers a creative and complex articulation of Whig Revolution principles.

The key to Tyrrell's theory lies in his conception of an original Convention and his definition of 'the people'. In defending resistance and Whig revolution Tyrrell attempts to avoid placing constituent authority in the people but cannot assert parliamentary supremacy. Since power can be said to devolve neither to a representative body nor to the people, Tyrrell's Whig spokesman sets out to prove that the Convention of 1689 is acting within the traditions of England's ancient council, and that that council can be said to be composed of the 'original people'. The analysis of the identity of this people is essential to this theory and Tyrrell focuses again and again on defining and narrowing 'the people' in order to assimilate them to the Whig cause. In the course of these dialogues the argument points to an original body of the people both in contract theory and in England's past, and then conflates this original body of the community, the makers of a social contract, with the council or representative body that was part of the ancient government established by that community. This proof rests upon the manipulation of history and theory, and the exploitation of the myth of an original people and of an ancient council. In so justifying Whig Revolution principles James Tyrrell, and other Whigs, argued for resistance without dissolution, and conflated revolution and continuity – they made the case for revolution by degrees.

2
Exclusion and the Evolution of Contract Theory in James Tyrrell's *Patriarcha non Monarcha*

The story of the social contract, that exceedingly influential theory of the foundations and legitimacy of government, underwent crucial development in British thought in the seventeenth and eighteenth centuries. Embedded within this political theory was an important political fiction, the fiction of an original group or body of people who acted as primary movers in the founding story. This political fiction was to play an important part in the development of a Whig theory of resistance. Contract theory was certainly not new to Whig thinkers; there was a long natural law tradition in continental and British political thought that relied upon the notion of a founding community from which authority derived.[1] This image of an original people took on particular significance, however, in the political theory and historical writing of the late seventeenth century.

This origin or founding story of civil and political society was greatly elaborated in England in the 1680s in response to an insistent Tory defense of divine-right theory, and a strong articulation of the biblical story of creation. Confronted by a favored authority, Sir Robert Filmer's retelling of God's creation of the first man and monarch and his insistence upon the divine origins of human society and government, some theorists offered another explanation based on natural reason, consonant with but not identical to Scripture. The story of a social contract, of the creation of community and government by a legendary group of first men, was set forth in order to counter the absolutist interpretation of the biblical creation myth of man, property and authority. Political theorists offered another story of creation, an alternative explanation of the origins and evolution of government and society. This theory which posited the action and agreement of a founding people, and the continuing consent of their descendants to this agreement, provided some answers to the problems of contested succession and potential resistance at issue in the seventeenth-century crises of authority.

The argument against Filmer's version of divine-right theory was essential to the formation of a Whig theory of resistance after 1688 on two levels. First, theories of contract and consent were shaped by the need to answer patriarchal ideology. Ideas about a first people forming a social or political contract were clarified and elaborated; the spatial and temporal problems attending any conception of consent were addressed; and attention was given to the problem of representation, and the identity of 'the people'. Second, the Filmerian controversy was inextricably bound up with the question of the antiquity of Parliament, and the evolution of the historical debate with the Tory scholar Sir Robert Brady. Whigs such as James Tyrrell, William Petyt and William Atwood marshaled historical evidence in order to prove the true nature of England's ancient constitution, the antiquity of the commons in Parliament and the role of the people and consent in English government.[2] The singular mix of contract and ancient constitution that would characterize Whig theory after 1689 was already developing in the 1670s and 1680s. Conceptions of an original people and an immemorial council were being formed both in abstract theory and in an ancient, legendary, English history. Later notions of abdication and vacancy, and of an original Convention, were built upon this groundwork.

This combination of history and theory was one way in which the implications of contract theory were moderated by the Whigs. Moreover, the very development of a Whig version of contract was shaped by the need to contain some of the more alarming implications of this theory which posited the principle of popular consent. Whig theory relied upon the central role of the people against the assertion of absolute paternal power, but also offered a careful definition of that people. Expansive claims made in contract theory – claims about natural freedom, rationality and equality – were rendered acceptable because they could be shown to be based upon common assumptions about gender and property. This evolving delineation of 'the people' was crucial to the denial of the radical outcome of contract theory, the dangers of dissolution and popular sovereignty. And this initial development of a Whig version of contract theory was essential to the later justification of revolution. That is not to say that there was an inevitable course of Whig ideas and events leading up to the Revolution of 1688. However, it is certainly no surprise that questions about sovereignty and the religious settlement retained their force throughout the later Stuart period. The movement to exclude the Catholic James, Duke of York, from his accession to the English throne is one such expression of the continued controversy surrounding these issues, and the Exclusion Crisis of 1679–81 has long been recognized as a significant event in the development of Whig ideology and the emergence of early political parties.[3] Contemporary scholars have also surveyed the whole of the Restoration period, and the series of 'crises' that shaped English politics in the 1660s and 1670s.[4] The unsettled nature of the Restoration Settlement has been emphasized, as historians have focused on continuities between the religious and political struggles of the 1640s and 1650s, and the political crises of the later Stuart period. This attention to the whole of the later Stuart period is crucial for the analysis of the process by which political parties formed, yet the Exclusion Crisis may still be regarded as having special significance for the development of a Whig theory of politics and resistance. The early 1680s were a turning point: although there is continuity between the arguments of these first Whigs and the theories of their predecessors, the debate over Exclusion translated the problems and ideas of the 1640s and 1650s into a new Restoration context, and particularly focused on questions of succession and ancient constitution. The terms of debate were forged in the late 1670s and 1680s, and these languages of patriarchalism, English history and contract would shape the arguments and explanations offered after 1688.

The difference between Exclusion and the Revolution of 1688, between exhortation and justification, should not, however, be underestimated. This difference has often been noted in discussions of the Exclusion context of Locke's *Two Treatises* and the disjunction between his early 1680s 'radicalism' and the more moderate Whig defense of Revolution after 1688. Another, perhaps better indication of the relationship between 1680 and 1688 may be found in the works of James Tyrrell. Tyrrell's *Patriarcha non Monarcha* was also written during Exclusion, also in response to the publication of Filmer's works in 1679–80. An examination of Tyrrell's 1681 work in this chapter, in conjunction with an extended analysis of Tyrrell's 1690s dialogues in subsequent chapters, will afford us the opportunity to chart the development of Whig ideology and the theory of resistance. Unlike Tyrrell's later dialogues his Exclusion tract does not dwell for long upon the questions of justifiable political resistance and dissolution of government. Moreover, Tyrrell's ambivalence about excluding a legal heir is apparent in 1681, whereas in the later defense of the accession of William and Mary his discomfort is muted and rationalized. This difference between forcing and declaring, between 'exclusion' and 'abdication and vacancy' was real, and the worry that there might have been a valid heir born to James II continued to plague Tyrrell, and the Whig justification, long after 1688.[5] Finally, *Patriarcha non Monarcha* signals the beginning of Tyrrell's exploration of the history, and myths, of England as well as his formulation of a definition of 'the people' through his confrontation with the political and historical works of Sir Robert Filmer.[6] The questions framed in the early 1680s were familiar by 1689, but the contexts within which they were discussed made all the difference.

James Tyrrell, John Locke, and the first Whigs

What was the first of these contexts – what was Exclusion, and who were these first Whigs and Tories who take up the political debate? The political drama generally known as the Exclusion Crisis began in the spring of 1679 when critics of Stuart government gained new power: accusations that corruption and Catholicism plagued the court became more potent when evidence of a Catholic conspiracy, a 'Popish Plot', was deemed credible by Parliament and public. The sensational revelations of this supposed plot to assassinate the King, and to foment a Catholic terror, helped to promote the collapse of Danby's ministry and the dissolution of the Cavalier Parliament. Parliamentary elections, held for the first time in eighteen years, initiated a period of ferment in London and the localities; the increase in electoral contests was one important indication of reaction against the court. As Mark Knights has reminded us, this crisis was not simply a parliamentary contest over exclusion. Conflict between court and country, particular local contests, and general fears of popery and arbitrary government all contributed to a widespread 'crisis in politics and opinion'.[7] Agitated polling and propaganda surrounded the election of all three Parliaments summoned between 1679 and 1681.[8] Within Parliament, leaders of the opposition were not satisfied with the dismissal of Danby: some argued that corruption and conspiracy against the English government were far more widespread, and they pointed to an insidious foreign and Catholic influence dating as far back as the Restoration. Their attacks did come to focus upon James, Duke of York, most pointedly in the Bill of Exclusion proposed in order to thwart James's succession to the throne. The problem of a Catholic succession was not new, and Exclusion had been proposed as early as 1674, but with the Popish Plot scare the proposal received renewed and intense attention.[9]

Charles II attempted to deflect the movement to exclude his brother, and proposed limitations to be imposed upon a popish successor in order to safeguard the rights and liberties of the Protestant kingdom. Charles's motives were questioned, however, and it was unclear whether such limitations could legally bind James.[10] Against the proposed limitations some men argued that excluding James, Duke of York, was more 'royalist' than limiting him, since Exclusion would seemingly preserve all the powers of the monarch intact. The Earl of Shaftesbury may not have been completely disingenuous when he argued that a limiting statute would 'substitute democracy for monarchy'.[11] Although some Whigs wanted Exclusion to signal the beginning of more thorough constitutional reform, most regarded it as an expedient measure to preserve England's traditional constitution.[12] The debates over the extent and possible limitation of the king's prerogative, and over the implications of altering the succession, naturally led to discussion of the location and nature of sovereignty itself. Questions left unresolved at the Restoration now became critical.

The first Whigs were not simply nor necessarily champions of parliamentary sovereignty or of popular power, and the divide on constitutional issues between Whig and Tory was not as sharp as historians once thought. Scholars have attempted to correct the older historiographical tradition which depicted this birth of Whig and Tory in terms of parliamentary and popular versus absolutist and conservative. Although the language of party, indeed the very epithets Whig and Tory, became fixed in the political vocabulary during Exclusion, political allegiances and the definitions of these nascent parties remained fluid. The struggle to describe and define these early ideological and political groupings has led to the recognition of a wide range of positions and significant agreement between Whig and Tory; there has been retreat from the idea that the crisis over the succession did in fact produce clear party affiliation and polarization.[13] Moreover, reexamining the nature of these first parties has led to an emphasis on the religious, social and economic, as well as the constitutional dimensions of political conflict. The very terms of reference – Whigs branded by association with Scottish Covenanters, and Tories with Irish Catholic bandits[14] – may indicate that the religious dimension was of the greatest importance. Polarization between Whig and Tory often reflected different attitudes towards the Church and Dissent as much as different attitudes towards the balance of king-in-parliament; the division was one between a Whig sympathy towards Dissent, and a Tory defense of 'intolerant Anglicanism'.[15]

This explanation helps to make sense of the support for Exclusion on the part of a man like James Tyrrell. His adherence to the policy of Exclusion is as much in accord with his religious as with his strictly constitutional beliefs. Although Tyrrell joined Locke in favoring contract and natural law theories, he was much more cautious about admitting the consequences of ideas about consent and natural liberty. Other Whig Exclusionists set forth constitutional proposals ranging from republicanism to a defense of limited monarchy to a preference for a strong Protestant monarch and indefeasible hereditary succession, and these beliefs were not necessarily mutually exclusive. In his view of England's constitution Tyrrell often had more in common with moderate Tories than with some Whigs; the image of Tyrrell as a radical Whig, proposed by some scholars, is exaggerated.

At the same time that Locke's friend and patron, the Earl of Shaftesbury, was championing Exclusion, Locke spent a great deal of time at Tyrrell's house at Shotover, near Oxford. While there Locke worked on a defense of toleration, with Tyrrell's assistance, in response to Edward Stillingfleet's *The Unreasonableness of Separation: Or, An Impartial Account of the History, Nature, and Pleas of the Present Separation from the Communion of the Church of England*. Stillingfleet's sermons preached uniformity and adherence to the Church of England against toleration of dissent.[16] The height of the Exclusion Crisis thus coincided with a period of close friendship and frequent contact between the two men.

James Tyrrell recalled meeting John Locke at Oxford in 1658. Tyrrell, age 16, was then a gentleman commoner at Queen's College, and Locke, at 26, had recently been elected a senior student of Christ Church. Tyrrell evidently admired his older, accomplished friend. 'Mr. Locke,' he later told Lady Masham, 'was then looked upon as one of the most learned and ingenious young men in the college he was of.'[17] James Tyrrell himself came from a learned background, as his mother Elizabeth was the only child of James Ussher, Archbishop of Armagh and primate of Ireland under Charles I and James I. Ussher was a highly esteemed, if controversial, authority on matters of Church doctrine, ecclesiastical history, and political obedience.[18] James Tyrrell participated in the later dissemination of his grandfather's work, contributing a dedication to Charles II for Ussher's *The Power Communicated by God to the Prince, and the Obedience Required of the Subject*, and writing a defense of Ussher's opinions against Peter Heylyn for Richard Parr's *Life of Archbishop Ussher*. Tyrrell's other publications, and his relationship with Locke and other Whig polemicists and historians make clear, however, that Tyrrell did not share his grandfather's views concerning absolute monarchical authority.

While a student at Oxford, and for many years thereafter, James Tyrrell was a part of Locke's close circle of friends. Tyrrell was also a member of a group that began meeting in 1668 in Locke's rooms at Exeter House[19] in order to discuss religious, philosophical and scientific questions. Other members of this club included Locke's school friends, and students of law and medicine, John Mapeltoft and Thomas Sydenham as well as Anthony Ashley Cooper, later Earl of Shaftesbury.[20] The continued intimacy and affection between Tyrrell and Locke is apparent in letters they wrote after leaving the university. They addressed each other with friendly nicknames apparently adopted from French literature – John was 'Carmelin' and James was 'Musidore'.[21] A good deal of their correspondence is taken up with mundane matters of health and personal favors. Locke's medical advice was often sought for the afflictions and distempers suffered by Tyrrell's wife and children, while Tyrrell's estate at Oakley in

Buckinghamshire provided stables for Locke's horse, and storage space for many of his books, papers, chairs, carpets, linens and various personal effects (including, among other things, a telescope, a barometer, a collection of specimens in glass bottles and boxes of seeds).[22]

But tensions over the location and condition of some of these goods was one reason for a growing estrangement between Tyrrell and Locke over the years. In 1686, for example, when Locke removed his manuscripts from Tyrrell's estate and entrusted them to another's care, Tyrrell was insulted. Tyrrell noted, somewhat acerbically, that Locke still trusted him enough to continue storing many of his other possessions at Oakley: 'I doe not speake this that I desire such a charge; since I am trusted by you with enough already. onely it vexed me a little to see another hand perhaps not so long knowne; so much preferred before mine.'[23] And in 1691, when Locke finally attempted to retrieve the rest of his possessions from Tyrrell's estate, Locke became annoyed at the many delays and excuses Tyrrell offered.[24] There were also disputes over money between the two men, and here too there were damaged feelings on both sides. The balance of payments between Tyrrell and Locke, always complicated by various purchases each made for the other, is a constant theme in their correspondence between 1683 and 1693. A debt of ten pounds, incurred by Tyrrell in 1683, appears to be a particular problem and may have been a catalyst in the cooling of their friendship. At the same time that Locke removed his manuscripts from Oakley, he demanded repayment and (perhaps intentionally) further alienated Tyrrell by making 'the calling in of [his] money almstot the onely subject of that letter'.[25]

Material goods were not, however, the sole cause of contention. There was also an intellectual rivalry between Tyrrell and Locke, and it is probably not a coincidence that Locke finally decided to retrieve all of his possessions from Oakley – setting in motion the final round of accusation and bargaining between them – soon after he defended his position on natural law against Tyrrell's critique. In a letter of June 1690, Tyrrell had pointed out an apparent contradiction between conceptions of natural law and the definition of morality in the first and third books of Locke's *Essay Concerning Human Understanding*. A number of other contemporary, and later, commentators also objected to Locke's relativist definition of virtue and vice in Book III, which appeared to conflict with his insistence in Book I on moral certainty and a 'Law knowable by the Light of Nature'. Locke was open to accusations not only regarding the uncertainty of his proof of natural law but also concerning the 'Hobbism' of his discussion of morality in Book III.[26] The undercurrent of intellectual and professional rivalry in Locke and Tyrrell's tense exchange of letters between July 1690 and March 1691 is made manifest by Tyrrell's frequent references to his own works on natural law and politics.[27] Tyrrell only exacerbated Locke's anger at being criticized by insisting that Locke brought this confusion upon himself.[28] And Tyrrell incurred Locke's further displeasure by openly discussing the question of the authorship of the *Two Treatises of Government* and pressing Locke on this point.[29] Certainly Locke was the older, and much more worldly figure, but the growing estrangement that so many scholars have noted was not simply due to Locke's boredom and Tyrrell's sycophantism. Although an intellectual disparity between Locke and Tyrrell has traditionally been emphasized, their relationship was much more complex, and more equal, than that of a master and his disciple.

Not only was James Tyrrell for many years a part of Locke's intellectual circle, but he was also in close proximity to the politics and excitement which surrounded the sitting of the Parliament at Oxford in March 1680. Tyrrell divided his time between his boyhood home at Shotover, and the family estate at Oakley that he had inherited in 1670. Tyrrell was involved in local governance at home in Buckinghamshire, serving as a justice of the peace and a deputy lieutenant, before he was finally ousted from his posts by James II for refusing to subscribe to the Declaration of Indulgence. Locke was at Tyrrell's Shotover house and in contact with Shaftesbury and his supporters in the late 1670s and early 1680s. However, James Tyrrell does not seem to have been closely involved in the parliamentary, and extra-parliamentary, actions of Shaftesbury's followers. One indication of this lack of involvement is the fact that during the crucial period between 1677 and 1683 political events and ideas are infrequently mentioned in the letters to Locke from Tyrrell.[30] In order to explain such silences, and to provide evidence of underground political activity surrounding the Rye House Plot, Richard Ashcraft attempted to identify a code language used by Locke and his friends and political allies. Ashcraft interpreted one of Tyrrell's later letters in light of this code, asserting that Tyrrell also sent political messages in disguise. Yet even Ashcraft discounted any radical political activity, or even specific knowledge, on Tyrrell's part, and retreated from the suggestion that this letter is proof of his political involvement.[31]

However, as *Patriarcha non Monarcha* attests, Tyrrell was certainly engaged in polemical activity on behalf of the Whig cause and he may have collaborated with Locke on the response to Filmer. Although Peter Laslett and John Gough asserted that due to Locke's characteristic secrecy there was literally no exchange of ideas, scholars have remained doubtful that no discussion would have taken place between the two men during these years of heated political debate. It is particularly improbable since Locke was working on a defense of toleration while at Tyrrell's house, and they engaged in discussion concerning the key political issue of the Exclusion period.[32] In fact, recent research has begun to explore the interaction between the two men, and the influence of Tyrrell on Locke, rather than relying on the familiar image of an isolated 'great philosopher' and his follower. It seems more than likely that these old friends who had shared ideas and opinions since their Oxford days, and who were together when possibly both of them were writing against Filmer, would have some knowledge of each other's work. Indeed, John Marshall and David Wootton have introduced some evidence in order to show that Locke, at least, knew of *Patriarcha non Monarcha*, and intended the *Two Treatises* to be a response to Tyrrell as well as Filmer.[33] It is also possible that Tyrrell later intended portions of his *Bibliotheca Politica* to be received as his response to Locke's *Two Treatises*. The relationship between Tyrrell and Locke and, I will argue, the ongoing relationship between *Patriarcha non Monarcha*, the *Two Treatises*, and *Bibliotheca Politica*, form a vitally important context for understanding both Whig and Lockean political thought.

The challenge of patriarchalism

In 1680, at the height of Exclusion, Filmer's *Patriarcha: The Naturall Power of Kinges Defended Against the Unnatural Liberty of the People* was published for the first time. A year earlier a collected edition of Filmer's other political and historical works had been republished as an instrument of Tory propaganda – launched, in Mark Goldie's phrase, as the 'ideological flagship' of Toryism.[34] Republication of Civil War and Commonwealth tracts was an established political strategy, and Filmer's work appeared as one part of a broad Tory defense of monarchy and church.[35] In attacks on their Whig opponents, Charles II and his Tory supporters reminded Englishmen of the dangers associated with attacks on the monarchy, including the loss of property, religion, and liberty. Tories alleged that the Whigs intended to revive the Commonwealth and to destroy the Church of England. Both Tory and Whig polemicists referred back to the 1640s and 1650s in warning, yet they were also drawing upon the authority of theorists such as Sir Robert Filmer, William Prynne, Philip Hunton and George Lawson.

Of course, republication was not a new idea. This political tactic, and the reissued political theories themselves, were part of a longer tradition of debate over the origins of government, the nature of sovereignty and the limits of political obligation. In the 1680s English theorists called upon their ancestors in political debate, and they reproduced the arguments of many English, Scottish and continental predecessors. Among the most important sources for the Exclusion debates were the works of French monarchomach and politique theorists. The works of Jean Bodin, François Hotman, Theodore Beza, and of the author of the *Vindiciae Contra Tyrannos*, were centrally important to the development of English political theory throughout the seventeenth century; the religious conflicts and disputed successions that had agitated France in the late sixteenth century appeared to be singularly relevant to the English crises of the 1680s. Moreover, since Filmer's work also called upon this longer tradition, setting forth a Bodinian as well as a patriarchalist conception of monarchical sovereignty, it made sense for Whig Exclusionists to return to French authorities, and their interpreters, in response.[36] The works of some of these controversialists were republished at the same time as Filmer: treatises of Beza and Bodin, Hunton and Prynne, and of George Buchanan and Robert Parsons also appeared during Exclusion.

Reference to these earlier controversies provided both sides with useful authority, but they could also encourage some harmful associations. Whig defenses of consent, limited monarchy and resistance were branded by association with Calvinist resistance theorists such as John Ponet or George Buchanan, or by association with Catholic resistance and the ultramontism of Robert Bellarmine and Robert

Parsons. The charge of promulgating 'popish' and 'Jesuitical' doctrines was also leveled against Tories: their defense of royal absolutism was branded by association with a Catholic (a French or Spanish, and not English) kind of despotism. There were, then, many layers of debate by 1680 as Whigs and Tories engaged with French monarchomach and politique theories, and reproduced many of the arguments of the Elizabethan and early Jacobean controversialists. Finally, English thinkers were also indebted to German and Dutch interpreters of contractarian and absolutist thinking such as Johannes Althusius, Henning Arnisaeus, Hugo Grotius and Samuel Pufendorf, those whom J. H. M. Salmon terms the 'intermediaries' of French ideas.[37] In taking on Filmer, a Whig theorist like Tyrrell contributed to this ongoing tradition, while at the same time participating in a debate over the meanings and legacies of the English Civil Wars.

Sir Robert Filmer's *Patriarcha* was initially composed in the 1620s and completed by 1630–31, after which time it circulated among the royalist gentry of Kent in manuscript form.[38] *The Free-holders Grand Inquest Touching Our Soveraigne Lord the King and His Parliament*, Filmer's pointed contribution to the controverted history of Parliament, was published in 1648 in response to the dissident lawyer and parliamentarian William Prynne's *The Sovereign Power of Parliaments and Kingdoms*. In that same year Filmer also published *The Anarchy of a Limited or Mixed Monarchy*, his reply to the seminal Civil War tract, *A Treatise of Monarchy*, written by the Puritan divine and parliamentarian pamphleteer Philip Hunton.[39]

The primary goal of all of Filmer's works was to destroy the notion of man's natural liberty, and the claim that the obedience due to rulers was based upon the grant of sovereign power from a naturally free people.[40] A simple synopsis of Filmer's main ideas is provided by Locke in the *First Treatise* where he reduces Filmer's work to these two essential propositions:

> His System lies in a little compass, 'tis no more but this,
> *That all Government is absolute monarchy.*
> And the Ground he builds on, is this,
> *That no Man is Born Free.*[41]

The 1679–80 republication and reaffirmation of Filmer's unyielding defense of absolute, divine-right monarchy presented an important challenge to supporters of Exclusion who opposed the Stuart, and High Church, drift towards absolutist ideology. The basic tenets held by seventeenth-century English absolutist theorists were that the monarch was above all human law and accountable only to God, his power supreme and irresistible.[42] This conception of absolute sovereignty was, like theories of limited sovereignty, based upon notions about divine law and human nature. There was broad agreement among absolutists that divinely inspired reason, or natural law, led man to create a sovereign power. Whether they contended that this sovereign power was established immediately by God, or conceded that it arose through the mediation of man, they agreed that sovereign power was derived from God alone and was accountable to God alone.[43] The patriarchalist version of this ideology of absolute power was founded upon notions of direct divine appointment and indefeasible hereditary succession. Patriarchalist ideas were meant to reinforce obedience to the absolute sovereign since the security of '[o]rder could only be maintained,' H. T. Dickinson explains, 'if subjects were in no doubt about who had the *right* to be king and hence who had the right to exercise this absolute authority'.[44] Patriarchalist arguments provided such certainty about divine appointment and succession. Theorists pointed to the divine origins of fatherly power, and explained how the authority of the father was based upon a divinely ordained law of nature. They asserted that the first fathers were absolute kings, and that the origins of government lay in the orderly succession of power rather than in free consent.[45] Indeed, Sir Robert Filmer attempted to prove these doctrines of divine appointment and indefeasible succession through arguments for the direct descent of rulers from Adam.

The prevalence – perhaps the very existence – of this kind of absolutist thinking in seventeenth-century England has, however, been disputed by some contemporary scholars. Glenn Burgess, for example, has advanced an argument in favor of abandoning the usual dichotomy between 'absolutist' and 'constitutionalist' when describing the political thought of the early Stuart period. An appreciation for the nuances of ideological consensus has led Burgess to some valuable suggestions about possible areas of agreement between Filmer and Locke, as well as areas of disagreement between Filmer and his Tory champions. Yet Burgess is too charitable in his assessment of Tory intentions in the republication of Filmer's work. The choice of Filmer was a deliberate choice of strong royalist and Tory principles. Filmer exemplified patriarchal theory and its uncompromising absolutist interpretation, and many other Tory treatises made similar arguments about natural subjection, patriarchal power, divine right, and the indivisibility of sovereignty.[46] Tory ideology was an ideology of absolute monarchy. There were, to be sure, aspects of Tory thought that might temper the stark principles of absolutism: some theorists allowed that the people might designate a ruler, although it remained true that the ruler's authority was derived from God; the Tory doctrine of passive obedience allowed that subjects might not be obliged actively to obey ungodly commands; and the emphasis upon the ruler's rational and moral obligation to obey natural law and human law allowed for the 'standard Tory paradox' of an absolute and limited king.[47] However, none of these concessions ultimately changed the Tory principle of absolute sovereignty, in which final authority rested in the king alone.

The Whigs perceived the move to republish Filmer as a display of rhetorical power, an unyielding and thus powerful statement of Tory principles. And so, in taking on Filmer, Locke, Tyrrell and others attempted to counter the development of English absolutist theory and to refute the entire group of 'ideologists of Restoration Royalism' who sought to enhance royal power.[48] These absolutist doctrines were especially prevalent among the clergy, those whom Goldie terms the 'agents of Anglican authoritarianism', and an attack on the Church of England's dissemination of the theory of royal absolutism is a critical element of the argument against Filmer.[49] Tyrrell, like other Exclusionists, criticized the Church for its failure to support Exclusion which he regarded as a failure to protect the Protestant religion. Indeed, Tyrrell cites the pernicious influence of the clergy as one of the reasons why his own work is necessary:

> And that this Notion of the Divine and Patriarchal Right of absolute Monarchy hath obtain'd so much among some modern Church-men, who cry it up as their *Diana*, and consequently hath so much infected our Universities, that are the Seminaries where the Youth of this Nation do commonly receive Principles both in Religion and Politicks, which if they have not a mind large enough to overcome the prejudices of Education, will mis-lead

them as long as they live, and so make them desire at least to alter that Government, and give up those Priviledges which their Ancestors were so careful to preserve and deliver down to Posterity: I thought my self obliged... to do God, my King, and Country this service, as to lay open the weakness of the Reasons, and the dangerous consequences of this Author's Principles.[50]

James Tyrrell certainly did not think that the Tories were blind to the implications of Filmer's writings, nor to the statement being made in republishing them. And so Tyrrell prefaces his response to Filmer with this equally potent rhetorical challenge, depicting himself not only as an opponent of absolutism but also as a defender of tradition and England's ancient government against these innovating High Churchmen.

Tyrrell is also thus seeking to turn unwelcome associations with Civil War and Commonwealth disruption back upon the Tories themselves. Whigs, like Tories, attempted to paint their opponents as dangerous radicals who would strip Englishmen of their liberties and properties, and return them to the dark days of the 1640s and 1650s.[51] In noting the difference between Filmer's original motivations and the intentions behind this republication, Tyrrell acknowledges that Filmer's works may initially have been written 'in defence of Kingly Government, and of his then Majesties lawful and just Rights, then trampled upon by a domineering Faction, and may contain some things useful enough to confute divers levelling Notions, then too much in fashion'.[52] Yet the republication of these tracts in 1680 is, he argues, of a more sinister political nature:

> [S]ince no man can imagine to what end this *Patriarcha* and other Tracts should come out at such a *Time* as they did, unless the Publishers thought that these Pieces, which printed apart could onely serve to ensnare the Understandings of some unthinking Country-Gentleman or Windblown-Theologue, could do no less, being twisted into one Volume, than bind the Consciences, and enslave the Reasons of all his unwary Readers.[53]

Tyrrell associates the loss of reason and conscience with Tory ideology and politics, while at the same time distancing himself from the 'levelling' principles of Filmer's opponents.

As his title makes clear, Tyrrell's *Patriarcha non Monarcha* seeks first to distinguish paternal from political power. The association of paternal and political power was a traditional argument used against consent and contract notions by absolutist theorists, but Filmer's literal patriarchalism made this association even more central. The nature of familial authority, and its relationship to political power, were the primary concerns of any critique of Filmer's identification of father and monarch.[54] Although Tyrrell allowed that paternal power provided a pattern for government, he insisted that there was an essential difference between them. The description of the king as father of his country, as captain of the ship of state, and as head of the body commonwealth were conventional images in the hierarchical, patriarchal culture of early modern England. In exploring the nature of paternal power Tyrrell contends that it is not absolute and arbitrary, so that theoretical similarities and even historical proof of the identification of father and king will not justify the doctrine of absolutism.[55]

Scripture afforded a potent argument against Filmer since critics could call attention to the distortion of Genesis 1:28 and the Decalogue in *Patriarcha*'s account of the divine grant and sanction of paternal power. Tyrrell and Locke criticize Filmer's convenient omission of the mother from the command to 'Honor thy father' and the exclusion of Eve from Filmer's narrative of the divine grant.[56] Thus Tyrrell denies that Adam was made an absolute and exclusive lord over all creation, and rejects Filmer's interpretation of Genesis and the command to 'be fruitful and multiply'. Tyrrell states:

> From which words I do not conceive that *Adam's* absolute power over his own Off-spring can be made out; for the words are spoken as well to the Female as Male of Mankind.... By which words *Adam* hath no power conferred upon him over his own Children (when he should have them) These words implying no more than a conferring of a power by God on Mankind, under these words of *Male and Female* (and not at all personal to *Adam* or *Eve* alone)....[57]

Both Tyrrell and Locke deny the absolute monarchical power of Adam by demonstrating that authority was placed in the mother as well as the father, thus creating parental, not absolute patriarchal, authority. Natural law arguments provided another essential language with which to refute Filmer. The notion of parental authority was founded upon ideas about natural reason and freedom, and drew especially upon the authority of natural law theorists Hugo Grotius and Samuel Pufendorf. The parental authority that Tyrrell recognized was based upon care and education, and not mere procreation, of the child. This power was linked to duty, and the child's obedience was tied to performance and gratitude for the care received. Tyrrell adheres to the notion of an 'age of reason'[58] and believes that the parent wields almost complete control until the child attains maturity and is able to exercise his inherent rationality and freedom. Yet like all dominion, this parental power is limited by the ends for which it is exercised; the supremacy and responsibility of the parent is based upon reason, and the natural law which enjoins preservation of life.[59] All subjection in the family runs according to the natural order apparent to reason, as the strong care for the weak, the parent for the child, the husband for the wife. This conception of a natural law, ordained by God and evident to reason, was an area of consensus between absolutist and consent theorists: the law of nature established the necessity of government, in the family and the state, in order to preserve human life.

The notion that this power, in parent or ruler, was directed towards the preservation of life and the good of those governed was the basis of Tyrrell's argument for limited, rather than absolute and arbitrary, power.[60] If subjection was not absolute but was limited according to reason and natural law, a wife or child could deny obedience to a father who ruled contrary to these imperatives. Thus Tyrrell recognizes a right of resistance in the family if the patriarch threatens the life of child, wife or slave. In the case of a father's madness, drunkenness or rage, resistance of his command is justifiable. The extravagant abuse of power puts father and son, husband and wife, or master and slave into a state of nature where each individual is judge and heeds the law of self-preservation. Tyrrell acknowledges the potential danger of disobedience in this defense of resistance, but maintains that the risk must be accepted in order to preserve natural law. Here Tyrrell recognizes a right of resistance in extremity in the family, but he is much more cautious with regard to resistance in the state.[61]

The fundamental goal of the response to Filmer's absolutist theory was to establish the consensual origins of civil society, and the limits on sovereign power. Whig theorists looked to reason and the law of nature in order to provide a sound hypothesis about the foundations of authority and government. Such an account was generally presented as an alternative to the Genesis story and was sanctioned by reference to divinely ordained natural law and natural reason. Indeed, Tyrrell comes to argue that Scripture is precisely the wrong place to seek an explanation of the foundations of dominion and property, 'the Scriptures not being written to shew us the originals either of Government, or Propriety, anymore than to teach men Chymistry or Astronomy, though there be some so sottish to think they thus find some grounds for their Fancies in those studies'.[62]

Instead, like other natural law theorists, Tyrrell depicted an original state of nature in which individuals, seeking peace and preservation and driven by necessity and reason, join together to create political authority.

> So every particular person having before, in the state of Nature, a Right to preserve himself and to govern his own actions, when many men joyn together to confer this care upon one or more, there arises a Political Power indeed more noble, yet of the same kind with the other: for if the singulars had it not before in some measure, the universal could not have it at all.[63]

Tyrrell conjured up images of a state of nature and the very first institution of government. In so doing, he drew upon important theoretical traditions of social contract and natural law, and he embraced principles of natural sociability, freedom, rights and contract. But there were ideological as well as theoretical motives for his recourse to such images and arguments. In responding to Filmer, Tyrrell was certainly taking part in a longer European theoretical tradition, but he was also appealing to his own contemporaries, seeking to provide a compelling alternative account of the origins of government in the tradition of the founding stories of cities and nations. Contract theory offered such an account of the beginning of time, of a natural state in which natural men discovered a need for community and created political society. Whereas patriarchalist, divine-right theory began with the creation of Adam and depicted political society as the work of God, contract theory rested upon another creation story and depicted a primordial time, peopled by men performing a sacred function. In this way, the story of the social contract exhibits some of the classic characteristics of myth: it takes place 'in the beginning', depicts heroic actors exercising a supernatural[64] creative force, explains how reality came into existence, and how to re-enact or recreate these origins when necessary.[65] Locke emphasizes these mythic connotations when he describes the first people that established the first commonwealths as living in a 'virtuous' and 'golden age'. Tyrrell, following Aristotle, calls these first father-kings 'heroical'.[66]

Absolutist theorists such as Filmer rejected the original contract, arguing that there was no evidence for this state of nature and this original body of men, and reasserting the natural and original subjection of man.[67] Their critique of an original popular contract, and of the foundation of government in consent, rested upon two cogent points: the impossible, and absurd, image of the whole congregation of humanity at one place at one time; and the fragility of any government based upon the free consent of so many individuals at one time and over time.

In response, natural law theorists insisted that natural reason demonstrates the origins of political society in contract.[68] Aristotelian notions of natural sociability, and a rational adherence to the natural law enjoining political society, could be proven by the exercise of this same natural reason. Samuel Pufendorf, for example, justified the story of the social contract through this evidence of reason:

> Now we would not have it thought that these remarks on the pacts which give rise to a state are a creation of our imagination, because the origins of most states are unknown, or at least it is not entirely certain that they were established in that manner. For one thing is sure, namely, that every state had at some time its beginning. ... Yet since it is impossible to understand that union and subjection without the above-mentioned pacts, they must have interposed, tacitly at least, in the formation of states. Nor is there anything to prevent men from being able to reason out the origin of a thing, despite the fact that there remain no written records upon them.[69]

Theorists defended their liberation from strict reliance on scriptural and historical testimony in favor of argument from reason and the law of nature. Many did, however, also offer some historical and anthropological proof. Locke and Tyrrell presented the fabled examples of Rome and Venice in defense of the possibility of an initial meeting of an original people and their consent to government; and the Indians of America were also depicted as a real example of the primitive, natural state.[70] It was conceded, however, that individuals must have first gathered into families and that in all likelihood authority and political society evolved from these families, from the natural affection and obedience given to fathers. Both Locke and Tyrrell acknowledged the long tradition and history of monarchical, paternal government. Both men also advanced a conjectural history of the transition from the state of nature to the commonwealth through the mechanism of the family.[71] In this way a moment of consent and a site of gathering and contracting became unnecessary, although consent remained the basis of authority.

For Tyrrell, the admission of this evolution from family to commonwealth solves the problem of fixing the moment of consent, and the story of the social contract is once again viable. He returns to the image of an original people meeting and creating government, and asserts that fathers and freemen were the original people, the creators of the commonwealth:

> So that Though I grant all Government might at first be instituted by Fathers of Families, yet this does not prove any despotick Power that such Fathers had over their Children or Descendants; ...since though there never was any Government where all the promiscuous Rabble of Women and children had Votes, as being not capable of it, yet it does not for all that prove all legal Civil Government does not owe its Original to the consent of the People, since the Fathers of Families, or Freemen at their own dispose, were really and indeed all the People that needed to have Votes; since Women, as being concluded by their Husbands, and being commonly unfit for civil business and Children in their Fathers Families being under the notion of Servants, and without any Property in Goods or Land, had no reason to have Votes in the Institution of Government.[72]

Kingdoms and commonwealths began when groups of men who lived apart and independent in the state of nature, or who were collected in one army or one city, agreed to set up a government.[73] This definition of the original people was formulated in response to Filmer's important concession to the authority of 'supream and independent heads of families' in case of a disputed succession.[74] Yet it was also based upon common social and patriarchal assumptions about the political nation which excluded women and propertyless men from participation in the contract. This definition of 'the people' is constant in Tyrrell's work. It is essential to his theory of resistance and his understanding of the original Convention and the political nation.

Defining the people: the question of women

The argument against patriarchalism and absolute power seemed to lead to a broad definition of 'the people', to a recognition of equality and full humanity in all individuals, male and female. Even more, during the Exclusion Crisis public debate came to focus on the nature of human identity and human relations within the institutions of family, marriage, inheritance and legitimacy.[75] In the course of denying the legitimacy of Filmer's absolute patriarch, Whig theorists such as Tyrrell specifically came to confront the issue of woman's identity, and to affirm her equal possession of natural freedom and reason. Yet at the same time, women were judged to be naturally subordinate to men, and incapable of participation in the social contract. There is an ambivalence in Whig theory between the recognition of woman's common status as a rational and autonomous individual, and the insistence upon her difference or exclusion, her fundamental lack of freedom or power.[76]

In *Patriarcha non Monarcha*, for example, James Tyrrell defends natural law and consent against a doctrine of absolute patriarchal power, and he affirms the individual's natural right of self-preservation and resistance. This right to act in order to preserve life and well-being was seen to be equally justified in the woman, since she too operates according to reason and natural law. Tyrrell maintains that as a rational being, as one who has attained the 'age of reason', a wife shares parental power with her husband, and she is also responsible to defend the well-being of herself and her family. For this reason a wife might even contradict her husband because 'it is evident', explains Tyrrell, 'she never so absolutely submitted her will to his, as not to reserve to her self the faculty of a rational woman, . . . So likewise if the Husband command her to do anything against her Conscience, or the Laws of Nature, she is not obliged to obey him'.[77] If the good of the family necessitates, Tyrrell allows for change in the natural order and asserts that the wife might even govern the husband.

> I have already proved that the Authority of the Husband over the Wife, commences from that Contract we call Marriage; and though by the Word of God the Woman is made subject to the Man, yet the reason of that subjection naturally depends upon the Mans being commonly stronger both in body and mind than the Woman; and where that ceases, the subjection will likewise of course cease, even amongst us: For we see that if a Husband be a foolish or a careless man, and either cannot or will not govern his Family and Estate, the Wife may and does, and oftentimes him into the Bargain: Nor does any one finde fault with her for so doing, since somebody must govern the Concerns of the Family; and if the man either cannot or will not, who hath more Right or Interest to do it, than her, who hath an equal share in the happiness and well-being of her Family and Children?[78]

The ends limit the exercise of power, and may even circumvent the natural hierarchy of husband–wife–child.

However, when Tyrrell envisions this possibility of women empowered, he simultaneously reaffirms the right order of things and clarifies the authority of husband over wife. Tyrrell acknowledges the occasional necessity of 'correction' or physical punishment, and sanctions the husband's right to 'put away' an adulterous wife or to refuse to support children he suspects are not his own.[79] 'In some cases, whig ideology promoted the freedom of women as individuals;' Rachel Weil explains, 'in others, it played into male anxieties about women's power. Often it did both.'[80] John Locke's discussion of parental authority and of the relationship between husband and wife follows a similar, although not identical, pattern. Locke attributes slightly more autonomy to the married woman and, unlike Tyrrell, even defends the reasonableness of divorce, yet he too acknowledges the natural subjection of woman.[81] In both of these theories of contract the analysis of woman's role in the family, and the admission of her natural right to resist a tyrannical husband, present problems. This is especially clear when seen in comparison to these authors' treatment of the familial role and natural rights of a child, or a servant, or a slave who, however temporarily, lacks rationality and full human equality. Within the family, the right of resistance is unambiguous in the son or slave because each is an equal individual in the state of nature. By contrast, men and women are not considered to be naturally equal.

Whig theory does, at times, attribute the natural characteristics of freedom, rationality and equality to all humans, yet natural capacities and attributes are also sexually differentiated.[82] Thus, at the same time that women are depicted as free and rational beings, they are also judged to be naturally subordinate to men. Since women are, then, naturally subject, it followed that they were incapable of consent or participation in a social contract. A depiction of the original contract, like that offered in Tyrrell's *Patriarcha non Monarcha*, involved a conception of the original people as masters or fathers of families and freemen which excluded women, servants and children. Children are excluded because they lack sufficient reason and, like servants, lack property and independence, yet this condition is neither permanent nor natural. Women, on the other hand, are 'concluded by their Husbands' and are 'commonly unfit for civil business' because they are subject by nature and by contract even in the state of nature.[83] There are obvious tensions in this social contract theory between woman's natural subordination and exclusion, and the claims for universal natural freedom, rationality and equality. Mary Astell was simply one in a long line of critics to point out the implications of consent theory that were deliberately ignored or denied by theorists like Tyrrell or Locke. 'If all Men are born free,' Astell pointedly queried, 'how is it that all Women are born slaves?'[84] The refutation of Filmer's natural subjection and absolute sovereignty was based upon the premise of natural freedom and individual consent to government. The exclusion of some individuals, that is if women were considered individuals, from the right to consent posed an inherent contradiction.

According to Margaret Sommerville, this contradiction is diminished once we understand such contractarian theories within the context of attitudes towards and theories about women in early modern Europe. Sommerville is quite right to argue for a contextual interpretation of contract theory, yet such an analysis makes contract theory explicable rather than coherent; the Whig ambivalence remains.[85] However, an understanding of popular and theoretical notions about women's nature and, especially, about the construction of marriage and family in the state of nature, does illuminate the reasoning underlying Whig theory. Of central importance was the common belief that the social contract was premised upon the marriage contract. Samuel Pufendorf's *De Jure Naturae et Gentium* provided an authoritative account of this idea. As Pufendorf explained, the very material of the state, that is people and property, stems from marriage:

> Finally, since it is impossible to conceive of families without laws on marriage, and of states without families, and so on them rests all that decorous order that should prevail in the life of man, it is clear that without marriage men would live a life of isolation little better than that of the beasts. ... A further consideration is that without marriage, nearness of kinship could not be sufficiently established, and there could be no bequeathing of estates, the elimination of which would mean the loss of a great part of the advantages which either maintain or adorn the life of men.[86]

Marriage is posited as the mechanism enabling humans to escape the isolation of nature, creating family and property. Pufendorf advanced the familiar argument that the paternity of a child must be certain so that man has an interest in the survival of his offspring. This question of paternity, Rachel Weil has observed, 'exposed the fact that men are only fathers because they control women, and thereby forced onto the whig agenda questions about the particular character of the power of husbands over wives'.[87] Some theorists, like Tyrrell, argued that if the human species was to endure female sexuality had to be controlled so that children would survive and property interests would be protected and inherited.[88]

Within this postulated marriage contract male authority, of husband and then father, is created before sovereign authority. Tyrrell characteristically states that 'the Authority of the Husband over the Wife, commences from that Contract we call Marriage' and, like Pufendorf, he asserts that the husband's authority is based upon the natural and scriptural subjection of woman to man. Tyrrell and Pufendorf set forth three generally accepted reasons for a wife's subjection to her husband: the biblical evidence and divine command of woman's subordination; the practical reasoning against divided sovereignty, that a family cannot have 'two heads'; and finally the natural inferiority of woman in body and mind.[89] Because of this divinely ordained, rational, and natural inferiority, woman must be subject and she enters a marriage, before any other contract, as a subordinate to her husband.

Woman in this state of nature is both free and unfree. She is envisioned consenting to marriage, capable of entering into this contract, yet she is unable to join the social contract.[90] In seeking to explain woman's consent to this marriage contract, Tyrrell incorporates Pufendorf's image of the married couple as confederated empire – an image which affirmed the identity of the law of nature and nations. Tyrrell depicts the marriage contract as a tie of friendship, a treaty between sovereign, albeit unequal, individuals: 'of which Compact the Husband being Principal, does imitate that of an unequal League between Civil States, in which the Husband being the head, the Wife owes him all due respect and observance; and he on the other side owes her maintenance and protection.'[91] Thus within the marriage a woman retains the natural right of self-preservation and may resist a tyrannical husband. There is a parallel between the subject's release from obedience to a ruler turned tyrant, and the woman's freedom from subjection to a husband who either will not or cannot rule.[92] 'So that even this subjection of the womans will to the mans, commanded by Scripture,' explains Tyrrell, 'is still with a supposition that the man is capable or willing to govern: for if he be not, he loses this Prerogative of course.'[93] The woman is accorded some autonomy and humanity, and operates according to reason and natural law. Yet she is naturally and necessarily subject to her husband; in this sense her consent to the marriage compact is lacking a crucial element of freedom or choice. Recognizing this conceptual difficulty, Pufendorf attempts to explain the conjunction of consent and constraint:

> This merely means that a husband's sovereignty is not produced by the consent of his wife, but is already ordained by the

44 *Revolution by Degrees*

> command of God, and consented to by the wife.... And yet it should be carefully noted that the sovereignty, as a moral entity of one man over another, does not exist without a human act and is not intelligible without obedience. And no obligation lies upon a woman before she has with her own consent subjected herself to a man.[94]

The key to this paradox lies in the distinction, simultaneously underscored and undermined, between the paternal and the political, between the family and the state. Since the wife's subordination is not political, it is not seen to contradict the doctrine of natural freedom and consent to government.[95] Along these lines Tyrrell, again following Pufendorf, asserts that the ends of the state and of the family are separate, and that the wife is able to contribute to one but not the other:

> [S]ince Families (especially those who consist of a good number of Children and Servants) may have a twofold end: the one peculiar to it self, the other common with that of Civil Governments. The common end is considered in that defence and security resulting from the conjunction of many into one Body; in which, although an absolute Empire be necessary, yet since the Wife being but one weak woman, can contribute but very little to this end, it may very well suffice to the peace and unity of the Family, if she be tyed to her Husband onely by a simple Compact by way of Friendship, without any despotick power over her. But the peculiar ends of Matrimony, which are the procreation and breeding up of Children, and providing things necessary for the Family, may well enough be obtained, although the Husband be not invested with this despotick power (which supposes that of life and death, or other grievous punishments) and though the Wife be tyed by her Compact only and the Bonds of Amity....[96]

The woman belongs to the family, she is fit for private affairs but is 'unfit for civil business'. Thus, she has the natural right of a rational woman to resist a tyrannical husband, but has no right or identity as an individual outside of the family, in the state. The woman is excluded from political society because she is not capable of self-government and she cannot contribute to the power of the sword; she is allowed the rationality and ability necessary to govern family concerns, 'the procreation and breeding up of Children'. Theorists tended not to consider the question of an unmarried or childless woman in their analysis of the transition from nature to society, yet this woman too might plausibly be excluded by her natural inferiority in reason, property and biology. A more important issue was the status of a female ruler: although according to Whig theory a woman was essentially incapable of participating in civil society, a female successor to power might be endowed, as heir, with the attributes of an individual, that is property, power and the rationality of her ministers.[97]

Woman is excluded from the definition of 'the individual', and of 'the people', because her natural capacities are deemed insufficient and she is portrayed as fundamentally unequal to man. The natural equality between men, as described by a theorist like Locke, was not an equality of talent, or intelligence, or physical strength. It was, rather, an equality of reason, of adherence to the law of nature, and of freedom to consent to the authority of a sovereign power.[98] And yet this seemingly broad definition of equality delineates precisely those areas of perceived fundamental inequality between male and female.[99] Since sexual difference was said to connote intellectual difference, women were believed to be deficient in natural reason. Perhaps even more important, women were believed to be hampered by the deficiencies of female biology, and so crucially restricted in their ability to possess property. Whether in a state of nature or in civil society, the ability to bear children was understood to render woman weak and in need of support both during pregnancy and in rearing her offspring.[100] Further, this natural weakness was understood to make a woman's possession and control of the property in her own body tenuous; any ownership of real or moveable property, through labor or occupancy, was regarded as insecure and untenable. By demonstrating that marriage, and male authority, was thus a natural and necessary and reasonable state, theorists confirmed that the social and political order was indeed based upon the law of nature. The appeal to natural law was employed both to challenge and to reaffirm subjection. Although at times depicted as endowed with natural reason, rights and freedom, woman was in the end naturally unequal and unfree.

Defining the people: the question of property

The depiction of the acquisition of property, like the conception of marriage, was a vital element in the story of the social contract and the definition of the original people developing in Whig thought. Within this natural law tradition theorists analyzed the origins of private property in order to elucidate the origins of community and government. The acquisition of property in the state of nature was understood to exemplify man's natural freedom and rationality. Moreover property was believed to provide the impetus for the creation of community and government. The need to safeguard and regulate property arrangements was said to engender the necessity of a social contract. Property also explained the endurance of that contract, since the security of this property interest over time could be shown to lend proof of stability and continuity to the argument for government by consent.[101] The notion that people first entered society as property holders also helped to delineate just who was included in Whig theories of consent and contract. At the same time that a theorist like James Tyrrell excluded women as 'unfit for civil business', he also excluded unpropertied men from the social contract. Tyrrell asserted that children, servants, those 'without any Property in Goods or Land, had no reason to have Votes in the Institution of Government'.[102] Once again, theoretical claims about natural rights, freedoms and equality were contained and moderated, as Whig theorists sought to demonstrate the consistency between principles of natural law and the established order of English society.

In seeking to legitimate private property and the status quo and in founding government, in part, upon property rights, Whig theorists again worked within a well-established natural law tradition.[103] Seventeenth-century analyses of the origins of private property relied upon a theory of property primarily associated with St Thomas Aquinas, and developed by later jurists such as Hugo Grotius and Samuel Pufendorf. Property theorists, Thomas Horne notes, generally focused their attention upon a few fundamental questions. The first concern was to define the nature of God's grant of the earth to man: what was 'property' before the advent of 'private property'? Second, theorists questioned how private appropriation first took place, and how and why ownership was acknowledged. The problem of necessity was an abiding issue: once private property has been established, they wondered, what are the rights of the propertyless; do those in need still have any claim to the divine grant? Finally theorists considered what, more precisely, was the relationship between the development of property rights and the creation of a contract of government.[104]

The initial position taken by adherents of the Thomist tradition was that the earth was bestowed on all men in common, to be best used for human preservation and benefit.[105] Most theorists also continued to reaffirm the Aristotelian notion of the productivity of private property, and they concluded that reason dictates individual possession for the common good. Along these same lines James Tyrrell asserted that, for the benefit of mankind, rational management of resources naturally leads to the creation of private property:

> Therefore, if it be rational for me to desire my own preservation, and to enjoy the means to do it, it is likewise rational to permit another man to do the like, since he hath as much right to his being as I have to my own; so that if a man have already seised any of those common things for his own use, though he does not actually use them, those things cannot be taken from him without injury; and if any man will call this first principle of natural Justice, a true agreement of Mankind, I shall not gainsay it, since such an agreement is but a rational assent of every particular mans understanding that the abstaining from doing such a thing is every private mans interest, and likewise for the good of humane society.[106]

The right to private property was said to derive from possession, use, but most of all from rational agreement and consent. According to this view, property rights were firmly founded upon the law of nature and not uncertainly based upon the condescension, and ultimate possession, of the divine-right king. This Whig theoretical conception of property rights thus also ran counter to the legal-historical understanding of the feudal basis of property and power in England. The analysis of the origins of property and the principle of preservation accords with what Richard Tuck has identified as a Grotian shift towards a theory of natural rights, and a reading of the law of nature as an injunction to respect human rights.[107]

Tyrrell's analysis makes it clear that he, like Locke and other consent theorists, was participating in a well-established tradition, seeking to refine and to reaffirm the insights of predecessors like Hugo Grotius, Bishop Richard Cumberland and Samuel Pufendorf. At the same time, property was central to the Whigs' particular concern to refute Filmer, and the Filmerian controversy had both broadly continental and specifically English dimensions. The conflict between Grotius's theory of property and Filmer's pointed criticisms of rights and consent was inextricably bound up with the troubled legacies of the English Civil Wars. In particular, Whig analyses of property rights had to avoid that dangerous association with Leveller ideas. The assertion that property rights were natural, and that a system of private property was based upon consent, raised the possibility that consent might be revoked; or that any individual might lay claim to a natural right to property; or even that some men might seek to restore an original community of goods. Leveller theories of the 1640s had indeed affirmed principles of natural right and of popular consent. And their critical document of 1647, *An Agreement of the People*, included a proposal to abolish property qualifications for the franchise, that is, for the exercise of consent.[108] These theoretical possibilities, and this Civil War precedent, help to explain James Tyrrell's ongoing concern with defining the people of the social contract as masters and freemen. In the end even though unpropertied men may be regarded as excluded from his original contract, Tyrrell still faces the charge of 'levelling' – that his theory of consent opens the door for those with merely some property (the lower orders, the 'rabble') to political participation.

One of the Tories' purposes in reprinting another of Filmer's works, the *Observations Concerning the Originall of Government, Upon Mr Hobs 'Leviathan', Mr Milton Against Salamasius, H. Grotius 'De Jure Belli'*, was, of course, to exploit this possible connection between Whig theories and Leveller ideas. Filmer had insisted that if his opponents did not accept the account of an original divine grant of property to Adam, they were necessarily adherents of communal property, proponents of 'levelling' estates. In defending this notion of absolute monarchy and Adamite authority, Filmer easily attacked the conception of the divine grant as it had been articulated by Grotius. Filmer claimed that any acknowledgement of private property would necessarily contradict Grotius's initial assumption of an original community, the grant of the earth to all men. 'Doth it not derogate from the providence of God Almighty to ordain a community which could not continue?' Filmer criticized, 'Or doth it not make the act of our forefathers, in abrogating the natural law of community by introducing that of property, to be a sin of a high presumption?'[109]

In the response to Filmer, Tyrrell took care to avoid such Leveller associations. And he relied, in great measure, upon two works of the 1670s that defended the theory of natural property rights against critics like Filmer and Hobbes: the *Treatise of the Law of Nature* by Bishop Richard Cumberland, which Tyrrell later edited and translated, and Samuel Pufendorf's *De Jure Naturae et Gentium*. Tyrrell's property theory begins with a refinement of the concept of original community, drawing upon Pufendorf's essential distinction between 'positive' and 'negative' community.[110] The divine grant did not establish a 'positive, unalterable community of things', Tyrrell explains, since this would make private property impossible to introduce and would thus contradict the command to self-preservation and propagation:

> Therefore, it follows that God bestowed no more upon any particular man than what would serve for the preservation of himself and propagation of his species, and only in that manner as might prove subservient to that design, which being supposed it is evident that before compacts there might be a negative, though not a positive, communion of things; that is all things being exposed to all men (as meat is at an ordinary) they did not belong to this person more than to another.[111]

Since neither community nor private property was established absolutely by the law of nature, property could develop as was necessary for each community. '[F]or the Psalmist saith, God gave the Earth to the Children of men,' states Tyrrell, 'that is, not to any one man, nor yet absolutely in common, but to be either divided, or used in common, as they should find it stand best with their convenience and way of living.'[112] The options available in this 'negative community' are illustrated by the contemporary symbol of the state of nature, the example of the inhabitants of America: whereas the Indians have a system of communal property, the English planters in America divide the land into private shares for individual families.[113] Tyrrell, like Pufendorf, does retain the Grotian idea that more populated and 'civilized' communities would necessarily develop a system of private property. In this way, Tyrrell justifies English settlements in North America, assuming that the land they settled was previously unoccupied, and that sufficient land and resources were left. As Thomas Horne notes, the theoretical analysis of property became a 'political necessity' not only because of conflicts over the nature of government and constitution, but also because of European expansion in the sixteenth and seventeenth centuries. Conflict over colonies and trade stimulated the articulation of theories of legitimate and illegitimate acquisition, slavery, and just war.[114]

Consent remains the key to Tyrrell's argument against Filmer. The transition from negative community to private property is based upon the consensual actions of an original people, but Tyrrell must once more modify the image of the moment of consent and contract. Here Tyrrell continues to rely upon Pufendorf's modification of Grotius's theory. Grotius's description of the division of property through a communal compact, an instant of unanimous consent in that remote time when 'the human race could assemble', had been sharply and effectively ridiculed by Filmer.[115] In response to Filmer's critique Tyrrell points to the variety of ways in which property rights develop; Locke, in the *Second Treatise*, will adopt a similar approach. Both theorists follow Pufendorf in arguing that private property may arise either from an express division or from tacit consent to the occupation of property. The problems posed by Grotius's insistence upon original consent as the sole means of property acquisition are generally resolved in Tyrrell's and Locke's treatises. In addition to occupation, or use, Tyrrell and Locke introduce the notion of labor as a means of acquisition of property, but Tyrrell does not place much emphasis upon the importance of labor value in the creation of property rights. Whereas Tyrrell ultimately reaffirms Grotian ideas of consent, Locke emphasizes labor in property acquisition and then proceeds to an exploration of the role of money in the development of property rights and of inequality.[116] Both theorists do remain true to the traditional theoretical recognition of the validity of 'necessity' as a limitation on property rights. Tyrrell and Locke endorse the idea that private property is established as the best use of the divine grant for the common good, and they maintain that private appropriation remains valid only as long as there remain sufficient resources to provide for the necessities of others.[117]

The notion that a system of private property was based upon rational consent, and was established for the common good, provided Tyrrell with an answer to Filmer's critique of the stability of consensual theory:

> To which it may be answered, that the same reason that made men institute civil Government, and Property at first, the same likewise obliges them to maintain it, being once instituted in the state in which they find it: For since the Common good of Mankind, is the highest end a man can propose to himself, and the common good of the City, or Commonwealth where he lives, the greatest subordinate end next to that, and that both Government and Property were at first introduced by common consent for the good of those humane societies that first agreed to it, every succeeding member of that Commonwealth, or civil society, though never born so many ages after, is as much obliged to the observation thereof, as they that first instituted it.[118]

In addition to the laws of nature, civic duty and public utility dictate obedience to government and the division of property. Like Bishop Cumberland, Tyrrell here emphasizes the principle of common good more than the idea of fidelity to contract.[119] Tyrrell insists that private interest must yield to public good, and indeed that maintenance of the public interest and order is to the benefit of each private individual. As long as government and property exist for the public benefit, consent is the course of reason and civic responsibility. This emphasis upon consent and the common good also enables Tyrrell to avoid the 'levelling' implications of his property theory. He continues:

> [A]nd though some men either by their own fault, and the carelessness or prodigality of their Ancestors, may perhaps be now under such Circumstances by reason of their poverty, as that civil Government may appear inconvenient for them, and the Property now establisht contrary to their interests, ... he is not therefore at liberty to resist the Government and to change the course of this Property already establisht; and this is by the laws of

nature, without any Divine revelation: since no man can disturb the general Peace of humane society for his own private advantage, or security, without transgressing the natural laws of God, by bringing all things so far as in him lies out of the setled course they now are in, into a state of Anarchy and confusion... and consequently can never be in security until he have again entered into the same compacts for establishing both Government and Propriety, which his Ancestors did at first....[120]

In this way Tyrrell ensures the acceptability and stability of a system based on consent. Yet he treads dangerously close to natural subjection when he asserts that succeeding generations are bound to obedience and can never disturb the order established by their fathers, nor question the public good. However, this assertion is in accord with the particular definitions of the individual and the people upon which much of contract theory is founded. Those original men who formed the social contract were understood to be acting to protect their own lives, liberties and estates. The definition of the people as fathers and freemen, those who share this property interest and this independence, ensures stability by excluding more individuals from the right to consent. Men lacking property and autonomy are added to the list of women, children and servants. The people are fathers, masters and freemen, those who continue to have good reason to maintain civil government and private property. Tyrrell's version of contract thus supports the status quo and preserves England's ancient government.[121]

The power of the original people, and the initial contract, to bind successive generations is even more pronounced in Tyrrell's analysis of inheritance and possession. He argues, in effect, that obedience is tied to the possession of property:

[E]very Possessor of a propriety in Land or Goods in any Government is not onely bound to obey, but likewise to maintain it; since those that first instituted the Government, did likewise tye themselves and all those that should at any time possess those Lands or Goods, to the maintenance of the Government which they had establisht: And it is just and reasonable, that those that claim under such first possessors, should if they like to enjoy the Lands or Goods, perform the Conditions they annexed to them....[12]

The transmission of property thus also guaranteed the continuity of consent and the stability of political society. Indeed, not only possession, but even enjoyment or use of any of the common benefits created by the state was understood to imply a tacit consent and necessary obedience to government. 'As for all the others who possessing no share in the Lands or Goods of a Kingdom, yet enjoy the common benefits of the Government,' Tyrrell adds, 'I conceive they are likewise bound to obey and maintain it as first instituted, for the reasons before given.'[123]

Potentially controversial claims about natural rights and equality were continually and carefully modified. Most Whigs like James Tyrrell did not advocate an expanded franchise or a redistribution of property when they advocated a theory of consent. John Locke's intentions are, perhaps, not quite as clear, and the relationship between Locke and the Levellers is a matter of ongoing scholarly dispute.[124] Unlike Tyrrell, Locke does not offer a clear definition of the people as masters and freemen. However, much like Tyrrell, Locke does acknowledge some measure of obligation tied to inheritance and even enjoyment or use, and he employs a similar distinction between express and tacit consent.[125] Although Locke admits difficulty in determining what acts should imply consent, and how far a tacit consent binds the subject, he too concludes that 'whether this his Possession be of Land to him and his Heirs for ever, or a Lodging only for a week; or whether it be barely travelling freely on the Highway', possession or enjoyment are indications of consent and obedience to government.[126] The belief that 'barely travelling freely on the Highway' indicates tacit consent demonstrates the ways in which the obligation of those excluded from the contract, from the body of 'the people', is secured. The conception of tacit consent enables the theory of contract, of original freedom, equality and rational consent, to be gradually assimilated into the natural hierarchy of property and power among Englishmen.

There is no necessary contradiction, however, between the assumption of tacit consent and the doctrine of natural freedom. Indeed both Locke and Tyrrell reiterate the individual's right to refuse consent. They insist that there is no native allegiance or natural obligation to the place of one's birth; emigration and forfeiture of inheritance are possible and indeed reasonable for all citizens. Express consent alone, given rationally and freely, was understood to make man a full member of society. Once this consent is given, however, they maintain that the citizen's obligation and obedience to his state can no longer be easily terminated through forfeiture or emigration.[127] These theorists' emphasis remains upon rational action for the common good. Having consented freely and rationally, man is obliged to preserve the state and to submit his individual interest to the greater interest of public peace and welfare.

What if this greater public peace is destroyed by tyranny? Locke's *Second Treatise* does conclude with a recognition of a right of resistance, but Tyrrell's *Patriarcha non Monarcha* generally avoids any confrontation with this case of extremity. For example, when he affirms natural freedom and acknowledges a right of emigration, Tyrrell insists that such a right posed no threat of depopulation or weakness to good government. But he leaves open the question of what right – of emigration, or perhaps even of resistance – might be claimed against a repressive regime.

> And if it be objected, that upon these terms the major part of a people may go away and leave the Country without defence; that is not likely, nor so much as to be supposed, as long as the Country continues habitable, and the Government tolerable for the Subjects to live under: which if it prove otherwise, I see no reason that God should have ordained any Country for a common Bridewel, where men should be obliged in Conscience to drudge, be oppressed, and ill-used all days of their lives without remedy.[128]

If tyranny and oppression are widespread, perhaps even the citizen who has given express consent has some remedy, some right of self-preservation. This ambivalence towards resistance in Tyrrell's theory stems, at least in part, from the tension between the absolutist connotations of a strong rights theory, and the emphasis upon the public good articulated in a strong consensual theory.

Resistance and representation

In the theories of government and contract set forth in the *Two Treatises* and *Patriarcha non Monarcha* Locke and Tyrrell diverge as to what denotes the end of obligation. In the *Second Treatise* Locke imagines the possibility, even the likelihood, of misgovernment and the dissolution of the state. He envisions the end of obligation, justifiable resistance, and freedom to create and consent to a new state. Although Tyrrell has some notion of general oppression and the end of obedience, it is only fully explored in the context of the family and the right of a child, wife or slave to resist paternal tyranny. Official tyranny and the dissolution of the state are seldom touched upon in *Patriarcha non Monarcha*, and then mainly in response to Filmer's analysis of Aristotle and critique of Philip Hunton.[129] Throughout, Tyrrell emphasizes that private injury is to be suffered, and that the kind of general oppression that would justify resistance in theory is almost impossible in practice.

Tyrrell does slightly expand his own view of resistance in the course of defending Philip Hunton. Hunton's *Treatise of Monarchy* was one of the Civil War tracts republished during Exclusion, and reissued again after the Revolution. First published in 1643, at the outbreak of civil war, Hunton's *Treatise* was a response to the dilemma of allegiance facing Englishmen; it was an attempt to find a middle way between royalist and parliamentarian positions.[130] In *Patriarcha non Monarcha* Tyrrell affirms Hunton's search for accommodation. He claims, quoting Hunton, that when Englishmen are confronted by tyranny, redress is properly sought through petition, '"if the Monarch's Act of Exorbitancy or Transgression be mortal, and such as suffered, dissolves the Frame of Government and publick Liberty"'.[131] According to Hunton, however, if such petitioning fails, then,

> prevention by resistance ought to be: and if it is apparent, and appeal be made to the Consciences of Mankind, then the Fundamental Laws of that Monarchy must judge and pronounce sentence in every mans Conscience, and every man (so far as concerns him) must follow the Evidence of Truth in his own Sense, to oppose or not oppose according as he can in Conscience acquit or Condemn the Act of the Governour or Monarch.[132]

Hunton thus abandons hope of a constitutional remedy and concludes that final authority resides in individual conscience. Although Hunton maintains that fundamental law and ancient constitution continue to be valid, his recognition of an individual right of resistance tended toward a principle of popular sovereignty.[133] Against Filmer's critique of this principle, Tyrrell attempts to assimilate Hunton's position to a much more tempered view of resistance. In a limited monarchy such as England's, Tyrrell asserts, the people are able to judge when government exceeds its bounds and acts contrary to fundamental law and the common good. Moreover, the judgment of the people is generally reasonable and easily communicated. Tyrrell thus agrees with Hunton's conviction that the people may judge and that their judgment may be known, but he does not conceive of the kind of active resistance depicted by Hunton, and later by Locke. The people may judge but they may not execute that judgment; they may not oppose or condemn in a show of public resistance.[134]

The recent experience of civil war made it clear to many like James Tyrrell that most people were better off even under the worst of rulers. It was often claimed that opposition to the king was only ever contemplated for private ends, and that the kind of general oppression that would require resistance never really takes place.[135] This kind of reasoning led Tyrrell to abandon Hunton's defense of a right of resistance:

> [A]s for Mr. H's conclusion, that every man must oppose or not oppose the Monarch according to his own Conscience, when he can have no other redress, I do not approve of it. For I will not suppose any time (in which this Nation is not oppressed by a standing Army, or men of different Principles in Religion and Government); but the Subject may find redress, if not at one time, yet at another.[136]

The exceptional prospect of a standing army led by a Catholic king was still far off, and the example of royalist and parliamentary armies in the field was a vivid memory. In the early 1680s Tyrrell sought to preserve the continuity of reasonable and justifiable consent.[137]

The advantages conferred by the state are believed to warrant obedience and consent, and Tyrrell regards those who disown and resist government as hypocrites and enemies to the common good.[138] For Tyrrell, the motivation behind consent reveals a strong mechanism for ensuring the continuity of consensual government: adherence to the established order is obligatory because the original reasons for instituting government remain. Indeed, Tyrrell comes to assert that that original people who established and consented to government still endure:

> So that those that first instituted Government in any Country, have no necessity expressly to promise or engage for the Subjection and Obedience of their Children, or those who should succeed them.... for the People being once entred into Society, can never be supposed to alter their Judgments all at once without very good cause, much less to die, though the particular persons that constituted it do: for as a River is still esteemed the same as long as the water runs in the same Channel, though the same individual water never stays in the same place, but one part still pushes out another; so those are not less to be esteemed in the politick capacity (of a Civil State) the same people, than those by whom the Commonwealth was first founded.[139]

Employing water imagery most famously associated with Aristotle, Tyrrell offers a traditional image of the continuity of the state.[140] This is also an image typical of the 'common-law mind', of continuity and antiquity as articulated by John Selden and Matthew Hale.[141] Finally, this image serves to counter Filmer's analogy of mankind and the sea: 'ever ebbing or flowing, ... [t]hose that are the people this minute, are not the people the next minute.'[142] The image of the river or the sea was used both to exemplify the changeable nature of the people and consent, and as a symbol of continuity and the slow evolution of custom. Here Tyrrell mixes immemorial custom with original contract and affirms that England's ancient constitution is secure because her original people, and their property and reason, existed at one time and through time.

Custom and consent offer a solution to the problem of discontinuity and questioned succession at issue during the Exclusion Crisis. Contract theory, as articulated by Tyrrell in 1681, does not lead to the conclusion that resistance is legitimate, but it does allow for the abiding role of consent in government. In response to Filmer's assertion of indefeasible Adamite succession Tyrrell contends that the succession of rulers is customary, formed by the joint will of prince and people; it is a product of historical practice and subject to alteration.[143] He reaffirms that any change in the line of descent is properly referred to the people in that assembly of fathers and freemen who created and consented to government. The succession is not casually altered, however, for the descent of the crown to the next heir is a fundamental law of England. This fundamental law might be changed only as it was instituted, through the action of prince and people. Tyrrell explains:

> For we own no right of alienation in the People, as long as there is a lawful Heir remaining and succeeding in his right, to whom the Crown was first legally settled; nor yet does therefore the succession diminish the right which the People had at first, but that it may arise and take place again if the King should die without known heirs.[144]

A change in the line of succession, that is the exclusion of the Duke of York, would be possible with the consent of Charles II. It might also become possible if the king's death created a situation in which there was no known or competent heir. The issue of competence is left unresolved by Tyrrell, but there are indications that a line of descent may be altered if the heir to the throne is incapacitated by illness, madness or, perhaps, religion.

Tyrrell attempts to disarm Filmer's objections to this devolution of power and choice to the people by referring to Filmer's admission that power may escheat to the 'fathers of people'.[145] The disjunction between this common definition of the people as fathers and freemen, and the implications of a Whig theory which posited the freedom, rationality and consent of all individuals, male and female, rich and poor, was addressed by the fiction of the 'original people'. Like many Whigs, Tyrrell denies that in founding the state upon the consent of the people he provides an endorsement for democracy and an appeal to the rabble.[146] Instead in seeking to define the people, he identifies them with fathers, masters and freemen, the 'original people'. The tension in this identification remains, however, and Tyrrell cannot fully escape the element of representation in his equation of 'people' and 'original people'. 'I see no reason why these should not be looked upon as representing the whole promiscuous body of the people,' Tyrrell argues, 'to whom the Power devolves upon the want of a Successour.'[147]

The identity of the people is blurred even further in Tyrrell's examination of the question of the succession. When 'Power devolves upon the want of a Successour', Tyrrell asserts that the people or their representatives are required to act.[148] There is an elision between people and Parliament, and the contradiction between them is not confronted. The exclusion, or representation without consent, of certain individuals from the body of the people was vindicated by the fiction of the 'original people'. The exclusion of most men from membership, or even representation in Parliament was not equally justified. This disjunction between the role accorded to the people, even narrowly defined, in contract theory and the power accorded to their representatives in Parliament was obvious. Just as Civil War royalists had attacked parliamentarian doctrines of representation, this Whig incoherence on 'the people' was a target for Tory critics.[149]

Captain Thorogood, one such Tory contributor to the Exclusion debate, dwelt upon the injustice of England's narrow franchise in an attempt to discredit Whig arguments. If government was truly based upon the Whig principle of popular consent, he declared, then this equation of Parliament and people was absurd. Thorogood lists the number of those excluded from political participation by the forty-shilling freehold: '*Lessees* for Years, *Grantees* of *Annuities* for Years: *Men* that live upon the Interest and Product of their Money', clergy, soldiers, seamen, younger sons, '*Labourers, Servants, Artificers*, and *Tradesmen*'.[150] He rails against this discrepancy between people and Parliament in high-flown language drenched in irony:

> And what can be more unequal, not to say unjust, then that a numerous and upon due computation the far greatest part of the Nation, that are Passengers in the great Ship of the Commonwealth, as well as the rest, should be debarred their right of choosing a *Master* or *Pilot*, to whose Skill and Care they commit their common safety? Have they not their *Liberty*, their *Property*, their *Religion*; and in a word, the present enjoyments of this, and in some measure the hopes of a future *Life* to be secured or hazarded by the good or ill Conduct of their *Governour*? And must this, all this be left to the Arbitrary Power and Discretion of such, as by chance, perhaps more then merit, have acquired the Possession of some Land, or are free of Boroughs and Cities?[151]

Thorogood seeks to expose the traditions and assumptions upon which Whig theory was founded. The very core of the Whig accommodation between consensual theory and parliamentary power is attacked, as he states:

> That the supposition, of the Parliaments representing the People, is a fiction of Law, well devised by the Wisdom of our Ancestors, for quieting and appeasing the minds of all particular men, who could not have a stronger Motive of Submission, or of not believing themselves injured then their being accounted parties and privy to all Acts of Parliament.[152]

This fiction will not stand when there is crisis within government. In case of conflict between king and Parliament, and the potential dissolution of government, Thorogood concludes that "'tis but reason that the common concernment of the ruine or happiness of all, should be left, not by fiction of Law, but in reality', to be judged by the people themselves.[153]

Thorogood's criticisms give us insight into the ways in which a theory of popular consent, and the popular foundations of government, came to be shaped by rhetorical strategies and political needs. In the 1640s royalists like Dudley Digges and John Spelman also challenged the claim (or fiction) that Parliament directly represented the people; another royalist, John Maxwell, anticipated Thorogood's argument with the claim that parliamentarian theories of consent must eventually result in a recognition of popular sovereignty.[154] In the 1680s and 1690s it was Tories like Thorogood and Sir Robert Sawyer who openly articulated the implications of consent, and who pressed home the logical necessity of an expanded, popular franchise. They did this in order to achieve political and pragmatic goals: Tories attempted to discredit the opposition by depicting Whigs as either hypocrites or radical republicans; and they challenged the authority of an unrepresentative Parliament by pointing out fundamental inequalities in the franchise, and in the geographical distribution of seats.[155] At times, Tories also sought to portray themselves as the true champions of the people and defenders of the public good. The impact of these Tory critics was equally varied, and was not the simple disparagement of the Whigs and notions of popular sovereignty. The elaboration and clarification of a theory which based the legitimacy of government on the consent of the people, whether achieved through criticism or justification, was part of the evolution and transmission of the idea of the sovereignty of the people.

Despite Tyrrell's narrowing of the definition of 'the people' – despite his additional fiction of the 'original people' made up of fathers, masters and freemen – he was not yet able to equate Parliament with people. Tyrrell still had to confront the legal fiction of representation and to supplement it with an historical fiction. The notion of an original Convention, an ancient and legendary council composed of the body of the people, was not yet employed as a solution to the problem of the identity of 'the people'. It is this representation of Parliament as Convention, and the conflation of Convention with 'original people', that will be developed by Tyrrell in his contribution to the debate over the antiquity of Parliament, and in his justification of the work of the Convention after 1688.

3
'To preserve the Original Constitution of Parliaments': Revolution and Preservation in James Tyrrell's Whig History

In 1681 James Tyrrell was unwilling to endorse Philip Hunton's defense of resistance, but after 1688 Tyrrell deliberately set out to construct a justification of resistance. In the 1690s he, like other Whigs, argued that resistance to James II had, in fact, preserved England's ancient constitution. 'I think I shall be able to make out,' Tyrrell wrote in 1693 '... that all Resistance of the King, or those commissioned by him, is so far from being Treason, as you suppose, that it is every mans duty to oppose him in case he goes about to set up, instead of a Legal Monarchy, a Tyrannical Arbitrary Power in this Nation, since this is but to preserve the Original Constitution of Parliaments, which in some cases cannot be maintained without such a Resistance be allowed.'[1] A central goal of Tyrrell's work after the Revolution was to prove that the end of resistance, as it was envisioned and enacted by the Whigs, was to preserve and defend England's ancient government of king-in-parliament.

These claims of continuity and conservation – indicative of a common-law mentality – were a vital part of Whig Revolution principles and essential to the success of the Revolution Settlement. The very concept of the ancient constitution was formed by this 'common-law mind'; as J. G. A. Pocock and Glenn Burgess have shown, this concept was based on a complex understanding of custom and continuity, encompassing both immemorial stasis and evolutionary change. This way of thinking about English politics, this language of custom and prescription, was crucial to the Whig contention that the Revolution had preserved the ancient constitution. A Whig interpretation of history was, then, inextricably bound up with their theory of resistance. Moreover, Whig historiography was vital to the acceptance of the Revolution Settlement and the veneration of 1688–89. It was that set of assumptions and traditions associated with the ancient constitution, or common-law mind, that enabled Whigs to articulate, and enabled Englishmen to accept, a justification of resistance and moderate revolution.

While Whig arguments favored history and embraced ancient constitution, their version of history was contested in the 1680s and 1690s in much the same way as their version of contract was attacked. Indeed a contentious debate over the English past developed even before 1688, during the Exclusion Crisis, as part of the response to Sir Robert Filmer. The republication of Filmer's works included not only *Patriarcha* but also *The Free-holder's Grand Inquest* which was a study of parliamentary history and the scope of parliamentary authority. The first Whigs were anxious to discredit the historical as well as the patriarchal aspects of Filmer's theory.[2] The first salvo in this debate was William Petyt's *The Antient Right of the Commons of England Asserted* which sought to prove the existence of fundamental law and an immemorial Parliament. Another important early contribution was made by the Whig lawyer and historian William Atwood in his *Jani Anglorum Facies Nova*; Atwood was a friend and student of Petyt, a fellow controversialist deeply engaged in responding to Tory political and historical claims.[3] In response Sir Robert Brady published *A Full and Clear Answer to a Book written by William Petit... Together with some Animadversions upon a Book called Jani Anglorum Facies Nova*, his first attack on the Whig conception of the ancient constitution. Brady was an influential figure in the historical debate. A physician, professor of physic at Cambridge University, master of Caius College, keeper of the Tower records, and champion of the royal prerogative, Brady played a prominent role in criticizing and thus shaping Whig theory and historiography.[4] Indeed, ever since J. G. A. Pocock focused attention on Brady's history and influence this debate over the ancient constitution has been known as the 'Brady controversy'.

Although his main contribution was historiographical, Brady well understood the link between history and theory in Whig thought. In another response to Petyt, Atwood and other Whig historians, his

Introduction to the Old English History, Brady disposed of the theoretical aspect of Whig argument, the theory of contract, before turning to the problem of Whig historiography.

> One of these sort of Men preach to the People, That the Origin of all Power and Government is from them, That Kings or Magistrates derive their Authority from them; That they have none, nor more than what they give them; That they are their Servants, Instruments, Executors and Trustees only, and accountable to them for Male-Administration, and may be Tryed, Sentenced, Deposed, or put to Death by them, or such as shall Impower or Authorize to that purpose, that is, themselves. These Men are Pretenders to *Platonic* and *Eutopian* Governments, such as never had a *Real Existence* in any part of the World, nor never can be practicable amongst any People, or in any Nation whatsoever; yet are specious *Baits* to hook in *Unstable, Unwary, Fluttering* and *Malitious* Men.[5]

Whig theorists of contract were thus painted as republicans and regicides, as Brady played upon the danger of any association with Commonwealth doctrines, whether the theories of Levellers or Rump Parliament men.

While critics like Brady pointed to the dangers of leveling and the actions of the rabble, the Whigs were careful to found their theory of contract upon a fairly narrow definition of people as propertied men. A definition like that offered by James Tyrrell, who defined the people as 'masters and freemen', was consistent with a theory of natural law and contract and was a plausible, indeed a standard, contemporary definition. Ideas about the origins of government in contract became more acceptable when the people was so identified. This definition of the people also enabled Whigs to identify abstract theory with England's history, to combine the theory of contract with the tradition of ancient constitution. It became possible to approximate this body of the people to the ancient council of government envisioned as the whole community of freemen.

And so, the Whig reliance upon notions of contract, law and trust was tempered by an appeal to history. It was through the appeal to English history that Whig theorists sought to prove that resistance would not result in change, but was rather mounted in defense of the constitution. This defense of resistance acquired legitimacy by emphasizing the tyrant's violation of fundamental law, as Whig history traced the foundations of that law and explored the role of the people and Parliament in England's ancient constitution. Brady was well aware of this Whig historical strategy and identified these ideas with the second sort of 'turbulent men' he was eager to disprove.

The other sort are such as hold forth to the People, *Ancient Rights* and *Privileges*, which they have found out in *Records*, and *Histories*, in *Charters*, and other *Monuments* of *Antiquity*; by these Men the People are *taught* to prescribe against the Government for many Things they *miscal* Fundamental Rights; by these Men 'tis averred ...That all *Proprietors* of Land, all *Probi Homines*, or *Bonae Conversationis*, came to great Councils as Members, in their own Persons; That all such were *Nobiles*. That *Ordinary Freeholders* often came to *General Councils* of the Kingdom, without *Special Election* or *Representation*; That upon a *Change* in the *Succession* to the Crown, there might be *Extraordinary Conventions* of the People to *declare* their *Universal Consent*, for better *assuring* such *Successors*; and That this was an *Elective* Kingdom, which as often as they have opportunity they cunningly insinuate, though they do not plainly *assert* it in terms.[6]

The conflict with Brady centered on the interpretation of England's social and constitutional history. Here was a royalist who was an accomplished historian as well as an effective polemicist, and Whigs such as Tyrrell and Petyt and Atwood were determined to provide an answer to his powerful historical critique of an Englishman's ancient liberties.

The political and rhetorical strategy of these Whigs was to offer revolutionary arguments about contract and resistance while championing tradition. Brady's invective against the 'turbulent' Whigs is aimed at unveiling this strategy which he regarded as their deceptive, two-faced plan. 'Any Man,' concludes Brady, 'that shall observe, what the last Men craftily drive at, and *compare* it diligently with what the former assert, will not find much *Difference* in their *Principles* and *Designs*.'[7] Brady's conclusion pinpoints the characteristic attempt of Whig theory to harmonize contract and ancient constitution.

As he developed and defended Whig principles, James Tyrrell became engaged on both fronts of this debate. Before 1688, Tyrrell's *Patriarcha non Monarcha* had explored the contractual origins of government but did not defend resistance or dwell upon the potential for a dissolution of government. This early work also offered some reflections on English history and the ancient constitution but again Tyrrell stopped short, acknowledging that the task was better left to other men, such as William Petyt, who were engaged in more extensive historical research.[8] By the 1690s, however, Tyrrell was making numerous and wide-ranging contributions to the historical as well as the theoretical debate. The *Bibliotheca Politica*, a series of fourteen dialogues that composed his 'political library', was written in the early 1690s as a compendium of Whig constitutional history and theory in defense of the Revolution Settlement. Tyrrell became deeply engaged with the Whig historical argument in this work, in his *A Brief Enquiry into the Ancient Constitution and Government of England, As well in Respect of the Administration as Succession Thereof*, and in his *The General History of England, Both Ecclesiastical and Civil; From the Earliest Accounts of Time, To the Reign of His Present Majesty, King William III*. He kept the Brady controversy alive throughout the 1690s until his own death in 1718.[9]

Tyrrell conceived of *Bibliotheca Politica*, his major work of the early 1690s, as his reading of the post-1688 debate. The 'Dedicatory Epistle' to the collected dialogues begins with his account of the genesis of this project and its basis in contemporary debate. Tyrrell makes the claim that his own curiosity led him to read all the treatises published on the subject of government 'for some years before the late wonderful Happy Revolution, as well as since'.[10] His professed method of reading included copious note-taking, 'commit[ting] to writing the most considerable Arguments on both sides'.[11] From these notes, evidently, Tyrrell crafted his dialogues, believing that 'impartial Collections of this nature' might be beneficial to others. It was his hope, Tyrrell concludes in his dedication, that such a collection 'might prove of great use for the satisfying of some mens doubts and scruples concerning Lawful Obedience to the Government of their present Majesties'.[12]

In the end, Tyrrell produced some one thousand and fifty-two pages of debate between his imagined characters 'Mr Freeman' a gentleman, and 'Mr Meanwell' a civil lawyer. Meanwell, cast as a civilian, was immediately identified with the defense of royal prerogative; under the Tudor and Stuart kings, civilians had become increasingly associated with prerogative rather than common-law courts, and with a university education and the separate corporation of Doctors Commons, rather than with the social and educational community of the common lawyers at the Inns of Court.[13] As the name Meanwell indicates, Tyrrell intends to depict this character not as a virulent opponent, but rather as a well-meaning if misguided friend who might be brought round by rational and impartial discourse. This character might be seen as Tyrrell's appeal to those in his audience opposed to his views. The other participant in these dialogues, Mr Freeman, is clearly a Whig defender of revolution. Obviously the name signifies liberty, but Freeman's social standing is also an important indicator of Tyrrell's intended audience and relates to Tyrrell's definition of the people as 'masters and freemen'. It is hoped that the reader will identify with this gentleman, Mr Freeman, and that he will appeal to those addressed in the dedicatory epistle: 'To all Impartial and unprejudiced readers, especially those of our Hopeful and Ingenious Nobility and Gentry'.[14] Again, Tyrrell emphasizes the hope that his dialogues, as collections of contemporary debate, will prove useful to other gentlemen, saving them time and expense, and offering clear and convincing argument.

Separate title pages, publication dates and publisher's notices suggest that each dialogue was published separately in 1692, 1693 and 1694, although surviving evidence of separate publication is less conclusive.[15] A collected edition appeared in 1694, and a fourteenth dialogue was added in 1702. Collected editions of all fourteen dialogues appeared again in 1718 and in 1727. James Tyrrell's dialogues spoke to the pressing issues of the early 1690s, obviously concerned with the goal of satisfying men's consciences, and concerned with questions about the legitimacy and stability of the present government. From 1690 to 1692 much contemporary attention was focused on the problem of nonjurors, and on the related issue of abjuration; prominent clergymen like Archbishop Sancroft were deprived of their places for refusing to swear allegiance to William and Mary, while abjuration bills were repeatedly proposed and opposed in both the Commons and Lords. Another challenge to the security and legitimacy of the regime was presented by the potential for French invasion, intensified in 1692. The threatened invasion, coupled with the publication of a declaration and appeal from James II, engendered renewed disputes regarding allegiance and the basis of William's right to the throne.[16]

The first five dialogues of *Bibliotheca Politica*, from 1692, are largely concerned with the question of divine right and the doctrine of non-resistance.[17] As the Whig settlement continued to be precarious, contested by Tory critics and Jacobite plotters, Tyrrell and his publisher saw some value in continuing to publish these debates and defense of the Revolution. The sixth to the tenth dialogues, dated 1693, are largely concerned with the exploration of the history of England's ancient constitution and feudal law, while Dialogues 11 to 13, dated 1694, review the events of the Revolution, the actions taken by the Convention, and the immediate problem of the non-jurors. The fourteenth dialogue of *Bibliotheca Politica* is composed largely of a review of those terrible events that took place in the middle of the seventeenth century in England. This dialogue is focused on distinguishing Whig Revolution principles from Civil War and Commonwealth principles, distinguishing the murder of Charles I from the proceedings against James II. It is the last of Tyrrell's dialogues, a much later addition published in 1702, and likely part of a contemporary controversy surrounding the reputation of Charles I and the question of the authority of *Eikon Basilike*.[18]

These years 1692 to 1702, therefore, provide the context within which *Bibliotheca Politica* was published. The setting Tyrrell imagines, however, begins with the very moments after James II's flight in December 1688, the time before William and Mary were yet crowned. It is depicted as a moment of uncertainty, but also a time of liberty and possibility – 'a time when everybody not only thought but spoke freely'.[19] In these dialogues Tyrrell's Whig interlocutor acknowledges the consequences of contract theory as they were set forth in Locke's *Two Treatises*; he contemplates resistance of the whole people and a dissolution of government. The difference between Exclusion and the Revolution is apparent in the differences between Tyrrell's *Patriarcha non Monarcha* and *Bibliotheca Politica*: Tyrrell is no longer an anonymous critic of Filmer but is now a Whig spokesman, mounting a defense of resistance and willing to consider the implications of that defense. Although these dialogues provide an ample and generally fair hearing of Tory arguments, Tyrrell makes his own Whig affiliation known in his prefaces and in the fact that it is so often the

Whig, that 'Freeman', who is convincing the well-meaning but misguided Tory 'Meanwell'. In seeking to persuade, James Tyrrell moderated some of the more troubling aspects of Whig resistance theory by offering an interpretation of English history – one that carefully manipulated powerful traditions about an original people and an ancient constitution. The conventional belief in England's ancient constitution, and ideas about the composition and history of the council of government, were important parts of this construction of an acceptable theory of the Revolution. The justification of those Revolution principles of abdication and vacancy relied upon a particular interpretation of the development of constitution and society in England; and it relied upon a reasoned and scholarly, as well as emotional, defense of inherited ideas about England's past. In time Whig thought proved to have a powerful appeal, in part because it was based upon deeply held beliefs about English history and society.

The nature of the ancient constitution

Just as contract theory sought to elucidate the origins of legitimate government, the argument from history was similarly concerned with the source and true foundations of England's constitution. The theory of contract placed the origins of government in an agreement of the people and asserted that rulers were bound to a fundamental constitution at the very inception of government; persistent violation of this constitution signaled a tyranny that must be resisted. Yet Whig theorists frequently confronted the charge that their image of contract and the constitution was premised upon the impossibility of a divided sovereignty or, even worse, placed ultimate sovereignty in the Parliament or in the people.[20] The Whig history of the origins, composition and development of the ancient council was set forth in order to counter these criticisms. Some Whigs, like Tyrrell, identified the theoretical original contract with the ancient constitution and fundamental law, and at the same time the original people and the original council came to be conflated.

That Whig combination of contract and ancient constitution is pronounced in the fifth dialogue of *Bibliotheca Politica*. Here Tyrrell's focus on the origins of government shifts from a theory of contract based solely on reason and natural law to an investigation of the

English past. Tyrrell's Whig spokesman describes the original formation of limited and mixed governments. Tyrrell tended to view England's government as limited and did not often refer to the king as one of the three estates in a mixed constitution. Instead Freeman depicts the fundamental and perfect balance of the ancient constitution as a balance of prerogative and liberty, and asserts that the various parts of government had a 'cooperative' rather than a coordinate power.[21]

Tyrrell's exploration of the English constitution confronts the problem of maintaining monarchical prerogative while at same time defending liberty and limits. This is especially true in Dialogues 9 and 10, where Tyrrell explores the statutes and oaths against resistance to the king established during the reign of Charles II. In the fifth dialogue Tyrrell's Whig spokesman also defends limited monarchy, and insists that 'at the *Institution* of the Government, [a Prince] may be *limited* by those who are neither superior, nor *Inferior* to himself; but only *equal* in the *State of Nature*, as I suppose the *People* to be with a *King*, before he was *made* so by them'.[22] The theoretical state of nature, in which free and equal individuals form a social and governmental contract, is here reiterated in a defense of a right of resistance to tyrants.[23] Freeman then turns to a description of the institution of Saxon government in order to provide the clearest proof of the original contract and fundamental law:

> But to come to the matter in Hand, I shall shew you that it is not at all *impossible* or *improbable* that without any *hinderance* of that *Power*, which is *necessary* to the *King* as *Supream*, that he might for all that have bin *limited* as to the *Legislative* at the *first Institution* of the Government, which I shall thus make out.
>
> I do therefore in the first place suppose, that the *English Saxons* being a *free People*, after their *Conquest* of this Island, as well *Nobles* as *Commons* did agree by their *free consents*, and *publick Compacts*, to set over themselves a *Prince* or *Sovereign*, and to *Resign* up themselves to him, to be governed by *such* and *such Fundamental Laws*: *Here* is a *Supremacy* of *Power* set up, though *limited* as to the *manner* of its *Exercise*.[24]

As in his *Patriarcha non Monarcha*, Tyrrell is here again relying upon Philip Hunton's *Treatise of Monarchy*, and seeks to support his definition of limited monarchy with evidence from the institution of English government. He adheres to Hunton's conception of the Saxon 'conquest' as an expulsion of the Britons and a continuation of the Saxon constitution on English soil. This explanation was offered in Hunton's *Treatise of Monarchy*:

> For that of the Saxons was an expulsion, not a Conquest, for as our Histories record, They coming into the Kingdome drove out the Britaines, and by degrees planted themselves under their Commanders; and no doubt continued the freedome they had in Germany: unless we should think that by conquering they lost their own Liberties to the Kings, for whom they conquered and expelled the British into Wales. Rather I conceive, the Originall of the subjects libertie was by those our forefathers brought out of Germany:... Their Kings had no absolute but limited power: and all weighty matters were dispatched by generall meetings of all the Estates. Who sets not here the antiquity of our Liberties and frame of Government?[25]

Hunton's theory of expulsion allows him to trace England's ancient constitution back to the free and self-governing Saxons. As Samuel Kliger notes, Hunton 'established by this ingenious argument the continuity of Saxon democracy'.[26]

Many Whig historians, including Tyrrell, cast back to Saxon and even pre-Saxon England in an attempt to describe the ancient Gothic constitution. The Saxons and the Angles were considered to be branches of those Gothic, or Germanic, nations that settled over Europe after the fall of Rome. Englishmen looked back to this invasion of England, and the introduction of the Gothic constitution, as they called upon the Tacitean tradition.[27] Tacitus' accounts of these ancient nations in the *Agricola* and *Germania* had been manipulated for their constitutional and political significance ever since the 'recovery' of these texts in the fifteenth century. This historian's overarching theme of Germanic liberty, and his depiction of elected German kings ruling with advice and consent, were taken up and debated by French and English historians in the sixteenth century.[28] Tacitus was frequently exploited as the source for a national history. One of the most influential continental examples of this practice for later Whigs was provided by the French Hugenot, François Hotman.

Hotman's *Francogallia* was a celebration of the Gothic heritage in France, and a defense of resistance aimed to preserve that ancient Gothic liberty. English historians in the sixteenth and seventeenth centuries also adopted Tacitean history, creating that story of Gothic liberty instituted by Anglo-Saxon founders.[29]

The tradition of Gothic liberty was the cornerstone of Whig history. The political institutions brought to England by the Saxons, their customary law and tribal assemblies, were considered to be the source of England's ancient constitution.[30] This reliance upon the Saxon institution of government did not, however, contradict the idea and authority of an immemorial constitution. If the beginning of the constitution in England could be fixed at the entry of the Saxons, its history stretched far back into the mists of ancient Germanic liberties. The ancient constitution of king and council, existing since time out of mind, merged imperceptibly with an image of the state of nature and the original contract of king and people. Tacitus' account was important in inspiring this conception of foundations, this myth of origins – what Donald Kelley terms 'speculative soundings in the deep past'.[31] For these Whigs history and theory equally confirmed the contractual origins and the essential continuity of the ancient constitution. This emphasis upon historical continuity, and this appeal to immemorial Gothic liberty, is a strong indication of the persistence of the common-law mind.

Whig history relied upon both the cultural and political aspects of the Tacitean tradition in order to argue that a public assembly or council was a part of the institution of Saxon government. This idea that the council or assembly of the people was coeval with the institution of monarchy was a central part of the Whig argument from history.[32] Tyrrell's Freeman is representative when he asserts that councils were an integral part of the fundamental constitution, and he even goes so far as to suggest that this council originated before the monarch. In opposition to the Tory notion of an original absolute monarchy Freeman insists that the council's existence was prior to, and indeed acted in, the creation of the king.[33] He is careful to distinguish the council and its inception and evolution from the king's other courts which derived all their authority from him.[34] The image of an original, coeval council was a key element in the defense of the ancient constitution of king-in-parliament. The conflict with Brady's interpretation of the antiquity of Parliament was a contest over the role of Parliament in sovereign power.

This Whig account of the origins of Saxon government is ridiculed and opposed by Brady's supporter in *Bibliotheca Politica*. 'I confess you have given a long and plausible account of the *Original* and *Form* of our Government,' Meanwell begins, 'though if it come to be examined I doubt it will prove a *meer Romance*, and not at all agreeable to true History, or Matter of Fact.'[35] Here the Whig version of early English history is labeled an historical fiction in much the same way as Brady had depicted the theory of contract as a 'Platonic and Eutopian' myth of government. Freeman and Meanwell echo the contentious debate over the ancient constitution, as Tyrrell attempts to develop a definitive answer to the challenge posed by Brady and the historiography of early England.[36] In order to counter the royalist and absolutist versions of the nature of England's constitution, Tyrrell follows the Whig antiquarian William Petyt's focus upon the commons, and its part in the original council. Petyt, Tyrrell and others wanted to prove that a free people had created the English constitution, and had a place in that government. These Whig historians defended their notion of the ancient inclusion of the commons for three reasons: to deny the absolute, arbitrary power of kings; to affirm the ancient liberties and fundamental rights of Englishmen; and thus to contend that the Whig defense of contract and resistance was a defense of tradition and immemorial custom.

The appeal to immemoriality and continuity was central to the Whig refutation of their opponents' position. Royalist and absolutist versions of history and theory asserted that the king was the original and sole locus of sovereignty in England's constitution. All laws and liberties enjoyed by Englishmen were said to be granted as favors and concessions of their kings. The institution of Parliament was also regarded as a grant of the king, and not a result of immemorial custom and fundamental liberty. According to this view, most famously articulated by Sir Robert Brady, the ancient constitution could be traced back only to the Norman Conquest; this not-so-ancient constitution rested upon the absolute sovereignty of William I. The most powerful element in this historical defense of monarchical power was the focus on the Norman conquest, and the associated claim that feudalism had accompanied the Norman settlers to England.

Antiquarian scholars in England had long been demonstrating that the Norman constitution was a feudal constitution, in which all land and power emanated from the king, but many of the implications of this knowledge of feudal England were first pursued by Robert Brady.[37] The recognition of the feudal was now used to demonstrate that there had been significant change in the constitution of English government: the ancient constitution could not be an unchanging expression of the agreement of free men, but rather had been based at one time on feudal relations of dependence and obedience. And so English laws and liberties, and the role and power of the people in Parliament, had evolved out of the institutions of feudal obligation and were the work of benevolent kings. According to this account of the past, Parliament was understood to have begun as a meeting of the king's advisors or great men, summoned at the king's discretion, composed only of those tenants-in-chief and excluding any representation of the 'commons' below them. Moreover these great men's feudal holdings, this property, entailed obedience not rights.[38]

The feudal interpretation of history was thus a severe blow to the Whig depiction of England's ancient constitution and the immemorial continuity of Gothic liberty. The focus on the Norman Conquest was the most powerful element in the historical defense of absolute power. Further, Tory investigations into the nature of feudal tenures threatened the image of an unchanging limited monarchy based on prescriptive and immemorial rights and liberties, and it undermined any Whig defense of a right of resistance. Tyrrell affords the reader clear recognition of the strength of this challenge, as he allows Meanwell to point out the futility of the Whig claims regarding early England:

> let the first institution of this Government have been what it will in the Saxon times, and what original contract soever you may please to fancy between them and their Subjects, yet this was all gone, and out of doors, by that absolute Conquest which K. *William I* made of this Kingdom for himself; and his heirs who do not at all claim under the Title of our English Kings.[39]

James Tyrrell's evident appreciation of the strengths of the feudal interpretation, and his insight into the flaws in Whig history, are among the most interesting aspects of his contribution to Whig historiography in *Bibliotheca Politica*. Here Tyrrell undertakes a defense of Petyt's *Antient Right* in the light of Brady's criticisms; Tyrrell endeavors to present a revised and improved version of Petyt's argument, and to reconcile feudalism and the ancient constitution.[40] In so doing, Tyrrell comes to use some of Brady's own techniques and arguments against him.[41] Of central importance is a focus on feudal terminology. Brady had undermined the very foundations of Petyt's work by showing that the entire argument rested on anachronistic definitions. He exposed the erroneous assumption that titles, such as baron or thane, or phrases such as *liberi tenentes* or *clerus et populus* had a singular meaning that remained static over time. Tyrrell is aware of the problem of anachronism, and sees that the contextual definition of these terms is the key to the Whig argument. 'But since this is a Dispute about the Signification of Words,' agrees Freeman, 'in what sense they were used in that Age we are now treating of, it will not be inconvenient to examine from the most Learned Glossarists, the Ancient Signification of those Words, which are in dispute between us.'[42] Tyrrell employs the same authorities used by Brady, such as Sir Henry Spelman, William Lambarde, Sir William Dugdale and William Prynne, in order to refute the critique of Whig history.[43] He believes that he can establish the true ancient meanings of these terms, and thus provide incontrovertible evidence for the inclusion of the commons. This awareness of possible differences in definition stems not only from the study of Brady's critique and an appreciation of the feudal, but was also realized through a comparison of England with other 'Gothic' nations.[44] Studying the Gothic heritage in Tacitean history inspired this comparative approach; reading Tacitus on ancient language, law and place also fostered an interest in philology.[45]

In order to prove that the commons were included in the ancient council, Tyrrell fights for an expansive understanding of the ancient terms. His Whig interlocutor demonstrates that titles of nobility or military tenures, such as baron, thane, magnate and *fideles*, were anciently used in a broader sense, signifying commons and freemen as well as nobles.[46] Freeman contends that contemporary distinctions between nobles and gentlemen, or commons, were not the same in early England and he charges the Tory Meanwell with the anachronism of reading modern meanings into ancient terms.[47]

Meanwell's assertion that the term *populus* was anciently used only to refer to nobles and military tenants is likewise criticized as a distortion. Here Freeman repeatedly points up the contradiction between his opponent's definitions of *clerus* and of *populus*: Meanwell's admission that inferior clergy were encompassed by the term *clerus* should, it is argued, logically lead to a similar understanding of *populus* having been used to denote commons as well as nobles.[48] Finally, Tyrrell provides a justification of Petyt's definition of *liberi tenentes* as ordinary freeholders, rather than tenants by military service, based upon evidence from the most highly respected antiquarian source:

> But that these Words *Liberi Tenentes*, do not here signifie *Tenants by Military Service*, pray see Sir *Henry Spelman's Glossary*... which upon every one of these Titles he makes to signifie all one and the same thing, *viz.* an ordinary Freeholder. And therefore it is a very forced Interpretation of yours, to limit these Words *Communitas Populi*, only to the Community or Body of the Earls, Barons, and *Tenants in capite*.[49]

Tyrrell deliberately relies upon the authority of Brady's predecessor in medieval studies. If the whole of Brady's history was, as J. G. A. Pocock tells us, founded upon Spelman's earlier insights into feudal tenures,[50] then the most effective response to Brady must call upon that same work. Tyrrell's goal in focusing upon these definitions, and centering this attention upon terminology, was to demonstrate that the people were a part of the constitution, integral to the founding of England's government. In order to confirm that the ancient constitution was made up of king and council, and that England's founding was based on contract, Whig historians like James Tyrrell sought to prove that early England was made up of independent property-holders who created a monarch limited by a popular council.

It was commonly agreed that the right to appear in the ancient council was based upon property qualifications, but Freeman asserts that even lesser landholding was a basis for inclusion. Freeholders of less extent and wealth than the king's great lords were said to have a right to a place in the council. In order to undermine the Tory history of a council of tenants-in-chief even further, Tyrrell also suggests that feudal tenures pre-dated William I and thus did not originate in conquest. These arguments are typical of what D. W. L. Earl has identified as 'Procrustean feudalism', a 'stretching' of feudalism in order to assimilate Brady's findings to the Whig cause. Tyrrell concludes that a right to appear in William I's council of government was premised upon possession of these more ancient estates, and not upon the grant of the Norman king.[51] Moreover, Freeman adds that 'there were besides all these [feudal tenants] several *Alodarii*; who held their Lands, discharged from all Services, and could sell or dispose of them without the consent of the King, or any other inferior Lord'.[52] These were men who held property independent of feudal services and fees, and these allodial tenures were another, equal basis for inclusion. Finally, the power and wealth of cities and boroughs is emphasized by Freeman as proof that propertied citizens and burgesses were of sufficient estate to be freemen, and were also an ancient part of the great council.[53]

In Tyrrell's analysis the definition of an English freeman, a man with the right to appear in council, was gradually expanded to include pre-Norman feudal tenants, allodial tenants, burgesses, and lesser as well as great freeholders.[54] The debate between Freeman and Meanwell came to be centered upon the identity of this ancient freeman, and the identity of the legal community or political nation. Freeman gives voice to the Whig view of the man whose property and independence gave him an equal right to a place in the council.[55] Tyrrell's work is clear confirmation that Robert Brady's observation was accurate: these Whig historians did claim that 'all *Proprietors* of Land, all *Probi Homines*, or *Bonae Conversationis*, came to great Councils as Members, in their own Persons; That all such were *Nobiles*. That *Ordinary Freeholders* often came to *General Councils* of the Kingdom, without *Special Election* or *Representation*.'[56]

Although the Whig argument for ancient feudal tenures, predating William I, had some merit, their claim that all men were anciently called to great councils was more of a distortion of the past. Broad assumptions of property, independence and equality led to the Whig vision of a vast council composed of all freemen. Brady also noted that these '*sly* and *malicious*' ideas were suggestive of popular sovereignty, and he accused the Whigs of attempting to '*undermine* the Government, and so infuse Dangerous Notions of *Sovereignty* and *Power* into the Peoples Heads'.[57] Tyrrell's dialogues allow a harsher name to be attached to such ideas: the Tory Meanwell attacks the 'Republican, levelling opinion, who do suppose that all the Freeholders of *England*, had an ancient indisputable right of appearing in Parliament by reason of their propriety in Lands, or other Estates'.[58]

The very task of the Whig historian was to deny the impact of Norman feudalism and the change in property ownership that would result from total military conquest.[59] In response to the Tory historian's acceptance of conquest and Norman feudalism, the Whig Freeman reaffirms his expansive definition of the ancient freeholder:

> But to come to the main Design of your present Discourse, which is to shew that none but Tenants by Military Service *in capite* were in the first times after the Conquest properly the only true *Freemen* or *Freeholders* of the whole Kingdom. I shall shew you that first the Notion is quite new, and never heard of, ... neither Mr *Lambard*, Mr. *Sommer*, nor Sir *Henry Spelman*, nor any of our *English* Antiquaries or Lawyers ever discovered any such thing, before your Dr. arose to disperse these Clouds; every man of the Kingdom, who was no Villain, being look'd upon as a Freeman, and every Owner of Lands of Inheritance, though of never so small a proportion reckoned a Freeholder, and his Estate called his *Franc Tenement*, or Freehold, as well in our Ancient, as Modern Laws; and that Freehold was not restrained only to Military Service, within a hundred years after the Conquest, appears by King *John's Magna Charta*.[60]

Like William Petyt and William Atwood, James Tyrrell provided an alternative to Brady's interpretation of the Domesday Book and argued that feudal tenures were only a minor portion of landholdings in England under William I.[61] By contesting the assertion that William I was an absolute conqueror who established a new feudal society in England, Whig historians countered the claim that Parliament was a creation of the king, a result of the decay of a pure form of feudalism in the thirteenth century.

The significance, and even the authenticity, of the Norman Conquest had long been contested by historians and theorists of English politics and society.[62] Whig historians of the 1680s and 1690s set out to reinterpret the Norman Conquest in order to deny the introduction of feudalism and to reaffirm the continuity of ancient political freedoms; again they relied upon the work of earlier antiquarian scholars such as William Lambarde and John Selden. Whereas some writers denied that any conquest had taken place, others insisted that it was a conquest of no force. Tyrrell and others insisted that continuity was evident in William I's confirmation of the Confessor's law, while any later breaches were considered to be rectified by confirmations of Magna Carta. The coronation oath was regarded as constant proof of the reaffirmation of the ancient constitution.[63] In order to call into question the military and feudal basis of William I's rule, evidence was also adduced to support the legitimacy of his claim to the throne.[64] This argument for William I's legitimacy was, in fact, also assayed by Brady in his attempt to deny that a *de facto* king was a fundamental part of the English constitution.[65] Whig historians added the claim that William was a legitimate king because he had been accepted and elected by the majority of Englishmen who had never opposed him. Finally, it was posited that the Normans who accompanied William would have reestablished a Gothic constitution in England, preserving the laws and liberties they had enjoyed at home.[66] This provides echoes of the argument that the Saxon conquest was an expulsion and that the invaders established Gothic liberties. All of these arguments underscored the role of contract and consent, and strengthened the image of a governmental contract rooted in English history and law.

Immemorial, original, ancient

Tyrrell's response to Brady in the *Bibliotheca Politica* is typical of Whig history. As he provides a defense of the antiquity of the commons in Parliament, Tyrrell develops an expansive definition and role for the ancient freeholder, and denies conquest and the imposition of feudal tenures. His Whig spokesman insists that no change has affected the Saxon constitution and that ancient Gothic liberties have continued unabated in England. Now the theoretical image of all men coming together to form an original contract could be confirmed by this Whig history of the English freeman. Whig history and theory depicted free individuals creating and consenting to government, and the theoretical image of all men forming an original contract was confirmed by the history of the Germanic and then the English freeman.

80   *Revolution by Degrees*

Tyrrell maintained that at this first institution of government all freemen had an equal right to appear in the council.[67] The culmination of the expansive definition and public role of the Saxon freeman lies in this conception of a council composed of all freemen. Tyrrell reproduces, from Spelman's work, what he alleges are the earliest extant records of the great council, 'held at *Canterbury*, A.D. 605, by King *Ethelbert*, not long after the settlement of Christianity in this Island', as evidence that the people were a considerable part of the council from the very beginning of Saxon government.[68] The right of all freemen to appear in the Saxon council forms the basis of the Whig claim for the antiquity of the commons. The force of prescription, the fact that this role in the council had been claimed since the very institution of government, since time out of mind, lends authority to the claim.[69] Here is the Whig belief in continuity, the timelessness of England's ancient constitution, and the ancient and immemorial rights of the freeholder.

It is at this point in Tyrrell's Whig history, with this conception of an original council, that a conflation of people and council occurs. At the first institution of government king and council are depicted as coeval, essential parts of England's ancient constitution, and all free men are seen as eligible to sit in this council.[70] This ancient council could, then, be associated with the whole body of the people since all freemen had a right to consent and contract; here the original people, that community of freemen who create and consent to government, become a part of the government they have created. Tyrrell exploited this blurring, or conflation, of people and council, yet he was well aware that this image of a vast council made up of all English freemen was open to criticism, and certain fundamental objections are voiced by his Tory spokesman. It is objected that a meeting of such a council, made up of tens of thousands of men, would have been impossible; and it is objected that contemporary parliaments could in no way be seen as identical to ancient councils.

> What then? do you suppose that all the Freeholders in *England*, by whatsoever Tenure they held, appeared in Person in Parliament, before the time Sir *H. Spelman* in his Glossary, and Dr. *B.* Assign for the summoning of the Commons to Parliament? At this rate every Yeoman, or Petty Freeholder was a Baron; so that this Assembly might then consist of above 50 or 60 Thousand Persons;

Since *Spot* in his Chronicle tells us, that *William* the Conqueror reserved to himself the service of about 60000 Knights fees, which by the time, I suppose, might have been divided into many more lesser ones,... And these, besides the Tenants in Socage, must needs have been so numerous, that what Room, nay what Field or Place was able to contain so great a Multitude? Or how could any business have been transacted therein, without the greatest confusion imaginable?[71]

This challenge echoes Filmer's objections to Grotius's theory of an original contract, citing the logistical problems of time and space in the conception of a meeting of the whole people.

Tyrrell defends the Whig position and reaffirms the ancient role of the people in great assemblies, but he also retreats from extreme popular sovereignty and introduces elements of representation into the ancient council.[72] The defense of an ancient commons, like the defense of resistance, easily led to greater claims about the extent and power of the people. Tyrrell must temper these claims by relying upon accepted legal fictions of representation. In theory he envisioned the people of the original contract as a contained group of masters and freemen. In history, at England's founding the people are also depicted as a group of freemen, a body numerous but manageable, who initially meet in person to limit their kings and preserve their fundamental rights and liberties. This original council lies somewhere between theory and history: it is the first meeting of all men, the body of the people who formed the contract of government; but is also an image of the Saxon founders, these freemen who met together in council. It is at times acknowledged that all the English freemen may have met in the person of representatives even in that first council, but more often Tyrrell maintains that the whole multitude of freemen appeared.[73]

The image of the great council is multilayered and as Tyrrell moves from the original to the ancient, and then to the historical council, he charts the process by which the literal body of the whole realm became a representative and symbolic body. 'I doubt not but our Common Councils or Parliament were in their first Institution, the main Body or Representative of all the Freemen of the Nation,' Freeman explains, 'and though it may by long continuance of time to deviate from that Institution; yet, that it is to be attributed either to some prevailing Custom, or else positive Law to the contrary.'[74] The foundations of the ancient constitution and the council lay in the people although their role became more symbolic and attenuated. Freeman explores the transition:

> [F]or it is certain that in the *Saxon* times, all the Freeholders of *England* had a right of coming to Parliament in Person; and hence it is that *Liber Tenes, Liber Homo & Ingenuus* were Synonimous, and of the same signification ... and hence it is, that the Members of those Councils were so numerous as they were in those times, and long after, till they became so vast and unmanageable, that they were fain by degrees to pitch upon this method, of sending Knights of the Shires to represent them, which is certainly a very ancient Institution;[75]

Originally all the freemen of England could meet in person, and even ancient councils were vast bodies, incorporating most of the people.[76] But, with the growth of cities and the increase in numbers of freemen, a system of representation came into use.

> ...and since all such Citizens and Burgesses, not being able to come in Person, as the Free-holders could, were represented either by their chief Magistrates, called their Aldermen, or else by Burgesses of their own chusing as at this day; so that all Freedom, or Ingenuity being in this, as in all other Common-wealths, reckon *per censum*, by the Estates of the Owners; our Common-Councils were, and that truly, the Representatives, not only of the Estates, but Persons of all the Freemen of the Nation, ... all Freedom consisting then in so much Freehold Lands, held in a Man's own right, or being Freemen of some City or Burrough Town.[77]

Although it is acknowledged that some men appeared only by their representatives, these ancient councils are still portrayed as huge assemblies, composed of most freemen. King John's council at Runnymede in 1215 was often employed by Tyrrell, and other Whig writers, as an example of the ancient meeting of all freemen.[78] The practice of electing representatives, rather than personal appearance in council, is perceived to be fairly common by the reign of Henry III, but the final and greatest change in participation is said to accompany later changes in landholding. Here Freeman recounts the declining participation of the people or freemen:

> Freedom anciently consisted in the Inheritance or Free-hold Estate of Land, or in Riches, in Trade or Traffick; Leases for Life and Years, being not known, or at least not commonly in use in those days; and hence it is, that when Estates of Free-hold came to be divided into small Parcels, all Free-holders till the Statutes of *Henry* IV. and VI. (which we have before cited) were as much capable of giving their Votes at the Election of Knights of Shires, as the best and greatest Tenant *in Capite* in *England*, till it was reduced by those Statutes to 40 s. Freehold *per Annum*; these Free-holders and Burgesses of Towns being anciently looked upon in the Eye of the Law as the only Freemen.[79]

The introduction of the forty-shilling franchise is portrayed as a narrowing, and an exclusion of the people, in contrast to the Tory version which depicted this as an expansion of popular participation granted by the king. According to Whig history, in the beginning every freeman, measured by his independence rather than the extent of his free holdings, had a right to appear in council; in the end, lesser freeholders were excluded from citizenship, joining women, children and the poor in the system of virtual representation.

This account of the transition from the original council of all Saxon freemen to a representative estates assembly affords a recognition of change that is seemingly atypical of Whig historiography. However this change is not constitutional, and the fundamental role of the people within the ancient constitution remains the same. The Whig belief in continuity and immemoriality is not impaired by this acceptance of the evolution of the great council. The theory of the ancient constitution was premised upon custom, the continuity of the common law, and custom could be understood to evolve so as to preserve the past constitution within the present context.[80] The significance of the original and the ancient councils lay in the fact that they were inclusive, and the examples given of ancient councils emphasize their vast size, depicting a gathering of all the people. Since the people were always a part of the ancient constitution, the 'commons' were always present in a literal or a legal sense.

In defending the Whig position, Tyrrell engages in some inventive manipulation of ancient constitutionalist language. Here, in particular, he draws upon that other element of the common-law mind, the belief in the evolution of custom and the essential preservation of the past in its present context. Tyrrell acknowledges the Tory criticism of any simple continuity between the ancient and the present constitution; his admission of change is then used to the Whigs' advantage, furthering his conflation of people and council. *Bibliotheca Politica* presents a variety of Whig arguments in defense of the antiquity of the commons and the role of the people in the ancient constitution. It is argued that the commons are 'ancient', a part of the council long before Brady's date of 49 Henry III, existing since 'time immemorial'. The commons are also placed in the 'original' council, fixed in the Saxon institution of government, but also associated with immemoriality and 'time out of mind'. The origin of Saxon government in England is in some ways fixed, but it is also linked to the Gothic constitution and the prehistory of Gothic liberties; the Saxon founding itself occurred before legal memory begins, and in this way too might be associated with 'time out of mind'. In addition, the very notion of origins is linked to the theory of an original contract and an image of a state of nature, existing before time.[81] Tyrrell's conception of time is both linear and cyclical, incorporating evolution and recurrence, and offers a complex vision of the relationship between the past and the present.[82]

The subtlety and nuanced meaning of these terms was crucial to the Whig defense of continuity. Tyrrell's history delineated the gradual change from an original council of all freemen, to an ancient popular assembly, to an historical representative body. He charts the process by which a literal body of the whole realm might become a representative and symbolic body. But the emphasis upon continuity and the immemorial made possible, and plausible, the identification of the later representative council with the first assembly of the whole realm. The notion of the immemorial lent itself to a blurring of terms and contributed to the conflation of people and council. The idea of an assembly of all the people had both a literal and a legal meaning, and this duality was useful to Tyrrell. He contends that an ancient council was a meeting of an infinite multitude, and at the same time he acknowledges that the presence of the 'whole people' occurred in a legal sense, in a meeting of lawful representatives.[83]

This duality will recur in Tyrrell's defense of resistance and his explanation of the role of the Convention in 1689. A Whig theory of the Revolution, such as Tyrrell's, posited both that the people have a right to resist tyranny and that the great council, or Parliament, has the right to fill a vacancy in the throne. The Convention's declaration of abdication and vacancy established this ambiguity, asserting both that James II 'abdicated' by breaking the contract of government between king and people, and that the government itself had not dissolved but was merely suffering a 'vacancy'. There was a right of resistance and a devolution of power to the people, but there was in fact no dissolution and no return of power to the people.

Tyrrell's recourse to duality in his idea of the assembly of all the people – his conflation of people and council – is an attempt to explain this Whig defense of resistance. If the people are identified with the council, and the Convention is that council, he might justify resistance and yet not end with dissolution. Thus, in adhering to the sense of 'immemorial' as unchanging, Tyrrell's theory and history posit that the Convention is, literally, that original assembly of the people. Yet the 'immemorial' has another meaning, denoting tradition and evolving custom, and in this sense Tyrrell does not literally identify council and people but rather he sees the Convention figuratively, and powerfully, acting according to precedent and prescription. Tyrrell depicts the Convention acting in the stream of English history, on a continuum with the first body of the people that formed the council. The Convention is assuming the identity of the original council, that immemorial body, and is an extraordinary body acting in extraordinary circumstances as occasionally occur in English history.[84] According to this vision of history that confirms and perpetuates the ancient constitution of government, the Convention may be identified with both the body of the people and the original or ancient council. These shades of immemoriality, this blurring of people and council enabled Tyrrell to justify abdication and vacancy, resistance without dissolution or popular power.

Tyrrell's analyses of the Convention, of English government, of the Revolution, contain all the hallmarks of the common-law mind as it has been defined by Pocock and Burgess. It was, to quote Burgess,

> a complex fusion of the growing knowledge of change with the persistent idea of continuity. . . . The idea of custom that underlay

> this view of the English past was, thanks to antiquarian scholarship, not a piece of simple-minded myth-making. It was a complex and subtle piece of historical imagination, capable of recognizing change while seeing the basic form of the constitution (the nature of kingship, the role of parliament) handed down from generation to generation since the Saxons[85]

Burgess's definition of the common-law mind renders Tyrrell's insistence upon change and continuity, and his use of both a literal and a figurative identity between the past and the present, much more comprehensible. This balance of continuity and change was also based upon complementary notions of reason and custom which Burgess has depicted at work in the common-law mind.[86] For Tyrrell the ancient constitution was understood to be made up of fixed principles of natural law and reason which were worked out over time and in time, according to contemporary situations and needs.

There is in this balance of reason and custom, however, still some residue or suggestion of the immutable nature of the ancient constitution since all laws and institutions adhere to the same natural law and reason. For example, even though Tyrrell does not insist that the ancient constitution has remained literally unchanged since the era of the Britons, his *General History* does portray their government in a manner similar to England's ancient Gothic constitution. The Britons suffered no tyrants and their estates assembly had the power to resolve questions of succession and to elect rulers; and Tyrrell claims that it was their departure from this constitution and this society ruled by law that led to their downfall.[87] The emphasis on reason allowed for some acknowledgment of continuity between the ancient Britons and England's Saxon ancestors, and some idea of the fundamental constancy of the constitution.[88]

The insistence on continuity indicates what Glenn Burgess terms an 'evolutionary theory of history'. Whig history 'did not assert the identity of past and present,' Burgess explains, 'but it did assert that a continuous process had transformed the former into the latter in such a way that they were in essence the same.' In the end, Burgess concludes, the 'ancient constitution was not a state to which the English ought to return ... it was a state in which they still lived'.[89]

One way in which Tyrrell's thought differs from this 'classic' common-law mind lies in the role of contract theory in his conception of immemorial and immutable. Although laws and institutions may be seen as customary, and part of England's historical evolution, the original contract remains the same and provides another element of literalism in Tyrrell's use of the immemorial. Within his history of England's laws and institutions there is a recognition of change along the continuum between past and present, but there is also some reliance upon the immutability of the ancient constitution. Tyrrell purposely draws upon these two versions of the ancient constitution, and these two meanings of immemorial. The identification or conflation of past and present was useful to Tyrrell, and he relies upon this mentality, this common-law mind.

Methodology and the 'common-law mind'

The Revolution Settlement was far from secure in the 1690s, and in defending the Whig order Tyrrell relied upon common beliefs and traditional ways of thinking about English history and law. The eventual success of Whig history and theory lay in the exploitation of fabled traditions about an original people and an original council, as well as the manipulation of certain convictions concerning property, citizenship and representation.

Thus while Tyrrell relies upon the common-law mentality he also demonstrates an awareness that this was one way of thinking, one argument to be used among others. Although Glenn Burgess exaggerates the 'death' of the classic common-law mind in the 1640s, he is correct in perceiving that it is not a hegemonic worldview in the late seventeenth century.[90] A recognition of the variety of possible interpretations of England's ancient constitution is what leads Tyrrell to allow Meanwell to ridicule and challenge Freeman's conceptions of immemorial and immutable:

> [W]hat were the Commons of *England* as now represented by Knights, and Citizens, and Burgesses, ever an Essential *Constituent* part of the Parliament from Eternity, before man was created? Or have they been so ever since *Adam*? Or ever since *England* was Peopled? Or ever since the *Britains*, *Romans* and *Saxons* inhabited this Island? Certainly there was a time when they began to be so

represented, and that is the Question between us, concerning which, whether you or my self be in the Right, I durst leave to any impartial Judge.[91]

Here, directly quoting Brady, Meanwell objects to the manipulation of 'the immemorial' to mean ancient, original and even timeless. The Whig response is again twofold. On the one hand Freeman offers a fixed point for the participation of the commons, beginning with the institution of Saxon government. Yet he still employs the definition of the immemorial as timeless and eternal; the argument from prescription, the claim to participation beyond any time within memory, is a powerful element of the Whig argument. At this point in the debate, Tyrrell does call upon the authority of Coke for the definition of prescription and a claim to custom as 'time beyond memory' and 'continual peaceable usage'.[92] Freeman insists that this right of the commons has always been avowed and has always been believed, and that such belief is more persuasive than the arguments of antiquarians.[93] This reliance upon prescription and tradition in order to prove the antiquity and the character of the constitution is a reliance upon belief, opinion and common knowledge.

Tyrrell's strategy is effective as he challenges, adjusts and reaffirms Whig arguments. His imagined dialogues are particularly important because they demonstrate Whig self-awareness and the self-conscious desire to construct a persuasive history and theory. This self-consciousness is another way in which Tyrrell's political argument diverges from the 'classic' common-law mind depicted by Burgess and Pocock. This difference is linked to that typical Whig incorporation of contract with ancient constitution, to Tyrrell's use of other languages in conjunction with the language of the common law. A final, again related, difference lies in the fact that Tyrrell and his fellow Whigs used this language in order to defend resistance to – and not just limitations upon – a tyrannical monarch.[94] Yet despite these differences, Tyrrell's work is indicative of an enduring Whig tendency to think within the paradigm of custom, prescription, and immemoriality. Ancient constitutionalism was a central and necessary part of the justification of the Revolution of 1688; after 1660 the common-law mind may not be the only, but it was perhaps the most important set of conventions for the conduct of public debate.[95]

A self-consciousness with regard to method also permeates these dialogues. Tyrrell attempts to avoid anachronism in his writing of history, yet in so far as the Whig defense of the ancient constitution was a defense of the present constitution of government, the problem was inevitable. Again, Meanwell is given room to attack the anachronistic reading of the past according to the present.[96] Although Freeman is at times guilty of this distorted reading of the past,[97] Tyrrell ensures that both men display an awareness of historiographical changes and methodological critiques. Tyrrell's historical writing employs a mix of old and new methods: he relies on the medieval chronicle model of history as a compilation and conflation of different sources but he also demonstrates that Renaissance historical sense, that awareness of historical context and the differences between past and present.[98]

Indeed, humanist advances in historical criticism are evident in this debate. The problems of missing and corrupted sources are foremost, as Whig and Tory accuse one another of accepting 'monkish blunders' or fragmentary evidence.[99] The problem of bias and factional interest in interpretation is also acknowledged by Tyrrell, and charges of manipulation and distortion of evidence are traded. Tyrrell takes to heart the challenge of historical method, and is not simply allowing his Tory interlocutor to mouth the sentiments of Robert Brady.[100] These dialogues of *Bibliotheca Politica* are certainly an attempt to refute Brady but the work also seeks, in some fashion, to rise above polemic and to settle on some historical truth. This goal informed Tyrrell's choice of the dialogue form as a way to determine the truth through a comparison of opposing biases. In that dedicatory epistle, where Tyrrell presents *Bibliotheca Politica* as the fruit of his wide reading, he also promises to set down the arguments on both sides without prejudice or favor. 'I have carefully avoided all bitter, & reflecting language on either side,' Tyrrell insists, 'since I designe these Discourses for common places of Arguments, not forms of Railing; And I have also declined shewing myself a Party, or giving my own Opinion in any Question proposed, and therefore I have not made either of my Disputants converting each other to his own Opinion.'[101] Tyrrell proposes to leave the reader to come to his own conclusions, 'since I freely declare my design is not to write against any man's Opinion, as they are his', he adds, 'but only freely to examine them, in order to an impartial discovery of the Truth'.[102]

These claims about impartiality, rationality and active reading are repeated in subsequent dialogues. One good example is the author's preface to the sixth dialogue, which concludes with this guidance to the reader:

> All that I shall farther desire of you is, carefully and diligently to peruse the Arguments and Authorities, and to examine the truth of them your self, if you doubt any thing in them, weighing and comparing Historian with Historian, and Record with Record, and sometimes both together, as the Subject-Matter requires, and then I hope you will be able to make a right and impartial Judgment on the whole; For I have made it my Province fairly to report other mens Arguments and Notions, so it is yours to judge of them, which I heartily desire may be without any unjust Byass or Partiality to either side.[103]

This exhortation to the critical reader contains echoes of Bodin's advice to students of history in the *Methodus*: if the reader can recognize the interests of each author and compare both sides, he will come closer to an unbiased, true account.[104] Tyrrell also highlights the connection between the methods of history and law, conceiving of his dialogues as a trial of the evidence on both sides and of his reader as an 'honest unbyas'd Jury-man'.[105] By means of this careful and rational method, and the contest between these representatives of Whig and Tory, a complete Whig account should emerge from Tyrrell's dialogues, a justification of the Revolution and the Revolution Settlement that both sides might accept.

The proper Whig understanding of English history, and the belief that the Revolution had in fact preserved the ancient constitution, were vital to this acceptance. Tyrrell is positing, then, that the impartial reader who compared Brady's and Tyrrell's accounts might fairly be convinced by the Whig version of the past. Tyrrell's claim was not a disingenuous one. Certainly Brady's Tory history was advanced.[106] Brady's, and Spelman's, investigations into the impact of the Norman Conquest paved the way for a deeper understanding of feudal England, and of the administrative, conciliar, and judicial origins of Parliament in the thirteenth century. Yet Brady's history was also, like the Whigs', motivated by political concerns, and like Tyrrell's work it must be understood in that political context.

'[Brady's] argument and his evidence, though remarkably sophisticated, were not well integrated;' R. J. Smith cautions, 'moreover, he did not apply his analysis evenly, for his was an era which still thought the past in some sense controlled the present, and yet also thought in terms of sovereignty.'[107] Smith concludes that Brady's history of Conquest and of the feudal origins of Parliament was premised upon the assumption that these insights provided a defense of royal authority and a justification for the subordination of Parliament. Moreover, when confronted by the victory of his opponents after 1689, and pressed by the need to offer proof of James's cause through a history of lineal succession, Brady too was not above manipulating his sources to serve his cause.[108]

Tyrrell's Whig history was similarly mixed, a history deeply engaged in debate. This debate over the origins and role of Parliament focused on whether the early English Parliament was a representative assembly or an enlarged session of the king's council, whether it was primarily a political or judicial body, and whether it had existed since time immemorial. Like other Whig historians, Tyrrell sought to combat the growth of arbitrary power and theories of divine-right kingship with historical proof that England's earliest government included a Parliament that was a broadly representative institution. To this end he made those claims against Conquest and in favor of the continuity of expansive Gothic liberty, and the antiquity and continuity of Parliament. Theories about an original, sovereign people were tied to related historical ideas about the antiquity of Parliament as a representative, political body.[109] This Whig history was defensible in some of its claims about Saxon institutions – in its notions about elective Saxon kings, or the role of the Saxon council – and in its recognition of important continuities between Saxon and Norman England. This Whig history was much less secure in its insistence upon the antiquity of Parliament and its depiction of Parliament as the successor to Saxon popular assemblies.

Whig theory was not pure logic nor was Whig history wholly accurate – but Whig history was persuasive. '[I]t was to be their mode of thought which left the strongest mark not only on the conduct of political affairs, but also upon the study of history itself, and even upon political theory', explains Quentin Skinner. 'The "whigs" managed either to suppress or to adapt both the historical and the theoretical views by which their own ideology could have been most severely damaged.'[110] Tyrrell's dialogues demonstrate this Whig strategy. Indeed in offering a full and self-conscious hearing of Tory and Whig arguments, Tyrrell's dialogues demonstrate a reliance more on adaptation than suppression. They reveal the construction of Whig ideology. They are important because they demonstrate Whig self-awareness, a comprehension of the arguments arrayed against them, and a conscious effort to adapt these arguments.

4
Whig Theories and Theorists after 1688: the Case for Resistance

The challenge of analyzing and defending the Revolution and Settlement addressed by James Tyrrell in *Bibliotheca Politica* was a task undertaken by other Whig polemicists even before the completion of William's landing and James's flight. It was a task that would continue well beyond the thirteen years of William's reign. A great number of men set out to contribute to the public and political debates and in doing so these lawyers, clerics, doctors and dons drew upon the theory of contract and the tradition of the ancient constitution.[1] This literature provides evidence of theorists' reliance upon common ideologies, those standard definitions of people and citizenship and the accepted beliefs and traditional ways of thinking about English history and law, upon which the justification of the events and ideas of 1688–89 was based. James Tyrrell's *Bibliotheca Politica* was a part of this Revolution literature and his dialogues reflect the rich variety of argument put to work in these years. The political literature of the 1690s provides a context within which to read Tyrrell, illuminating the strengths and weaknesses he shares with others, as well as those areas where he diverges from or improves upon his contemporaries' work. Certainly Tyrrell was not the only author defending the Whig order in these years, but his *Bibliotheca Politica* offers the most comprehensive statement of Whig theory. Yet even as Tyrrell draws upon common beliefs, definitions and traditions, he also provides some unique answers to the problems of justifiable resistance, dissolution and constitutional change.

Whig Revolution principles included not only abdication and vacancy but also contract and resistance, and the theory of resistance offered by Whig authors demands careful study. Many Whigs offered an explicit defense of resistance in the years immediately following the Revolution, and their interpretation of the events of 1688–89 reached well into the next century, clearly perpetuated in the case against Sacheverell and taken up by 'Real Whigs' and commonwealthmen.[2] These Whig authors often left ambiguities in their own thought, at times offering variety rather than clarity, and modern scholars are surely right to emphasize the tensions and troubles of this Whig theory. It is important, however, to understand and appreciate the historical traditions and legal and political fictions upon which their ideas were based, and which rendered some of their more controversial arguments acceptable. This is to explore rather than excuse Whig resistance theory, to study how and why and in what ways it was effective and not merely 'wrong'. Again this will involve reading Whig literature in the light of Tyrrell's, rather than Locke's, work. Some of these Whig theorists linked contract and resistance with conquest in order to avoid the argument from dissolution and popular sovereignty. Others defended resistance and adhered to the notion of vacancy, offering arguments along the lines of Tyrrell's original Convention. Whig authors set forth a number of arguments and ideas and their theory was rich, and complex, and appealing.

Politicking, debate and settlement

A settlement of the nation's affairs was achieved in a hastily formulated compromise reached by the Convention within weeks of James's flight to France. The debates that took place in the two Houses offer clues to the meaning of the Revolution, and scholars have carefully studied the political strategies of Tory and Whig, the influence of Williamites and Jacobites, and the pressure of international affairs on the nature of the Settlement.[3] The Convention debates were part of, and reflective of, the public discourse surrounding questions of legitimate government, allegiance and resistance, England's constitution and the succession of the Crown. These debates and the Convention's resolution also fundamentally shaped political discourse by setting out the thesis of abdication and vacancy. Subsequent writers and politicians offered a variety of interpretations of this resolution. Whig and Tory echoed arguments made in Convention and called upon the same precedents and authorities as they sought to defend or to challenge the Settlement. Moreover, changing events, contingent political circumstances and the fragility of the succession continued to have an effect on the nature and defense of the Settlement in subsequent years.

Despite the well-choreographed efforts of the provisional government, the early days of the Revolution were characterized by confusion, drama, and a sense of the danger of civil war or foreign invasion. Although most men involved agreed that a Parliament should be convened, serious legal, political and technical obstacles stood in the way. Various proposals were considered before the expedient of a Convention was adopted. Loyalists eager to protect James II's rights maintained that some form of summons under his authority could be arranged. It was suggested, for example, that those who had been or could be legally elected under writs issued by James in November should meet, and authorize elections to the remaining seats.[4] Soon after James's first withdrawal, however, a number of Williamites introduced the notion of abdication – the notion that James had ceded his crown, his authority and his rights – and this idea spread, following the King's second, successful, flight to France. Some lawyers advised William to follow the precedent of Henry VII and to take the crown as a conqueror:[5] if William thus declared himself king, he would be able to summon a legal Parliament. Such a claim would have entailed not only an admission of conquest and deposition, and a contradiction of his *Declaration of Reasons*, but would have provided a possibly fragile *de facto* right to the throne.[6] William rejected this claim, and sought further advice from an assembly of peers.[7] The peers offered one final option short of a Convention: it would be possible to construe the withdrawal of James and his 'pretended' son as a legal demise, and to have a Parliament summoned under the writs of the next heir to the throne, Mary, Princess of Orange. This was not an attractive compromise to loyalists or Williamites, and it seems clear that William would have rejected it as well.[8] William and Mary's own demands, in particular their unwillingness to consider the possibility of a regency or the title of consort for William, were crucial to the character of the Settlement. Thus the problems and proposals considered in calling a Convention involved the same groups and interests, and highlighted the very issues of succession, abdication, conquest and the potential dissolution of government – with no Parliament possible upon the absence or abdication of a king – that that assembly would have to address. Thomas Herbert, eighth earl of Pembroke, introduced the Convention solution to the assembled peers on 25 December 1688.[9] Herbert was a moderate Tory who, a year earlier, had been dismissed as lord lieutenant of Wiltshire for refusing to aid in the remodeling of the municipal corporations. After the Revolution Herbert was reappointed to the lieutenancy and held other important government posts, including that of Lord High Admiral, under William and Mary and under Anne.[10] Herbert's plan to have William call a Convention was adopted by the peers and was seconded by an irregular, and predominantly Whig, assembly of commoners convened by William and drawn from London aldermen, common councilmen and the surviving MPs of Charles II's last Parliament.[11] The prince issued letters of summons to a Convention on 29 December. The Convention that met on 22 January 1689 was neither a constitutional convention nor a regular Parliament, but was a legally defective Parliament since it was not summoned by a king's writs under the great seal. It was an irregular assembly, the result of circumstance and political compromise, and so great care was taken to make this assembly appear as legal as possible. The Convention was to meet in the same place and in the same form as a regular Parliament, with two separate Houses of peers and commoners.[12] The Convention was also consciously tied to a longer course of English political events, traditions and ideas. It was regarded not simply as the result of the recent experience of abortive elections and contentious political debate during James II's reign; rather, the decision to hold a Convention, and the course of elections to and debates within this Convention, was believed to reflect the influence of selected precedents in English history. Frequent references were made to the accession of Henry VII, or to the fall of Richard II, but the Convention of 1660 provided the most recent and important precedent, lending political actors in 1689 a valuable association with the establishment of a legitimate king, and contradicting an association with the events of 1649.

The process by which elections took place was also designed to emphasize legal form and to mirror past elections to Parliament as closely as possible. There were elements of unavoidable divergence from normal procedures, but for the most part legal forms were preserved, and irregularities were tolerated in the interest of moving towards a solution of the crisis in government. The relative calm of elections to the Convention offer an impression of overall political consensus, but it was the long preparations of previous months that helped these elections to run smoothly and created an illusion of consensus.[13] Only a few of the elections were contested, and few of these were divided along party lines.[14] Once the Convention met, however, contests and maneuvering over the election of speakers, and for control of debate, reveal that even if there were fewer electoral party contests there was strong competition between Whigs and Tories from the very outset of the meeting. Within this split between Whig and Tory three main groups – loyalists, adherents of William, and supporters of Mary's sole right to the throne – can be identified. Further complicating these alliances were the myriad past experiences and connections, both personal and political, that tied many of these men together.

For all that the Convention shared with a regular Parliament, important differences remained. The absence of a king meant not only that there could be no legal summons, but also that there would be no lord chancellor, no opening of the session with the king's speech, and no members' sworn oaths of allegiance and supremacy.[15] Such irregularities were significant. For example, a Speaker *pro tempore* had to be elected in the Lords, and instructions to the Commons to elect a Speaker came from the Lords rather than from a King. Such expedient measures provided occasions for party influence and contest, and played a significant part in the outcome of debate. In the Convention House of Lords George Savile, Marquis of Halifax, was chosen Speaker. Although Halifax had refused to join the 'Immortal Seven' in the invitation to William, and was the senior commissioner for James II at the Hungerford negotiations, he had long been a secret supporter of the Prince of Orange's Protestant policies. Halifax effectively joined the Williamite camp after James II's first flight from London, serving as chairman of the provisional government from 12 to 15 December. In the Convention House of Commons Henry Powle, a respected, well-connected moderate Whig, was elected Speaker. Powle was a critic of James and opponent of the spread of popery since the 1670s (although not an Exclusionist), and was associated with the Williamite group even before the invasion.[16] The election of these two Speakers sympathetic to William and the Whig cause provided the Whigs with an advantage. With Halifax chosen as Speaker in the Lords and Powle as Speaker in the Commons the Whigs were able to thwart Tory attempts to have the debate begin in the more conservative House of Lords.[17]

After this jockeying for advantage delayed debate for almost a week, the question of the state of the nation was taken up in the House of Commons on 28 January. The debate was managed by Richard Hampden who had been a vocal supporter of Exclusion in the Parliament of 1681. Hampden had served in Cromwell's second Parliament and was the son of John Hampden of Ship Money fame.[18] His election as chairman of the Committee of the Whole was another Whig victory. In general, the proceedings actively involved only a small number of experienced MPs, and were dominated by a Whig majority.[19]

The meeting of 28 January ended with a nearly unanimous vote on the abdication and vacancy resolution, but only after hours of intense and urgent debate.[20] During the course of the discussion members considered all of the essential issues related to abdication, succession, dissolution, and conquest that would appear in the political literature for years to come. The debate revolved around the interpretation of James's withdrawal, and the possible consequences of this action. If it were taken simply to be a legal demise, an interpretation proposed by the first speaker Gilbert Dolben, the Crown would devolve to the next heir resulting in the accession of Mary, or at the very least leading to a regency established under William.[21] Dolben, a young Tory representative for Peterborough, was perhaps influenced by the advice of his uncle Sir William Dolben – a prominent Whig judge who had been purged by James II but who would be restored to the King's Bench in March 1689. Like his uncle, Gilbert Dolben was trained in the law, and his opening speech to the Convention was founded upon arguments from English history and law.[22] Three speakers were quick to respond to Dolben's proposed 'legal demise': the former Tory and now ardent Williamite Sir Richard Temple,[23] the Whig MP John Howe, and Sir Robert Howard, historian, playwright and Whig politician. These men objected to Dolben's narrow focus on James II's final acts of fleeing and sinking the great seal, and they insisted that James's violation of the constitution, of fundamental law and liberties, were what led to his abdication and a vacancy in the throne.[24]

The potential consequences of such abdication and tyranny were very different. The ensuing debate over abdication led to the articulation of ideas about contract as the basis of legitimate government, and the question of resistance to illegitimate rule. Howard, an 'unrepentant Exclusionist' and supporter of William's placement upon the throne,[25] was the first to introduce the theory of contract to the Convention debates in an attack on the theory of divine right. Howard insisted that royal power was derived from a compact between people and king. 'This original of power, resistance or non-resistance, is judged by the power resolved by People and King,' Howard explained. 'The Constitution of the Government is actually grounded pact and covenant with the People.'[26] Other Whig speakers not only joined Howard in depicting all government as a mutual compact, and the king's power as a revocable trust,[27] but they also offered concrete examples of the contract, and its violation, in English and continental history. A favorite reference was to the deposition of Richard II.[28] It was argued that once a king breaks the fundamental compact he is no longer a king but is merely a tyrant who may be resisted like any other private man. The experienced Whig MP Sir John Maynard explicitly linked the events of the Revolution with this understanding of resistance. Indeed, he advised his fellows that if James II were still recognized as a legitimate monarch and allowed to return to the throne, they would then be guilty of rebellion. 'I think if the King should come back,' he warned, 'every one that sits here now would be equally Criminall with any one that should attemt the King's life with a dagger.'[29] Maynard, an influential lawyer and long an active politician, was surely referring to debates he had participated in roughly forty years earlier. James II abdicated, or 'deposed himself' Maynard added for clarification, when he broke the pact with his people.[30]

In arguing for contract some Whigs made broad claims regarding the role and power of the people; such claims would later be moderated. For example Howard asserted that the consequences of James's abdication was a devolution of right and power to the people. 'In my Opinion the Right is therefore wholly in the people,' he claimed, 'who are Now to new form themselves again under a Governor Yet to be Chosen.'[31] In Grey's record of Howard's statement this image of the diffuse people re-forming itself is somewhat softened by the identification of the people with the Convention; Howard is quoted voicing his opinion that 'here is an Abdication of the Government, and it is devolved into the People, who are here in civil society and constitution to save [Church and State]'.[32]

The former attorney general, Tory prosecutor, and MP for Cambridge University, Sir Robert Sawyer, latched on to this question of a return of power to the people. Sawyer quickly sharpened the debate with his focus on the difference between abdication as a 'demise', and such total dissolution and popular rights.[33] Sir Heneage Finch, a fellow Tory prosecutor, former solicitor general and MP for Oxford University, joined Sawyer in underlining the danger of dissolution and devolution to the people. Dissolution, Finch warned, would result in the negation of all hereditary rights and titles: 'For if you take it as a Dissolution, then wee that sit here have no right to our Estates, there is a dissolution of that Right too.'[34] Like Sawyer, Finch urged agreement on abdication as a demise, and insisted that a simple demise and a vacancy in the throne would not entail dissolution.[35] Sawyer and Finch were long-standing opponents of Whig proposals and actions. Although both men had recently been active critics of James II, serving as counselors to the Seven Bishops, they had earlier worked together on the Crown's prosecution of Edward Fitzharris and on the *quo warranto* proceedings against the city of London. As attorney general, Sawyer had also been involved in the prosecutions arising out of the Rye House Plot and Monmouth's Rebellion; his targets then included Lords Shaftesbury and Russell, Algernon Sidney and John Hampden.[36]

Sawyer now offered the most trenchant criticism of Whig proposals, highlighting the inconsistency between positing an abdication based on contract, which results in dissolution, and declaring a vacancy in the throne. If government was dissolved and power devolved to the people, he argued, there would be no simple vacancy in the throne to fill, and no Convention of Lords and Commons to fill it. Sawyer effectively underscored the difference between a devolution to the people and the meeting of this Convention:

> If the Government be devolved to the People, Copy-Holders, Lease-holders, all men under 40s. a year are People – What needs the advice of the Lords to reduce things to a settlement? Is it not then the right of all the People to send Representatives, and our

sitting under this frame of Government is void, as we ought not to be here, so it restores not the rights of the Kingdom ... If the Government be devolved upon the People, what do the Lords there? And we are not the People.[37]

The Whigs are directly challenged to reconcile the claims of contract and popular power with the notion of vacancy and the role of the Convention. Whig MPs such as Sir Robert Howard, the dissenter and suspected Rye House plotter Hugh Boscawen, and the prominent Whig lawyer George Treby, responded to this challenge and this criticism.

In considering these responses it is useful, again, to keep in mind the history of cooperation as well as dispute between the Convention MPs. For example, Treby was also involved in some of the major legal cases of the 1680s: with his cousin Henry Pollexfen he defended London, arguing against Sawyer and Finch in the *quo warranto* proceedings; Treby again opposed Sawyer and Finch in the Fitzharris case, joining Maynard, Henry Pollexfen and William Williams on the defense team. Treby served as solicitor general in March 1689 and soon after became attorney general, in May 1689. Finally, Treby was, along with his predecessors in these posts and former opponents Sawyer and Finch, a member of the defense counsel for the Seven Bishops.[38] Now in this debate with Sawyer over abdication and contract Whigs like Treby and Boscawen reaffirmed the standard definition of the people as 'masters and freemen', and insisted that the Convention could stand for this people. 'I think wee represent the people fully, who did indeed originally represent themselves,' Boscawen explains, '... but that cannot be now they are grown so numerous & therefore they chuse Representatives for them, who represent them all.'[39] The original people all met in council, and the Convention is associated with that council. There is some suggestion here of Tyrrell's conflation of people and council in order to vindicate abdication and vacancy. Howard, too, identifies Convention and people, arguing that this care for the vacancy and preserving the succession has obscured the real danger, posed by the Pretender and the French king, and the real remedy at hand. 'Much is said of the Succession,' Howard complains, 'but we are the people; and threaten ourselves by ourselves when the question is asked, shall we dare to chuse?'[40]

The debate ended rather abruptly, as the attempts of a few Tories to redirect the committee's conclusions were quashed.[41] The final resolution asserted

> That King James the Second, having endeavoured to subvert the Constitution of the Kingdom, by breaking the original Contract between king and people, and by the advice of Jesuits, and other wicked persons, having violated the fundamental Laws, and having withdrawn himself out of this Kingdom, has abdicated the Government, and that the Throne is thereby become vacant.[42]

Only three members, the Tories Edward Hyde, Viscount Cornbury, Charles, Viscount Fanshaw, and Edward Seymour voted against the resolution, yet this seeming unanimity was fleeting. The issues of abdication, contract and succession were taken up the next day by the House of Lords and then further contested in a joint conference of Lords and Commons.

The Lords first debated the issues of vacancy and regency, and then looked to their legal advisors on the question of original contract. Sir Robert Atkyns, a distinguished jurist and a frequent opponent of the court in the late 1670s and 1680s, provided a legal defense of contract.[43] Atkyns called upon the authority of Richard Hooker and James I to provide assurance that this theoretical contract referred to the first institution of government, and the agreement between king and people to form a limited monarchy. The noted antiquary William Petyt linked this original contract to the introduction of the Gothic constitution in England by the Saxons, citing Henry Spelman and John Selden.[44] In the Lords' debate, Whigs provided further proof of the contract through appeals to the tradition of the coronation oath and precedents in English history and law. The House eventually affirmed the existence of this contract.[45] The definition of contract endorsed in the Lords emphasized historical traditions and offered an image of an original people in England, reflecting continuity in the common-law mind. These historical representations of an original contract were also a standard part of subsequent literature justifying the Revolution and Settlement.

The Lords accepted all but the abdication and vacancy clauses of the Commons' resolution and proposed instead that James had 'deserted' the government. They rejected any mention of a vacancy.[46]

These amendments were rejected in turn by the House of Commons, and abdication and vacancy were again debated in a free conference between the two Houses on 6 February 1689. In this conference the Commons' representatives insisted that James's actions were evidence of an abdication and not a bare desertion; and once again they employed the language of contract, in history and in nature. Not only long-established Whigs like John Maynard and John Somers but also John Holt, a frequent defender of the Crown throughout the 1670s and 1680s, now advised the Lords that James's despotism and renunciation of his trust, his breach of the fundamental constitution, amounted to an abdication.[47] Although their main task was to convince the Lords that this abdication and the vacancy of the throne did not entail a change in England's constitution, some Whigs went even further in defending the contract interpretation of abdication. For example, Sir George Treby insisted that the King's violations were extreme and widespread, resulting in an extraordinary crisis:

> It is because the king hath thus violated the constitution, by which the law stands, as the rule of both the king's government, and the people's obedience, that we say, he hath abdicated and renounced the government; for all other particular breaches of the law, the subject may have remedy.... but where such an attempt as this is made on the essence of the constitution, it is not we that have brought ourselves into this state of nature, but those who have reduced our legal well-established frame of government into such a state of confusion, as we are now seeking a redress unto.[48]

Treby's statement could be construed as a defense of resistance, and this alarming view of James's abdication and the resulting state of nature could not be reassuring to the Lords. Yet it was repeated by Maynard in his appeal to natural law as he defended taking those actions necessary in this time of crisis. 'If we look but into the law of nature (that is above all human laws),' Maynard states, 'we have enough to justify us in what we are now doing to provide for ourselves and the public weal in such an exigency as this.'[49]

The opponents of the abdication and vacancy clause in the House of Lords objected to these implications of constitutional change. At its worst, abdication and vacancy raised the problem of an entire dissolution of government, and at the very least seemed to entail a change from an hereditary to an elective kingdom.[50] The Commons' representatives denied any breach in the ancient constitution, pointing to historical and legal precedents as they defended the right of the Convention to fill the vacancy of the throne. Sir Robert Howard, for example, insisted that all public acts since the abdication had been legal; he cited the precedent of the accession of Henry IV as he claimed that the power to fill the vacancy 'is still, according to the constitution, residing in the lords and commons, and is legally sufficient to supply the vacancy that now is'. Howard added that the Lords might even have acted alone in this crisis, assuming their role as the 'great council of the nation' in the absence of the king.[51] Another Whig MP, Sir Thomas Lee, traced this right of the estates to act in such emergencies back to the 'original constitution in all governments that commence by compact'. Lee demanded of the Lords 'Whether upon the Original Contract there were not a power preserved in the nation, to provide for itself in such exigencies?'[52] Whig arguments set forth that combination of contract and resistance in accord with the ancient constitution. The nation reserved a right to preserve itself, and that right resided in the original council. Again, here are elements of that conflation achieved by Tyrrell.

The spokesmen for the Lords and Commons reached no conclusive agreement in this conference. Many of the Lords insisted that filling a vacancy in the throne would constitute a change to an elective government; they received no satisfactory answer from Whig lawyers as to whether the vacancy applied to James alone or to his heirs as well.[53] Yet the Lords were hard-pressed to identify who now occupied the throne. They too were accused of proposing constitutional change, and were confronted with the consequences of denying the vacancy in a pointed challenge delivered by Henry Pollexfen. Pollexfen, like so many others, was well known to his Tory opponents. As already noted, he was part of the defense counsel in the proceedings against London, the trial of Lord Russell, and the trial of the Seven Bishops.[54] In this debate Pollexfen argued that if the throne was not vacant then James II retained the right to be king, and he cleverly demonstrated that any other rule would be established according to commonwealth principles. 'But the right to be still in [James], to have a regency upon him without his own consent, or till his return, we take it to be a strange and unpracticable thing,' Pollexfen asserted, 'and would be introductive of a new principle of government amongst us. It would be setting up a Commonwealth instead of our ancient regulated government by a limited monarchy.'[55] This criticism may be taken as a direct challenge to the unusual alliance forming between the royalist adherents of regency and the commonwealthmen, who also hoped to delay William's accession to the throne in the interest of forming a new contract and constitution of government.[56]

The stalemate between the two Houses, between the advocates of regency or of Mary's accession and the advocates of joint sovereignty, was ended mainly through the influence of outside forces. William had already made it known, in a private meeting of lords, that he intended to accept nothing less than joint sovereignty, and Mary discouraged Lord Danby and his supporters from pressing her sole claim. Hours after the 'free conference' the Lords received word from Princess Anne: in the event that Mary should predecease William, Anne would temporarily waive her right to the throne. On that same afternoon of 6 February the Lords voted, 65 to 45, to accept the abdication and vacancy clause.[57] The final agreement was a result of this balancing of interests and parties but it also rested upon a decided ambiguity, the possible interpretations of abdication and vacancy. Contract and resistance remained one of the viable interpretations of the Settlement, and was an important part of the Whig justification of the Revolution.

The Settlement was achieved in part because Whigs exercised constitutional restraint as they sought not only to compromise with Tory conservatives, but also to resolve the struggle within whiggism itself between radical and moderate groups. Thus they advanced a notion of abdication and vacancy that would justify resistance to a tyrant, but deny either parliamentary supremacy or dissolution and popular power.[58] The formulation of the Declaration of Rights also demonstrates this moderation as Whigs moved to deny the radical implications of their theory of Settlement,[59] yet also confirmed that contract and resistance remained part of Whig Revolution principles. The enumeration of the more radical 'Heads of Grievances', as well as any reference to an 'original contract', were struck from the final declaration, but those elements of misgovernment and the violation of the constitution that comprised a contractual interpretation of abdication were reaffirmed. The Settlement thus appears as a balancing act, and the question of intention and control over that fragile balance has been frequently debated. There is some scholarly consensus that the Revolution and Settlement entailed what Howard Nenner terms 'the triumph of restraint over radicalism'. But there is no similar agreement as to whether such restraint was a result of deliberate political vision or confused and hesitant hedging.[60] Whig politicians and theorists have often been depicted as deluded, or as deliberately avoiding the most difficult and important legal and political questions. It seems to me, however, that while the Settlement and Whig principles rested partly on luck and political expediency, they also relied upon careful strategy and the manipulation of generally accepted principles of English law and history. These ideological underpinnings might be viewed as an effective political vision as Whigs purposively employed compelling legal fictions and potent historical traditions.

After the Revolution: Whig theory 1689 and beyond

The issues of allegiance, legitimacy, the nature of England's constitution and the nature of the Settlement continued to be contested, and the political landscape remained crowded with competing interests, parties and personalities throughout William's reign. Those events of the summer and fall of 1688 indelibly marked the Convention resolution, but ongoing issues and demands also influenced Whig theory well into the next century. For example, the new connections between foreign and domestic politics in William and Mary's reign were soon felt: the Prince of Orange sent a letter to the very first meeting of the Convention which reminded them of England's obligations to the Dutch, as well as the 'dangerous condition of Protestants in Ireland'.[61] The theory, and history, of the Revolution continued to develop after the speedy deliberations and actions of the Convention and it is essential to understand this development within the context of European war, commercial development, the 'rage of party', Jacobite threat and renewed questions about regency and succession which characterized William's reign.

The period immediately following the Revolution was particularly uncertain and tense. The demands of foreign policy, and William's personal involvement in prosecuting the war in Ireland and France, ensured that the legitimacy of the regime and the stability of the succession would remain active issues. In the spring of 1690 Parliament was again openly considering the question of the location of sovereignty, prompted by the prospect of William's departure for Ireland. A grand committee took up a proposed regency bill, and debated the meaning of joint rule and the state of the nation and the Crown in the event of William's absence.[62] The Jacobite threat at home was also an abiding cause of concern which was heightened by England's military and naval defeats, and fear of a French invasion in 1692. Disputes about allegiance and the legitimacy of William and Mary's right to the throne were fueled by the French and Jacobite threats, by the tenacity of nonjurors at home, and by the ongoing struggles over abjuration and treason trial bills. Whig Revolution principles were attacked in the contentious parliamentary session of 1692–3, inspiring fierce polemical debate in the political press. These controversies continued throughout the 1690s as other events posed new threats to the stability of the Settlement. In 1694, for example, Queen Mary's death provided occasion for fresh questions and attacks on William's 'foreign' rule. In that same year the Jacobite 'Lancashire Plot' was exposed. Two years later a conspiracy to assassinate King William was revealed at the same time that there was a renewed threat of foreign invasion. Finally there were ongoing debates about the Settlement, and Revolution principles, as part of Tory and Whig conflicts over the prosecution and financing of war. The constitutional compromise enshrined in the Settlement was challenged not only by Tory and Jacobite critics but also by the more radical branch of the Whig party itself, as mainstream whiggism became increasingly conservative and more firmly entrenched as the party of government, war and commerce.[63]

   The close connection between parliamentary politics and published debate is not surprising since most Whig and Tory authors were part of the political nation, connected to one another and to Parliament. These authors of treatises, poems, dialogues and diatribes on politics, history and law were gentlemen, clergymen, lawyers, dons, political hacks and former MPs. They knew one another at university, through their professions and their publishers, in political clubs and social circles, and were frequently related by marriage. James Tyrrell's experience, like that of Howard, Sawyer, Treby or Pollexfen, was typical of these relationships and interconnections. Tyrrell was not only associated with John Locke, and a member of the club that Locke founded at Exeter House, but Tyrrell was also engaged throughout his life with other scholars like William Petyt, Thomas Hearne and

Roger Gale in formal and informal debate over questions of law, politics and history.[64] Tyrrell was surely acquainted with other lawyers and political actors through his affiliations with Oxford, Gray's Inn and the Inner Temple as well as through his engagement in local politics in Buckinghamshire. Finally Tyrrell was associated by his sisters' marriages to the Whig freethinker Charles Blount, and to the son of the radical Whig Colonel John Birch.[65] Professional and personal life, scholarship and politics were the bonds that joined the members of the political nation.[66]

In the continuing debate over the Revolution and Settlement Whig authors repeated some of the arguments laid out by the Convention Whigs and offered some clarification of Whig history and theory. These printed texts relied on many of the same sources cited in the Convention speeches, such as Grotius or Bracton, and they referred to familiar historical examples like the deposition of Richard II. As these authors explored the meaning of the abdication and vacancy resolution a Whig theory of resistance was elaborated. Practical political concerns in the 1690s, as well as the implications of arguments from contract and abdication, ensured that a Whig defense of Settlement included a justification of resistance.

The momentum and range of public debate also affected Whig doctrine as extensive press activity guaranteed that the Revolution involved a large part of the political nation. Moreover, the manipulation of the press and pulpit by William and his adherents influenced the course of Whig ideology since the Court sought to propagate a 'doctrinal middleground' by which Whig and Tory principles might be compromised.[67] Whig authors articulated a theory of resistance as they sought to respond to a variety of competing doctrines. They confronted familiar challenges, posed by ideas of divine right and passive obedience, while they defended the legal authority of William and Mary against the threat of James's return. Although some Whigs relied upon claims of possession, conquest or providence in order to justify the Settlement, such arguments entailed the unwelcome possibility of further upheaval or the defense of absolutist authority and were not effective in securing the principles affirmed in 1689. Thus, at the core of the Whig interpretation of abdication and vacancy lay resistance.

An understanding that James's abdication resulted from his violation of the constitution and contract of government was upheld by these Whigs. In an echo of Temple's comments to the Convention, William Atwood contended that it was certainly more likely that misgovernment ended James's right than a 'supposed faultless desertion'.[68] In order to justify allegiance to William and Mary it was necessary to demonstrate that James II was a tyrant to whom obedience was no longer due. Like continental theorists of the previous century, Whig authors employed ideas about fundamental, inviolable laws, mutual obligation and contracts formed between rulers and subjects. A Whig version of contract was a crucial element of the public debate, just as it had figured prominently in the Convention debates. Many authors offered a rendition of historical contractarianism and argued that England's ancient constitution of limited or mixed monarchy,[69] was founded upon an original contract.[70] The theoretical original contract was identified with the ancient constitution and fundamental law. These Whigs relied upon common beliefs about English history and law, providing evidence of this contract in the tradition of the coronation oath and in those acts confirming Magna Carta and the Confessor's law.[71] A characteristic example is provided by Daniel Whitby, a clergyman and anti-Catholic polemicist who published tracts in defense of allegiance to William and Mary.[72] In his *Historical Account of Some Things Relating to the Nature of the English Government, and the Conceptions Which our Forefathers Had of It*, Whitby summarized the significance of the coronation oath in English history:

> Here then you see that *William Rufus, Henry* the First, and *Steven,* get the consent of the People by virtue of this promise *to grant them their usual Laws, and ancient Customs,* that *Henry* the First, *Richard* the First and King *John,* and *Richard* the Second at their Coronations oblige themselves by Oath to grant them; And upon these Obligations the People, Nobles, Bishops, and Commons consent to own them as their King, ... that all of them at the beginning of their Reigns by Oaths, or Promises oblige themselves to grant these Laws and Customs to the People, and that if any scrupled to do so, the Nobles thought it their concern to hinder his Coronation, till he had either made, or promised this engagement.[73]

In addition, these Whigs insisted upon the immemorial nature of English laws and customs and argued that they were confirmed by

William I, who was no absolute conqueror. The story of William I's acceptance of the Confessor's law proved the continuity of England's original contract and ancient constitution against the apparent rupture of a Norman Conquest.[74] 'And such Oaths have been made here, and in all other *Northern* Nations from times immemorial,' explained the author of *The New Oath of Allegiance Justified, From the Original Constitution of the English Monarchy*, 'Nor did the People think them Complements, because they charged the Kings afterwards with the obligation of their Coronation Oath.'[75]

The unbroken origins of England's ancient constitution were thrust back in time and linked to the Gothic constitution introduced by the Saxons. In response to theories of monarchical descent from Adam, and the patriarchal foundations of government, Whig authors disseminated the history of those people who were the source of England's ancient constitution.[76] The original people, those Saxons from whom the English were descended, founded governments based on consent and preserved their 'Gothic liberties'.[77] This Whig history of the Germanic freeman and his English successors confirmed the theoretical depiction of free individuals creating an original community and contract of government. The historical record of William I's acquiescence to popular demands to confirm the Confessor's law was also adduced as a reenactment of the contract between king and people.[78]

Whig history posited that the original contract was established by the whole community; throughout this history, the people depicted are fathers and brothers, bearing arms and free.[79] Moreover, these English founders are depicted as independent property-holders, parties to a contract that created a monarch limited by a popular council. The law of St Edward the Confessor which ordained the annual meeting of the folkmote, the general assembly or common council of the people, is cited as proof of the role of the people in the contract and the establishment of the ancient constitution of king and council.[80] The idea that the assembly of the people was coeval with the institution of monarchy was an important part of the Whig argument from history. This council could be associated with the whole body of the people since all freemen had a right to consent and contract, and Whig authors exploited this blurring, or conflation, of people and council.[81] In these ways, Whig theorists gave historical support to the idea of an original contract, emphasizing certain traditions about coronation oaths and Magna Carta, and repeating certain myths about the meeting of the people at the founding and throughout the history of the ancient constitution. A Whig theory of the original contract was often presented in historical terms, yet some Whig authors did advance a natural law theory of contract. They asserted that reason and nature demonstrate that legitimate government is founded upon consent, formed by a contract of free individuals in a state of nature. In the ongoing campaign to refute patriarchalist and absolutist doctrines Whigs argued that man is not born into subjection. Even a cleric and antiquary like White Kennett offered a natural law version of contract. Kennett, a firm royalist and defender of Charles II during the Exclusion controversy, began to change his political views in reaction to the Catholic policies of James II. Like Whitby, he preached against 'popery' and refused to read the second Declaration of Indulgence in 1688. His defense of the Revolution of 1688 included this defense of contract: 'That Nature obliges you to Obedience, is a great Mistake,' he explained 'for she constitutes no Subordination among Men; as we are produced by her, we are all Equals; she ordains neither King nor Peasant, Lord or Slave.'[82] The true influence of nature, he added, lies in man's subordination to its laws which guide him, through reason, to create society and government. Kennett states:

> The Laws she designs for our Guide, are her own Precepts; (*viz*) those Innate Notions of Good and Evil, those Common Sentiments of Vertue and Vice that are proper to all men, as they are Rational Creatures. The Governour she appoints over us, is every man's own Reason, the Judge, our particular Consciences. 'Tis indeed by the Force or Energy of Nature we are made Men, but we are born Free. This is evident from the absolute Authority every particular Man hath over himself, (*viz*) an independent Power in disposing of his own person.[83]

Kennett's depiction of man's natural freedom and absolute authority comes close to Locke's conception of the executive power of the law of nature.[84] It is posited that men originally live together in a state of nature according to reason and natural justice without a common judge. It is when this natural law is abrogated, and human freedom and preservation are consistently threatened, that government becomes necessary. Some Whig authors identified this change from a state of nature to one of war with the Fall of man, that subjection of human nature to sin and depravity rather than reason, and the introduction of conflict and power.[85] The insecurity and instability of the natural state contradicted the 'grand Principle of Nature', human preservation, and made society and government necessary. 'The great and fundamental Law of Nature is *Self-Preservation*,' explained Kennett, "tis the *Magna Charta* of all Constitutions, and the very End and Design of the Government itself.'[86]

Thus the law of nature, reason, and a concern for human good dictated the formation of an original contract. Some Whig theorists described this contract as a two-stage process, beginning with a social contract creating community and ending with what they termed, following the Civil War theorist George Lawson and his continental predecessors, a 'rectoral contract' and the election of a governing authority.[87] The anonymous author of *A Discourse Concerning the Nature, Power and Proper Effects of the Present Conventions in Both Kingdoms* clearly set forth these stages of contract:

> You must then consider, that in all Common-wealths constitute by Men, there must be two Contracts and Agreements. *Express*, or *Tacit*, by Word or by Deed; One amongst these Families who unite themselves into one Body Politick, whereby they are incorporate, and become one People, and for distinctions sake this may be called the *Popular Contract*: the other is between the Soveraign Power and the Body Politick, which two makes up the Common wealth, and settle the Government of it in such Person or Persons, and with such Powers as they agree; this may be called the *Rectoral Contract*, by which the Soveraign Power is to govern and protect the People in all their Rights, and whereby they become Subjects obliged to Obey.[88]

Like Locke and Tyrrell, this author tempers the idea of a moment in which numerous individuals gathered to consent by offering a conjectural history of the evolution of society through the formation of families. 'The Popular Contract must have been entered by the Fathers of the Families incorporated,' he explains, 'for before the Erections of Common-wealths there was no other Government amongst Men, but the Patriarchal Government of the Fathers of

Families, over their Wives off-spring and Servants, which was no less extensive ... than many civil Societies that now be and comprehended all Authority, Sacred, Civil and Criminal ...'[89] Here the definition of a free, equal and rational individual as a father, master or freeman is made abundantly clear, and it is assumed that even within a natural law theory of contract some individuals are born to subordination. Although the author is not assigning absolute sovereignty to the father and husband, he is defending the natural hierarchy of domestic society and the exclusion of women, children and servants from the social contract. Legitimate government is based on the consent of the original people who were fathers of families.[90] He adds that this initial social or popular contract must be entered into freely and unanimously since an individual is only bound by the decision of the majority of the community after he consents. The rectoral contract is formulated only after an agreement with regard to the details of the suffrage is worked out; the relative weight of different members' votes are determined, and in this way too citizens are defined and delimited.[91]

Once this community is united by the social contract, government is established. Whig consent theorists asserted that the law of nature ordains society and government, but the specific form of government is open to popular choice. Monarchy is not erected by divine right, rather government is a creation of the people with a power derived from God. It is argued that man follows natural law, in the interest of the preservation of God's creation, and transfers his individual power to enforce that law to a common authority. Matthew Tindal, a notorious deist and critic of Tory, high-church principles, was one who clearly distinguished divinely-ordained natural law from divine right. 'God, who is the Author of every good thing, may be said in a more special manner to be so of Government, because it is absolutely necessary to the Well-being of Mankind,' Tindal explains, 'and He, by the Law of Nature, which obliged mankind to act for their good, has instituted it, and has since by his Positive Law ratified it and confirmed it.'[92] Although this possibility for government is given to man through the divinely-inspired law of nature, the plan of human government is undetermined and left to free human choice. Tindal states:

> But there is no Law of Nature for any one Form of Government, so as to make the rest unlawful; or that one person, rather than

another should have the Sovereign Administration of Affairs: Nor can there be any one Law of Nature urged, why any particular person should have a Power over so many Millions of different Families, with no manner of relation and dependence one upon another, and who are by Nature equal beings of the same rank, promiscuously born to the same Advantages of Nature, and to the use of the same common Faculties: And therefore, it remains, That Government Must be derived from consent.[93]

Man obeys governmental authority, and agrees to relinquish his absolute liberty, because it is necessary for security and prosperity, for human good and preservation.[94] Civil authority is conferred upon rulers through compact, and this authority is a trust to be administered for the common good. Thus the rectoral contract may result in the creation of a monarchy or a democracy, among other legitimate forms, but it cannot establish a tyranny. Indeed the little-known author of the tract *The Defence of the Parliament of England in the Case of James II*, Sir P. Georgeson, employs this natural law reasoning to defend past instances of the deposition of tyrants who pursued an individual good and brought about a common decline and destruction. '[T]he practice of turning out Kings, ... doth plainly argue that the publick Safety and Welfare is by all manner of ways possible to be defended and secur'd,' Georgeson asserts, 'and that one single Person should not be obeyed, at the cost of indangering the whole Nation, is a Law I think Nature itself hath enstamped upon the Hearts of all Men whatsoever, now where Divine Laws are silent, who questions but that Nature may be listened to as a Deity.'[95]

Georgeson reveals the radical potential in the Whig use of contract theory when applied to the question of illegitimate government and the violation of natural and fundamental law. Whig theorists employed many of the same arguments used by John Locke and James Tyrrell concerning natural law, social contract and sovereign trust in order to establish that all legitimate government was based upon popular consent. It was not inevitable, however, that this contract theory would result in a radical defense of resistance. Most theorists combined natural law with more restrained historical arguments which did not invoke a state of nature and new foundations. Whigs provided examples of justified resistance, and some did point to depositions of tyrants in English history, as evidence of the traditional and ultimately constitutional nature of the Revolution.[96] Moreover, Whig theory was based upon standard, accepted ideas about social and political life. Although a few more radical Whigs imagined that these social and rectoral contracts included a broad spectrum of men, most Whigs considered the people of contract to be a narrowly-defined group of interested and eminent men; the makers of the theoretical social contract were the same fathers and freemen of Whig history. In general this 'people' could be identified with the representative body,[97] and the threat of a truly popular resistance by the 'rabble' – and the threat of real constitutional change – was diminished. It is certain, however, that the Whig interpretation of abdication, which insisted that the foundations of government lay in contract and consent, did lead these writers to articulate a theory of resistance.

Contractual resistance was defended as both a natural and an historical right. As Georgeson, and others, argued, men regain the right of nature when sovereign authority violates its trust and contradicts reason and human good. Again, self-preservation is seen as the fundamental law of nature, and examples are proffered of a wife's, child's or servant's right of resistance against a tyrannical patriarch even within these relationships of natural subjection.[98] The right of resistance was also authenticated by the history of ancient, continental and English governments, and it was argued that in legitimate polities based on contract there exists a constitutional right to resist.[99] Since England's kings were limited by law it was believed that allegiance was at an end, and resistance was justified, once these kings repeatedly broke that law and violated their oaths.[100] Finally, many Whigs called upon the authority of Grotius in order to add a more conservative case for resistance, one separate from contractual arguments.[101] They affirmed that obedience and government are ordained by God and that the subject has a duty of non-resistance, yet they allowed that there may be extraordinary instances of lawful resistance.

The learned rector Richard Claridge reviewed those exceptional circumstances enumerated by Grotius: resistance is lawful in the event of the abdication or alienation of the kingdom; when a king wages war against his own people or their property; and in the interest of the 'great Principle of *Self-Preservation*' as proven by examples taken from Scripture.[102] White Kennett also pointed to Grotius's endorsement of resistance in exceptional circumstances, such as the Maccabean revolt,[103] and even provided an exegesis of Romans 12 and 13 in defense of this kind of resistance. 'The Duties of Obedience the gospel enjoyns, is to Lawful Authority, not to illegal or imposed Jurisdiction; not an Arbitrary Power,' Kennett asserts. 'It condemns not our defending ourselves from apparent ruine and destruction; and permits us to dispute our Rights with our Princes, without that infamous Character of Rebels.'[104] Resistance at the Revolution was here justified by reference to the case of extraordinary necessity, when traditional rules of non-resistance are suspended. The appeal to resistance *in extremis* was a popular argument, and one sanctioned by the authority of Hugo Grotius, William Barclay, Thomas Bilson and William Falkner.[105] White Kennett's statement exemplifies the way in which Whig authors combined evidence from Scripture, history and nature in order to justify resistance.[106] These arguments were often used in conjunction with one another and shared a common focus on self-preservation, but within these justifications there remains a difference between the definition of resistance as an ongoing right, enshrined in nature or in the ancient constitution, and as a temporary exception.

Whig theory also sought to address certain questions and criticisms regarding the extent and timing of resistance. In considering whether the right to resist a tyrant is only reactive or encompasses preventive action, most authors reaffirmed the image of a cautious and reluctant people responding to a dire threat. More important, and difficult, was the question of the parameters of action in resisting: if the violation of contract legitimates resistance to, and perhaps even the deposition of a ruler, what are the consequences of this lawful resistance, and where does it end? Once again the crucial issue is whether violation leads to dissolution, and whether those who have a right to resist are also entitled to refashion the rectoral contract.

At this point, the differences between the justification of resistance according to history, nature or extremity become more significant, since each argument has the potential to produce different results. The defense of resistance *in extremis* and the defense of an historical and constitutional right of resistance both offer some safeguards against an entire dissolution of government, but neither argument fully confronts the question of the location of sovereignty. The belief that the duty of non-resistance may justifiably be abrogated in extremity does not explain who must be passively obeyed once the danger is averted. The historical argument runs along the lines of violation and abdication, which results in a vacancy within government which can be filled. Yet this vacancy only makes sense with an admission of parliamentary sovereignty, because otherwise a vacancy would signify a rupture in the sovereign authority and the resulting dissolution of the entire government. This problem was evident to the author of *The Anatomy of a Jacobite-Tory: in a Dialogue between Whig and Tory*. 'If you urge the *Vacancy*,' the Tory interlocutor argues in this tract, '... you must grant *that the Government was dissolv'd, every thing reduc'd to its primitive state of Nature, all Power resolv'd into Individuals, and the Particulars only to provide for themselves by a new Contract*.'[107] This is precisely the danger in defending the right of resistance according to natural law that the historical justification seeks to avoid. A natural right of resistance entails the return to a state of nature, the potential for constitutional change and the accompanying danger of popular sovereignty.

Dealing with dissolution

Some Whig tracts ignore these implications while others openly confront the consequences of dissolution and the question of parliamentary or popular sovereignty. As they interpret abdication and formulate a theory of resistance most Whigs do deny dissolution, and confirm the public explanation of vacancy instead, and many authors then attempt to provide some explanation of this apparently changed resolution. Here Whig history, and ideas about the role and identity of the council and the people in case of a vacancy, become crucial. For example, the anonymous author of *The New Oath of Allegiance Justified, From the Original Constitution of the English Monarchy* avoids dissolution by asserting a constitutional mechanism of self-preservation, 'some Power in every Government to preserve itself'. In a mixed monarchy, this is a power all three of the components of government have:

> [I]f one of the Estates will trangress all its Limits, and swallow up the other Two, they must then have a right to prevent this intollerable Mischief to the Community; and where nothing less can secure the Publick, than taking the Forfeiture; there they may do

it, yea, must do it, or the Legal Government would certainly be dissolved.[108]

When one part attempts to usurp the whole power of government, and thus change the constitution, the other parts have a right to assume sovereign authority. The author denies an entire dissolution of government and also skirts around the claim of parliamentary supremacy, reaffirming the ancient constitution of king-in-parliament and alluding to historical precedents for this constitutional solution. The council enjoys only a temporary authority and cannot assume total power or change the constitution. Indeed the council would not effect constitutional change, but would be sure to preserve the mixed monarchy of which it is a part.[109]

This idea of a body within the ancient constitution entitled to preserve that constitution was an important part of the Whig approach to the question of dissolution, but it came awfully close to a bare assertion of parliamentary supremacy. In order to soften this association of council and Parliament some Whig authors deliberately identified this constitutional body with the body of the people who originally contracted. This identification might also serve to eradicate fully any possibility for dissolution and popular power. Here the language used by Whig authors may be consciously signaling, much like James Tyrrell, a rejection of Lockean and Lawsonian solutions. For example, the author of *A Discourse Concerning the Present Conventions* says that the Convention represents the body of the people 'such as might have been before these Bodies Politick entered in a Rectoral Contract with the first Kings of the Race that now Reigneth'. He continues:

> and they are no Judicial or Authoritative Judicatures; and ... will claim no Power to make Laws, to judge Persons, or to impose Taxes. ... but do proceed by the Judgment of Discretion, not as they are Subjects or Parts of the Commonwealth; but as they are the Parties Contracters and must be considered as unsubordinate; for they were not Subjects in that Contract and therefore they have the same native and inherent right to deliberate, and resolve how far they were obliged by that Contract, and how far the present King hath observed or violated the same.[110]

The anonymous author of *A Political Conference Between Aulicus, a Courtier, Demas, a Country-man, and Civicus, a Citizen: Clearing the Original of Civil Government, the Powers and Duties of Soveraigns and Subjects* also contends that this body of the people can declare that the rectoral contract has been terminated. This tract then explains that the popular contract endures and that the people, as a council, now assume the power to choose a new ruler. The moderate spokesman, Civicus, states:

> ...there have been, may, and must be Assemblies not only founded upon the rectoral, but upon the popular Contract, as if the Royal race should fail, the popular Contract is not thereby dissolved: therefore the Citizens may assemble by themselves or their deputies, they may by a new rectoral Contract constitute the Monarchy in another Family, and in the case of the infancy, fatuity, desertion, or renunciation of the King, and not by any Law of the Kingdom, but by the Body Politick in their own proper right, which is not authoritative ... but they can only by the judgment of discretion declare their own right, as they are a Body Politick.[111]

The popular contract endures, and the popular assembly meets, but Civicus does not address the question of whether the government itself endures or is dissolved. The author is sidestepping the issues of dissolution and popular sovereignty by introducing this image of an assembly created by the popular contract. Yet he certainly recognizes the problem of dissolution, and the possibility of Lawsonian solutions which are articulated and dismissed by the 'Country-man', Demas. Demas relies instead upon the principle of *salus populi*:

> I shall not fall upon these debates, whether the Sovereign Power be ever in the People, or that they be two Supremes in the Common-wealth, a Majesty real in the People, and personal in the Prince. ... but there is yet a more universally acknowledged Principle, *Salus populi suprema Lex*: this is ever understood ... in the Contracts within the Common-wealth, where the interest of the whole must ever over-rule the interest of any part. So that to me it is clear, that in the present conjuncture of these Kingdoms, the safety of the People doth require a change of the Person in the Sovereign Power; and therefore these Meetings of the Body

Politick may warrantably set the Crown on the Prince of *Orange's* Head, who best deserves it at their hands of any mortal....[112]

Demas calls upon this principle in order to defend the Settlement and the power of the Convention to place monarchical power in William.[113] Yet this solution is still too close to an acknowledgment of the dissolution of the monarchy and an assertion of a constituent, rather than merely declaratory, power in the Convention. In response, Civicus further moderates these ideas as he seeks to deny any challenge of dissolution, popular sovereignty, or potential for constitutional change. He dismisses Demas's 'popular principle' and insists that England's is a successive monarchy, where the assembly of the body politic has the power to declare the succession but not to alter the original contract or constitution.[114]

The ancient constitution is seen to regulate and preserve itself. These Whig authors allow only certain constitutional changes, such as the securing of the Protestant succession, a just liberty of conscience, and the Union of the two kingdoms, to be effected by the body politic in Convention.[115] There are elements of James Tyrrell's political theory evident in these two tracts, in particular the conception of the identity of the Convention. However, these anonymous Whig authors do not admit dissolution, and do not conflate people and council in order to disarm dissolution. By contrast, in Tyrrell's *Bibliotheca Politica* dissolution and vacancy are made to work through the link of council and people.

Another interesting attempt to avoid the conflict between dissolution and vacancy, and to explain where sovereignty devolves, may be found in Thomas Comber's argument for dissolution and conquest.[116] The just conquest claim was widespread in the early 1690s,[117] and was assayed by Whig divines and Williamite propagandists such as Thomas Comber and Gilbert Burnet. But it also involved problems for Whig polemicists with regard to theories of consent and resistance, and called into question the stability and legality of the Revolution Settlement and regime.

Comber, an established cleric and author of well-known religious literature in the 1670s and 1680s, was an outspoken defender of Protestantism against popery and a critic of James II. He became a public supporter of William and Mary, preaching sermons and writing pamphlets in defense of the new government, and was rewarded with the appointment to the deanship of Durham in 1691.[118] In *A Letter to a Bishop, Concerning the Present Settlement and the New Oaths*, Comber defends allegiance to the new regime by adhering to the Whig understanding that James's abdication resulted from his acts of violation and misgovernment. In particular, the abuse of the dispensing power and the granting of military commissions to popish officers are identified as actions which entailed the total subversion of law and the dissolution of the constitution.[119] Within the ancient constitution of king-in-parliament, Comber argues, if one part alone makes law 'then the Constitution is at an end, and our Legal Government does cease'.[120] The fact that subjects are no longer bound to obey when 'the government of that person to whom [an oath was] taken is at an end' is Comber's strong persuasive to the nonjurors. His analysis of misgovernment is in accord with the historical argument for contractual resistance.

Yet Comber does not pursue the implications for popular sovereignty in dissolution and resistance, nor does he suggest that James's abdication resulted in a vacancy in the throne which could be filled by a sovereign Parliament. Instead he posits that James was justly conquered by William of Orange, that Protestant deliverer. Comber proposes that even if the image of James's active and voluntary abdication is subject to debate, all sides might agree that this tyrant was legitimately conquered. Here he employs one of Grotius's criteria for a just war and the *jus gentium* right of conquest: even if subjects had no right of redress and resistance against James, Comber explains, William had just cause to punish him for his tyranny.[121] The idea of conquest does not negate Comber's prior assertion of abdication and dissolution, since it confirms the analysis of James's violation and misgovernment. Although a right of resistance is not granted in this theory of just conquest, the analysis of abdication and dissolution may be maintained.

Comber advances a variety of arguments to appeal to a variety of consciences, and this leads him to affirm and to deny resistance. Yet this reversal allows him to avoid affirming abdication and vacancy, and to offer a coherent statement of dissolution and conquest. Conquest provides a way out of the difficulties of the Whig position on abdication and vacancy. The tyrant's abdication, which results in the dissolution of government, concludes with the devolution of sovereignty to the conqueror; this precludes a return to the state of nature, or a denial of dissolution and an insistence upon vacancy. This is a legitimist version of conquest, based on the conqueror's claim of right in a just war, and not a *de facto* argument for obedience to power regardless of legality.[122] Moreover, this conquest by *jus gentium* may still be consistent with, and derive legitimacy from, contract and consent. Comber insists that James II alone was conquered, and that a 'true contract' was established between William and the nation.[123] This just conqueror rules legally and not simply with force in a perpetual state of war, but the image of a contract between the conqueror and the nation assembled in Convention does bring Comber closer to an assertion of vacancy and the attribution of power to the Convention. William and Mary's claim to the crown by hereditary descent is added to the arguments from conquest and consent, and Comber finally bases their lawful title on conquest, succession and consent:

> ...the Prince and Princess of *Orange*, by reason of this Conquest of the King, and by Vertue partly of their own Hereditary Right, and partly of the Consent of the Nation assembled in Convention, are in Possession of the Crown of England, and do Protect and Govern the Nation according to the Laws of the Realm, and have taken the Coronation-Oath, that they will always continue to do so [.][124]

The just war theory of conquest was a useful salve for the troubled consciences of nonjurors, and it seemed to offer a way out of the difficulty of dissolution. If it is clear, however, that Comber simply substituted one difficulty for another, perhaps he was prudent in offering a conquest argument that was, for some, more tolerable than the fiction of vacancy. Conquest was troubling, however, within the Whig justification of the Revolution because it denied Whig resistance theory, even construed purely as resistance *in extremis*.[125] It should be noted, too, that for Comber, who was actively engaged in resistance at the Revolution and participated in the takeover of Durham,[126] the abandonment of a theory of resistance had practical as well as theoretical meaning. Moreover, there were many other reasons why even a just war version of conquest was threatening to Whigs and the Revolution Settlement. In these years of Jacobite threat and fears of a French invasion it was essential to promote the stability of the regime, and not to disseminate arguments indicating that England's government might be vulnerable to future just war and conquest. The admission of conquest also tended to undermine consent and the tradition of the ancient constitution, even though it might be asserted, with an authority derived from Grotius, that a conqueror assumes only those rights and powers enjoyed by the vanquished monarch. Finally, the just war claim also involved certain fictions – of William's open declaration of war, his status as a sovereign prince and his limited conquest of James II – that opponents could attack.[127]

Thomas Comber admits dissolution, but at the price of abandoning resistance. Other theorists, such as James Tyrrell, maintain a right of resistance and acknowledge dissolution, yet still attempt to reconcile this with the thesis of vacancy. The key for Tyrrell lies in his conception of the identity of the Convention. Many Whigs share Tyrrell's ideas about the origins and history of the great council, and the definition of the people; a few others also make the move from dissolution to vacancy, but do not rely upon this conflation of people and council. A focus on the theory of resistance set forth in *Bibliotheca Politica*, and a comparison of Tyrrell's theory with the works of other Whigs who posit abdication and resistance, dissolution and vacancy, will provide greater insight into Whig Revolution principles. Finally, an appreciation of the Whigs' approach to dissolution, and their confrontation with the ideas of Lawson and Locke, should yield a better understanding of the proper context within which to read the theory of resistance set forth in the *Two Treatises of Government*.

5
Resistance in Tyrrell's *Bibliotheca Politica*: the People and the Convention

The debate of 28 January in the Convention House of Commons concluded with the famous abdication and vacancy resolution. It is clear from this debate and the subsequent literature, however, that other significant currents of thought were present in the Convention debates held that winter. Crucial issues and questions were raised to which abdication and vacancy were not the only answers. This resolution left intact the problematic, and potentially revolutionary, assertions of either parliamentary or popular sovereignty. Although the contention that James II 'broke' an 'original contract' was eventually denied, the implications of contract theory had to be addressed and rendered acceptable to members of the political nation.

Most historians agree that ideas about contract, whether of government or less commonly of society, were part of the ideology of 1688–89.[1] Medieval ideas about contract between ruler and ruled were set forth along with emerging theories of social contract; it was the interpretation and use of contract theory, and by implication the roles of the people and of Parliament, that were at issue. The Convention's use of contract theory in its resolution exemplifies what Harro Hopfl and Martyn Thompson have identified as the language of 'constitutional contractarianism', with its emphasis on fundamental law, original contract and ancient constitution.[2] When the explicit reference to contract was removed from the official declaration it remained, unspoken, in the notion of abdication: James II abdicated by subverting the constitution, violating the laws and withdrawing from England, all of which involved a failure of the contracted responsibility to govern. A rationalization of resistance was also an integral part of even a moderate formulation of the abdication and vacancy explanation. Whether James II abdicated willingly or willfully he ceased to be king, and by most accounts became a tyrant. At the very least, a king who deserts his kingdom was not believed to enjoy unconditional allegiance and might indeed be refused obedience.[3]

Theories of contract and of resistance were unavoidable in the debate over the events of 1688 but they were also unpredictable. Contract theory easily led to questions of dissolution, deposition, devolution of power to the people and even decapitation, the terrible example of 1649. The Convention was all too aware that with abdication and vacancy it left such consequences ambiguous and unattended. The dangerous implications entailed in advocating abdication and contract were easily underscored by a Tory like Sir Robert Sawyer. Sawyer's challenge to his colleagues in the Convention was pointed, and bears repeating as it appears in another record of the debates:

> I think the Disposall of the Crown is not in the people, for if it be, What do the 2 Estates do in the other House? Or what Do wee Do here? Wee are not the People collectively or representatively. . . . I say again that wee do not represent so many as the 4th part of the Nation, for there are freeholders under 40 shillings a year & all Copyholders, & Women & Children & Servants. All these have no votes in chusing Knights oth Shire or Citizens or Burgesses unlesse they are freemen, & I suppose nobody can deny that they are 3 times as many as those that do chuse us. Therefore they must be consulted before wee can take upon us to dispose of the Crown, if the Right of Disposing it be in the People. . . . If the People have the Power of disposing of the Crown, which I beleeve they have not, but suppose they had, Wee are not the People. [4]

Sawyer laid bare the radical conception of the role of the people and the nature of government towards which the justification of 1688 was tending. If it was acknowledged that contract was implied in England's system of government, and if versions of contract were familiar to contemporary minds, it was less apparent just how this contract operated in reality and what elements of society were involved.

James Tyrrell struggled with these questions in his *Bibliotheca Politica*. Indeed, these conversations between Freeman and Meanwell, Whig and Tory, may be seen as an extended, and extensive, Convention debate. Tyrrell deliberately framed these dialogues as first taking place during the uncertain days after 'the late King James' first Departure', and continuing through the troubled winter days of 1689 when the Convention was considering the state of the nation. In these dialogues Tyrrell incorporates Whig historiography and reconsiders the argument from contract and the question of resistance. In justifying resistance and contract Tyrrell constructs an interpretation of the identity of the Convention, and an assessment of its actions, that harmonizes the notion of contract and natural law with the traditions of the ancient constitution and England's social structure. In this explicit defense of resistance we see the final convergence of Whig historical and theoretical arguments.

The dialogues provide a justification of the Revolution which rests upon a conception of resistance as both a natural and an historical right. Contract theory and resistance to tyrants appear in Whig polemics such as Tyrrell's much as they informed the Convention debates. Tyrrell's theory of government begins with the premise that sovereign authority is a trust which is revocable if abused[5] and, like some other Whigs, he advances a natural law theory of contract.[6] He ensures that his Whig spokesman, Freeman, adheres particularly closely to Samuel Pufendorf's explication of the origins of civil government:

> First, It is without doubt that right Reason sufficiently taught Mankind when it began to multiply, and that they were sensible from the great wickedness and corruptions of mens Natures that their common peace and safety could not be well maintained unless Common-Wealths were instituted, which could not subsist without a Supream Authority placed in some one, or more persons. This being a dictate of the Law of Nature or Right Reason, and so highly conducing to the good of Mankind, it must needs owe its original to God the Author of all Truth, and the Giver of every good and perfect Gift.[7]

Here the original action and consent of the people is found consonant with natural reason and divine law, and divine right and absolute sovereignty are again negated.

The influence of continental thought is evident as Tyrrell, like other English theorists, relies on the monarchomach tradition that civil authority derives from God via the community.[8] Tyrrell emphasizes this role of the community in the origins of government, allowing Freeman to employ increasingly abstract language:

> This being setled, your Objection is easily answered, how Civil power can be conferr'd without an immediate conferring of it from God, since the people in the state of Nature had it not before; which proceeds from your not considering, that this Supream Authority is not like the Soul of Man, an immaterial form, that gives knowledge and understanding to the Body, and may be separated from it; but is only a moral quality which may be produc'd by the mutual consent of those that institute it, as the productive cause thereof, tho' they had it not formally in themselves before, just as from many Voices singing in Consort, though in different Tones there arises a Harmony, which was not in any single Voice alone.[9]

This explanation of the origins of civil government follows the account given by other theorists of social contract by positing an original state of nature from which reason led mankind to form a commonwealth. The social contract theory of James Tyrrell diverges from Pufendorf's analysis in its theoretical acceptance of this initial natural state.[10] However, in order to deflect critics' scepticism about a mythical moment of harmony and consent Tyrrell, like his friend John Locke and like other Whig authors, concedes that civil government might well have evolved through family government and consent to patriarchy.[11] Popular consent and contract are a constant feature of their founding stories of civil government, whether depicted in a moment of agreement between reasonable individuals or in the slow evolution of families.

The reality of an original contract is further defended by reference to the unwritten constitution and fundamental laws of England. Here Tyrrell exemplifies what other scholars also see as the Whig tendency to 'conflate the contract theory with the more conservative notion of the ancient constitution',[12] as he moves from a theory of contract based solely on reason and natural law to consider contract as an aspect of the ancient constitution. This theory of contract largely fuels his study of the history of limited monarchy and of the antiquity of the English Parliament. The Whig Freeman reminds his Tory friend that all Englishmen, including some of the Stuart kings themselves, have long recognized the existence of a fundamental constitution and contract:

> ... for as that Statute of King *James* I. sets forth ... and your self have already acknowledged, there are such things as Fundamental Laws, (that is, Laws that are as antient as the constitution of Government) there must have been also an implicit Fundamental Covenant or Contract on the Kings part, that he would maintain them, without any violation, and this is what we mean by an Original Contract.[13]

Like many Whig theorists, Tyrrell calls attention to the declarations of James I and the coronation oaths of England's kings in order to prove the existence of an original contract. When pressed to explain the substance of this fundamental law Freeman points to the immemorial rights and liberties contained in Magna Carta and the Petition of Right: life, liberty, property and religion. These abstract rights are made concrete in his subsequent elaboration of habeas corpus, trial by jury, consent to taxation and quartering of soldiers, and the election and meeting of Parliament.[14] Both the theory of natural law and contract and the tradition of England's fundamental constitution were adduced to prove that England was ruled by a monarchy founded in contract and limited by law.[15]

Dissolution and the people

These conceptions of contract, law and trust were vital to the justification of the right of resistance set forth in *Bibliotheca Politica*. Through his Whig spokesman Freeman, and through the revelation of his own position in his frequent prefatory comments, Tyrrell demonstrates that he is in agreement with those members of the Convention who asserted that a king abdicates his position when he violates his trust. In violation and abdication that king is considered to have become a man who may be resisted like any other. James II's extension of his prerogative, especially his thorough exercise of his dispensing power, was seen to be just such a breach of trust.[16] Once James II ceased to govern in accordance with law he became a tyrant and left off being king. Now, resistance to a tyrant may be lawful whereas disobedience to the king is not. This kind of resistance was deemed to be against illegal force, the kind of force embodied by the king's standing army, and was not strictly directed at royal authority.[17] Tyrrell cites the authority of Hugo Grotius and Samuel Pufendorf in order to confirm this right of resistance; like others, Tyrrell also points to the authority of the 'Romish author' William Barclay, a well-known opponent of resistance theorists like George Buchanan, in order to affirm this truth.

> Can there *no Cases* happen in which it may be lawful for the *People* by their *own Authority*, to rise up, and *resist* a King governing *Tyrannically?* [Barclay's] Answer to this Question is, there are certainly *none* as long as he continues *King*. ... Therefore the People can have no Power against him, unless he committeth something, by which he may *cease* to be *King*; for then he himself *abdicates* his Kingship, and becomes a *private Man*, and by this means the *People* being made *Free*, that Right returns to them, which they had before the King was made.[18]

This assertion that the king who rules tyrannically ceases to be the true ruler of the community lies at the heart of the abdication thesis. Indeed, part of this understanding of abdication is the idea that such a king deposes himself.[19] In exploring this connection between abdication and self-deposition Tyrrell offers an interesting challenge to the traditional image of the body of the commonwealth made up of head and members. Tyrrell explains that when a king sets up a separate interest contrary to the public good he ceases to be a true head. When associated with head and members imagery the notion of abdication might even recall decapitation, but performed by the king himself. Tyrrell's Freeman states:

> ... I affirm that a Natural and Political Body do wholly differ in this matter; for in a Natural Body, the real good of the head cannot be separated from that of the Body, nor the good of the Body from that of the Head, nor yet can the Body alone Judge of the proper means of its own preservation, nor when it is hurt or assaulted, but by the head, which is the principle of sense and motion; but in a Political Body it is quite otherwise; for first, the

Supream Powers of a Common-wealth, which you suppose to be the Head of this Political Body, do often pursue and set up an interest quite different from, (nay contrary to) that of the Body or People, and that not only to their prejudice, but also sometimes to their destruction; and that when they do this, the Political Body, or the People will in evident and apparent cases Judge for themselves, let this Political Head say or declare what it will against it, and will when they are thus destroyed, opprest, and inslav'd, by those that they have submitted to as their Political Heads, and in such cases of extremity, endeavour to free themselves from the severity of their Yoke.[20]

In this analysis such destruction and oppression constitute a war waged by the ruler against his own subjects. In cases of such extremity the people have a natural right of resistance for self-defense.

This natural right, 'that which is *Prior* to all Civil Laws, the Right of Self-defense, or Preservation',[21] is the essence of Tyrrell's justification of resistance. He is careful to have Freeman refute the Tory argument, given voice by Meanwell, that allowing this right of resistance implies recognition of a power superior to the king. Thus Freeman asserts that resistance for self-defense is not an authoritative act of punishment or judgment. Rather, it is a natural right conditionally given up upon entering civil government and resumed, by necessity, for the preservation of self and family.[22] This natural right of self-preservation follows from a state of nature which is now closer to a state of war than a sociable, reasonable existence.

It is at this point that Tyrrell confronts those consequences of contract and resistance – the threat of dissolution and popular power – which Sawyer had expressed so powerfully in his speech to the Convention. In the third dialogue of *Bibliotheca Politica* Tyrrell strongly affirms that the community possesses a natural right of resistance. Further, he contends that this right may be exercised once a prince tyrannically dissolves government and destroys the peace of civil society. Tyrrell's Freeman argues that when civil authority exceeds its bounds, the '*Civil Government* is as much *Dissolved* by such *Violent Actions*, as if a *Forreign* Enemy had broke in and *Conquered* the Country'.[23] Tyrrell is careful here to associate conquest with a tyrannical king, bolstering his arguments against Tory claims about the impact of the Norman Conquest, and also against current notions that William III's rule was justified by conquest theory. For Tyrrell, the Whig justification had to do with contract and consent, and not with conquest. Finally, the *Two Treatises of Government* are cited here as a source for Freeman's consideration of the dissolution of government. He states that

> the Question still is, whether, when a Prince makes *War* upon the *People*, or goeth about to *destroy* them, there is then any *Civil Power* in being; and whether the *Government* be not already *dissolved*, since the *main Ends* of Government, viz. the Good and Preservation of the Subjects, are quite destroyed. ... So then, if such *absolute Arbitrary Power*, in Princes, or States, can never consist with the *main Ends* of Civil Society, the Peace & Happiness of the Subjects, it is plain that when ever they are reduced to such a State, they will look upon themselves as again in the *State of Nature*. ...[24]

Although Freeman is questioned and challenged by his Tory opponent, he does not swerve from his defense of resistance or the terrible consequence of dissolution. He concludes:

> I do not in any Case whatever allow of *Resistance*; but only in these *three necessary* ones: When the Lives, Liberties, or Estates of the *whole People*, or the *greatest part* of them, are either *actually Invaded*, or else *taken away*, and when they are *Reduced* into so bad a Condition, that a *State of War* is to be *preferred* before such a *Peace*; and when the *End* of *Civil Government* being no longer to be *obtained* by it, the *Common-Wealth* may be lookt upon as *Dissolved*.[25]

This assertion of the dissolution of government raises questions about the devolution of power, the role of the people in the absence of government, and even the possible dissolution of society and reversion to a 'pure' state of nature. Tyrrell reaches dissolution in the third and fourth dialogues, and this theme reappears in later dialogues as well, but unlike Locke he does not end with the notion of dissolution. Tyrrell cites the *Two Treatises* but he doesn't rest with its authority, and instead he responds to and adjusts the conclusions drawn by his old friend.

In its entirety *Bibliotheca Politica* shows the whole conflict between contract theory and Whig problems of justification, and demonstrates the ways in which contract and resistance were tempered by appeals to history and to theories of representation. The movement of Whig theory towards recognition of popular power was generally unacceptable and subject to fierce criticism. The all too recent experiences of Civil War and Commonwealth were used equally to exemplify the terrors of popular sovereignty and the dangers of parliamentary supremacy. And so in the course of these dialogues Tyrrell affirms the devolution of power to the people and then tempers this conclusion with appeals to history, to the force of social order and custom, and with an analysis of the identity of 'the people'.

The critique of the idea of dissolution of government, as well as the attack on a natural right of resistance and return of power to the people, is openly addressed in the debate between Meanwell and Freeman. In dealing with this question of dissolution Tyrrell's dialogues explore the problem of the location of ultimate authority but consciously reject the solution of constituent authority of the people proposed by John Locke, or real majesty proposed by earlier continental and English theorists like George Lawson or Christopher Besold.[26] Tyrrell's response to Locke and Lawson on dissolution and resistance affords some insights into the contemporary understanding of these ideas.[27] Tyrrell has his Tory spokesman articulate the threat of this notion of real majesty implicit in the idea that power devolves to the people after abdication and dissolution have occurred. Meanwell warns his opponent that

> upon this Hypothesis of yours is founded that desperate Opinion concerning the real Authority or Majesty of the People; which the Common-Wealths-men suppose still to reside in the diffusive body thereof after the Government is Instituted; And by vertue of which they suppose there still remains a power in them to call their Kings or Governors to an Account, and punishing them for Tyranny or any other supposed Faults against the fundamental constitution of the Government, or the Original Contract, as those of your party are pleased to term it.[28]

This deliberate rejection of a distinction between real and personal majesty also appeared in Tyrrell's earlier work, *Patriarcha non Monarcha*, and is there identified with Samuel Pufendorf's critique of these concepts. In criticizing the absurdity of this distinction Pufendorf adds: 'There is no necessity to create a double majesty, for the reason that at the death of the king, or the extinction of the ruling house, the people regains its right, in so far that it may, as it sees fit, set up another king, or establish another form of state.'[29] Now that Tyrrell is defending resistance, Meanwell's accusation is contrived to go to the heart of the problem of defining and limiting 'the people' that plagues Tyrrell throughout *Bibliotheca Politica*.[30] The defense of a natural, universal right of resistance, and the notion of a devolution of power to the people, makes this definition the key to refining and resolving the dangers associated with the Whig defense of the Revolution.

Now Tyrrell also seeks to delimit the possible interpretations of his theory of resistance by focusing upon the definition of this people. First, he continually reaffirms that the right of resistance lies in the whole people, consisting of clergy, nobility and commons, and not in a mere faction nor simply in the 'rabble', 'vulgar' or 'mobile' part.[31] Moreover, the actions of this whole diffusive body of the people are said always to be commanded by the better sort, the more eminent members. Examples such as Wat Tyler's revolt, anti-popery riots or the English Civil Wars are used to distinguish between rebellions made by the rabble, or incited by faction, and justifiable resistance and change, led by nobility and gentry, the 'considerable part'.[32] This depiction of the people reflects the tension inherent in Tyrrell's attempt to reconcile the theoretical body of the people of contract broadly conceived, with the people recognized by English history and law. The familiar dual identity of the people, portrayed by most theorists as both subjects and citizens, is further complicated here by the practical distinctions made between subjects and those recognized as full citizens in England's system of virtual representation. Following established tradition, and echoing both mid-century parliamentarians and medieval conciliarists, Tyrrell assures his readers that when he posits the people as the primary source of power, he is referring to the '*sanior pars*', the responsible, rational and recognized members of society.[33] The admission of a right of resistance, and the possible devolution of power to the people, are rendered less threatening by Freeman's insistence that the whole people must act in concert, 'led by the Nobility and Gentry thereof'.[34]

Tyrrell builds upon the narrative and analysis of English history set forth in his previous dialogues and further circumscribes this definition of the body of the people by pointing to its identification with an historical people. Numerous examples of the exercise of power by the English people brought about by failed succession, breach of fundamental law, forfeiture or even deposition, serve to connect this notion of the 'whole diffusive body' to a coherent and comprehensible historical norm. Tyrrell points to the resistance of the English people against the evil ministers of King Richard I, against King John before that king's granting of the Great Charter, and the people's resistance against Kings Edward II and Richard II.[35] What the people have accomplished in the past, without anarchy or social upheaval, they may accomplish again. This constant movement between theory and history informs Tyrrell's conception of the people. Finally he turns to consider the original people, the body that first established civil authority and to whom this power returns, in order to complete the mixture of history and theory and render an acceptable solution to the problem of 'the people'.

Freeman, Tyrrell's Whig spokesman, initially posits that at the first institution of government the people reserved a right of judging 'concerning their own Preservation and Happiness and all means necessarily tending thereunto'.[36] This theoretical occurrence is confirmed by England's own experience as Freeman asserts that at the founding of England's limited monarchy this right of judging, of self-defense and the common safety, was indeed reserved.[37] Although he acknowledges that changes have occurred since 'the English Saxons did often exercise that Power they had reserved to themselves of Electing and Deposing their Kings', examples of resistance and deposition even from 'as high as the Times of the Kings of the West Saxons' are linked to the later examples.

> So that tho' I will not bring the Custom of the English Saxons as a precedent for the Parliament's deposing of the King; yet I think I may make use of it thus far, that this Nation has ever exercised the necessary Right of defending their Liberties, and Properties, when invaded by the King, or his Ministers, either by colour of Law, or open Force: And that this hath been the constant practice from almost the Time of the Conquest down to later Ages, I think I can make out from sufficient Authorities, both from Histories and Records.[38]

Freeman concludes this narrative with an account of his own times. He asserts that once James II violated the fundamental constitution legal authority devolved to this original people; it became 'forfeited to the People who at first conferr'd this Power on the first King of the West Saxons'.[39] Characteristically, Tyrrell here emphasizes continuity and immemoriality and denies the impact of the Conquest. However, the conception of the people offered here, although historically and theoretically grounded, will leave Freeman open to the charge that he ignores subject status and supposes a superior authority, or real majesty, in the people.[40] Tyrrell must have Freeman reject the claim that this Whig theory makes the promiscuous multitude superior to the king; he must disassociate himself from the view that the king enjoys personal majesty whereas the people possess real majesty or constituent power. And so devolution to the 'whole diffusive body of the people' is again defined:

> I do not suppose this forfeiture to be made to the people as Subjects, but to them as consider'd as a Community of Masters of Families, and Freemen, who as the Descendants and Representatives of those who made the first King upon a certain Contract, or Condition upon the non-performance of this Original Contract, do thereupon cease to be Subjects, as a Servant ceases to be so, and becomes again *sui juris* upon his Masters non-performance of the bargain made between them; and so this Authority thus forfeited, returns to the Community of Masters of Families and Freemen, who once conferr'd it upon the first King; nor needs this forfeiture any more suppose a Superiority in the persons who are to take it over the Prince that commits it, than when by the Law of *England* Tenant for Life aliens in Fee, He in reversion may immediately enter upon the Estate as forfeited to him, though the person that held it was perhaps his own Father.[41]

Power returns to the original people, yet this people is not thereby superior to the king. Rather, he explains, the people regains authority according to the original contract and those rights reserved in the beginning, when government was instituted as a trust or tenancy.

In this manner Tyrrell seeks to avoid placing an authoritative and constituent power in the people. He has Freeman articulate a stronger notion of the forfeiture, and not just abdication, of majesty, but here the association is with the language of property law more than constitutional law. The reference to property law – those notions of alienation, forfeiture and reversion of property, or power – is an important part of the denial of real majesty. Tyrrell builds upon his evocation of the origins of government as power derived from God and mediated by the people, and here sets forth the assertion that if power is forfeited and must return to the people it returns to them as mediators and not as authors. The people are 'in reversion', those who take on the tenancy but do not possess the fee simple, who form community and appoint sovereign authority with a power that originates with God.[42]

The references to estate and inheritance also highlight the fact that Tyrrell must take up the contested issue of the succession. Elsewhere, Tyrrell's dialogues explore the question of the royal succession and the reversion of power to the next heir, and Freeman is employed to marshal various arguments that prove that this reversion or devolution is instead to the people. The fact that England was originally an elective, and not a successive, monarchy is one such proof.[43] Even conceding the evolution and tradition of hereditary succession, Freeman also argues that James II's forfeiture created a situation equivalent to the death of a king without lawful heirs.[44] Finally, and most strikingly, he contends that although the legal and common course of succession should be followed, the right to the kingdom is not like a private man's inviolable interest in an estate and may be circumvented, since the public good is to be preferred to 'the Dignity or Authority of any particular Person whosoever, or howsoever nearly related to the Crown, when it is evident that the advancement of such a Person to the Throne, will prove destructive to our Religion, Civil Liberties and Properties'.[45] Here is an echo of Exclusion, as Tyrrell asserts that the principle of *salus populi* might override the normal succession of the Crown.

This introduction of ideas about inheritance and succession also plays a meaningful part in Tyrrell's campaign to define the people. The people 'in reversion' are naturally masters of families and freemen, those capable of property ownership and descendants of those who participated in the historical contract. Power devolves to the original people, those who possessed property and had a reason and a right to contract. These propertied men are 'the people' because they are the ones who exercised reason in forming society and civil authority. If rationality defines personhood, the masters and freemen who acted according to natural reason and divine law may be defined as 'the people'.

The original Convention

The whole body of the people – both the theoretical and the historical people – is now shown to be the masters of families and freemen, the descendants and representatives of those who first instituted civil authority. In challenging and ultimately adapting the notion of real majesty Tyrrell here accepts Lawson's idea of an initial community which entailed a distinction between *cives* and subjects. However Tyrrell goes on to conflate Lawson's effective distinction between the rights of the community and that of its representative.[46] The original people, to whom power returns, is allowed to be this group of masters and freemen who are representatives of a broader body of men, women and children. Power is said to devolve to this self-contained people, the propertied, who became a part of the government they created. The theoretical notion of a whole people, comprised of various individuals rationally coming together in community and instituting government, becomes intertwined with an historical, ancient constitutional account of masters and freemen, representatives of those people creating a government, until it is possible for an original people to become confused with an original council.[47] Once the people is narrowly defined and already involves some measure of representation it becomes easier to merge images of the body of the great council and of the people, so that assertions of devolution to the people or to the council become identified and interchangeable.

Through an emphasis on Whig history – an insistence upon the antiquity of Parliament and the role of the commons, a denial of Norman Conquest, and a focus on the role of the ancient great council in past instances of vacancy, devolution and resistance[48] – Tyrrell finds a way for the Whig argument to escape dissolution and popular sovereignty and to reaffirm the antiquity and power of England's representative institutions. Tyrrell essentially conflates the original body of the community with the council that was a part of the ancient government established by that original community. The extraordinary body of the Convention, conceived of both as the ancient great council and as the people (the masters and freemen, or their representatives), is the key to this solution.

Tyrrell pursues the ambiguities left by the Convention resolution, and yet still endeavors to steer clear of the fallacy of parliamentary supremacy in a mixed government and the radicalism of popular sovereignty. Merging contract, and its tendencies towards popular sovereignty, with the ancient constitution, interpreted in favor of parliamentary sovereignty, Tyrrell is able to avoid both claims. Sovereignty is at once located in the people and in its representatives. Through constant redefinition in these dialogues, resulting in images of the people as both community and council, the Convention could now be said to be the body of the people. It was a short step from the definition of the people as that community of fathers and freemen to the conclusion that the Convention was indeed that community, and was the people. Rather than resting with Lawson's innovative logic of dissolution, Tyrrell focuses instead on the means by which government is reconstituted through representatives, the *sanior pars*. He is in accord with the contemporary legal and theoretical distinctions being made between a Parliament and a Convention, and he insists that the Convention of 1689, like great councils of old, embodied the original community.

Freeman is now able to exult in the accession of William III to the throne, asserting that 'his present Majesty' has

> a Right to the Crown, from that inherent power which I suppose doth still remain in the Estates of the Kingdom, as Representatives of the whole Nation to bestow the Crown on every Abdication, or Forfeiture thereof, on such Prince of the Blood Royal, as they shall think best to deserve it; ... and therefore it is not at all to be wondered at, if the Convention hath in this case exercised that Original Power, which the People reserved to itself, at the first institution of Kingly Government in this Island.[49]

The tension inherent in Tyrrell's struggle to accommodate both the implications of contract theory and the tradition of Parliament and ancient constitution is apparent in this conclusion. Theory led him towards recognition of the constitutive authority of the people, whereas history and the demands of Whig politics pointed towards the power of the representative institution and tended to blur the distinction between Convention and Parliament. Tyrrell's Whig ends by arguing that power devolves to the great council or Convention which at the beginning and then throughout history was the people, as his argument shifts from devolution of power to the people[50] to devolution of government to the great council.[51]

This depiction of the identity and power of the Convention was, Tyrrell knew, a subject of some controversy. Echoing the criticisms leveled by Sawyer at the Convention Whigs some five years earlier, Meanwell reminds his Whig friend that this argument for dissolution will not allow for Conventions that are not popularly elected and properly representative of the whole community. Meanwell states:

> You have often talked of this forfeiture and extravagant Power of your Convention, by whom you suppose they are not obliged to place the Crown on the head of the next Heir by Blood, which I shall prove to be a vain Notion; for if there be an absolute forfeiture of the Crown, the Government would have been absolutely Dissolved; for since there is no Legal Government without a King, if the Throne were really vacant, and that the People might place whom they pleas'd in it, yet the Convention can have no power to do it, as their Representatives; since upon your suppos'd dissolution of the Original Contract between the King and the People, there was an end of all Conventions and Parliaments too. And therefore if a King could have been chosen at all, it ought to have been by the Votes of the whole body of the Clergy, Nobility and Commons, in their own single Persons, and not by any Council or Convention to represent them, since the Laws for restraining the Election of Parliament-men only to Freeholders are upon this suppos'd Dissolution of the Government, altogether void.[52]

The fiction that the Convention was the people assembled had been stretched too far to accord with reality. Even without mentioning Sawyer's reference to the glaring absence of 'freeholders under 40 shillings a year & all Copyholders, & Women & Children & Servants' from the definition of the people, Meanwell is able to challenge the notion that the Convention can or does represent the people. Here Freeman is confronted by a long-standing debate concerning the nature of parliamentary representation and the definition of the people. Similar attacks and answers were traded by parliamentarians and royalists like Henry Parker and Dudley Digges in the 1640s. Yet the growing certainty of Tyrrell's definition of the people as masters, fathers and freemen, as an original council, as both community and part of government, allowed for a reconsideration of dissolution. Freeman responds to Meanwell's critique with arguments from history and fundamental constitution; rather than insist upon the idea of devolution to the whole body of the people, he now asserts that government remained without the king and there was, in fact, no real dissolution.

Once again he puts forth a view of 1688 in terms of dynastic dispute and stalled succession. Freeman states that the ancient testamentary or elective kingdom of England is never subject to dissolution when the government is without a king, 'since in all those vacancies of the Throne, it is plain, the Government devolved of course upon the g[r]eat Council of the Nation'.[53] Tyrrell moves away from dissolution towards vacancy, and affirms that there can be no constitutional change since government endures. When confronted with the final consequences of dissolution and devolution of power to the whole people, with Sawyer's reminder that 'Wee are not the People', Tyrrell must emphasize continuity and ancient constitution and deny entire dissolution and resistance. Freeman, the conciliatory Whig, reassures Meanwell:

> And though 'tis true the Crown hath been long enjoy'd by those who have claimed by Inheritance, yet there is no reason for all that, if the like cases should fall out as have done in former times, why the Government should devolve to the mix'd Multitude now, any more than it did then; since it may well be supposed that the same tacit Contract still continues of maintaining the Original constitution of great Councils, which I have proved to be as Antient as Kingly Government itself. ... for it can never be thought to have been the intent of the People who Established this form of Government, that upon the extinction of the Royal Family, the Government should be so quite dissolved, as that it should be left to the confused Multitude to chuse what form of Government they should think fit.[54]

With this, Tyrrell's Whig defense came close to a simple affirmation of parliamentary sovereignty.[55] Yet the implications of this devolution of government to a representative council was still tempered by the ongoing emphasis on history and tradition – it was tempered by the association of this council with the original people, the

'Community of Masters of Families and Freemen', and the constant theme of the leadership of the 'considerable part' rather than the action of the rabble. Tyrrell's history and theory conclude that power rests with the original people who first conferred authority on the king, and themselves constituted a council, a part of the government created. Thus whether power is said to devolve to the people or the council, the ancient government is always in existence. This is the justification of abdication and vacancy: there may be violation of contract, justifiable resistance, and dissolution of power to the people, but there is no corresponding dissolution of government since the people, as the council, forms a part of that ancient government that endures.

During the course of presenting these arguments in debate Tyrrell again demonstrates his self-awareness in his attempt to present a strengthened and persuasive Whig argument. Tyrrell clearly recognizes that the identification of the Convention with an original council and an original people would be subject to criticism. He also acknowledges that the claim that the Convention was the body of the people assembled was far from reality. The conflation of people and council articulated by Freeman is less assured in the present than it is in his version of the past, in history and theory. And yet the necessary reconsideration of dissolution that appears in the later dialogues is not simply a contradiction of earlier arguments and logic. Tyrrell's attention to the definition of the people ensures that his Whig spokesman is not left merely asserting the devolution of government to an estates assembly and denying the return of the power of the people. The use of history, contract and the story of the origins of government in these dialogues enables Tyrrell to portray the people as both community and part of government. The attempt thus to define the people and the council allows the assertion of devolution of power to the council to take on a different meaning. Moreover, this original and historical identity of the people, which is worked out in the course of considering dissolution, is designed to render dissolution of government impossible and irrelevant. Tyrrell tries to accord the people a place within the constitution, to merge the community outside government with the council within, so that the ancient constitution would always be maintained and neither dissolution nor change in government could occur.

Continuity and the reaffirmation of the ancient constitution were, after all, the obvious answer to Tory or Jacobite charges of Whig radicalism or Williamite conquest. In this way *Bibliotheca Politica* is wholly characteristic of the Whig response to the Revolution Settlement in the political climate of the 1690s. It argues that if action is taken by the properly defined people, any breach in government caused by tyranny posed no danger to England's ancient constitution. Along these lines of reasoning, Freeman can justify resistance:

> For there may be a Common Civil Government without a King, but there can be no King without a People. Of this Opinion our English Ancestors always were, who though they often resisted, and sometimes deposed their Kings; yet they still maintained Kingly Government, though with the change of the person. And if it fail'd in the last Civil War, it was because it was at last managed by a faction of men of quite different Principles both in Religion and Politicks, and not by the Nobility and Gentry of the Nation, whose interest it was, and ever will be to maintain the ancient Government of a limited Monarchy; without falling into a Common-wealth or giving up their just Rights, and Liberties to an Arbitrary Power.[56]

Here is a defense of moderate revolution. It includes a repudiation of Commonwealth doctrine and an insistence that Whig principles, Whig revolution, was a safeguarding of English law, society and religion. It is shown that the admission of a right of resistance does not pose any threat to England's fundamental constitution. The people, here the rational and propertied, have an interest in the status quo and will always maintain the ancient form of government and society.

In the end, arguments for resistance, dissolution, continuity and ancient constitution exist side by side in Tyrrell's work. Drawing upon theories of contract and resistance, as well as upon tradition and English history, the consequences of Tyrrell's theory are activism and settlement, dissolution and non-dissolution. The key to Tyrrell's characterization of the events of 1688 lies in his definitions of the people and of the Convention. The ambiguous history and use of these concepts enabled Tyrrell to mount a politically and ideologically acceptable defense of the Whig cause.

Conceptions of Parliament and Convention

The identity and the history of the Convention, like that of Parliament, was an important part of this Whig argument, and Whig theorists could draw upon a variety of definitions of Convention. The simplest meaning, a convening, was most closely associated with the meeting of a regular Parliament. The term Convention was initially applied to instances when a Parliament assembled without passing any bills and was thus understood to be a mere meeting, or convention, rather than a session of Parliament. Over time, a more technical definition of Convention evolved in England. In particular, during the course of the Civil Wars, Convention became associated not only with the simple sense of a meeting but also with a special sense of a defective Parliament, lacking complete legal form.[57] The idea of a Convention as a legally defective Parliament, lacking the summons or concurrence of the king, was certainly relevant to the assembly that met in 1688.[58]

This change in definition may be due to the influence of Scottish constitutional thought, especially at the outset of the Civil Wars, and the Scottish recognition of a Convention of Estates as a less formal assembly with certain rights and powers.[59] Scotland had a richer tradition and conception of Convention than did England. There the definition of a Convention evolved from an identification with an ancient great council to a meeting approximating Parliament. Conventions were understood to have emerged originally as the successors to General Councils, those enlarged councils of the king which at their inception in the thirteenth century were made up of the same personnel as constituted Scottish Parliaments.[60] These General Councils came to be distinguished from Parliaments in respect of summons and in respect of competence as a court of law. Finally by the sixteenth century, the Scottish General Councils began to exclude members of the burgess estate, and so also became distinct in terms of personnel. However, in the years between the accession of James VI and the Civil Wars, as the composition of Conventions varied and came to include burgesses, they came to be associated both with councils and with Parliaments. The identification of Convention with Parliament was complete by 1643–4 when the personnel of the two bodies was identical.[61] These Conventions, whether associated with council or Parliament, were used to pass temporary legislation and were assumed competent for purposes of taxation.[62] The Stuart monarchs tended to summon Scottish Conventions, which could not make or repeal law or be prorogued to a second session, in order to grant taxes.[63]

An additional aspect of the history of Convention in Scotland, especially in the sixteenth century, was its involvement in the appointment of regents and in the recognition of new rulers.[64] This was also part of the experience of England's medieval Conventions that played a role in the abdication of Edward II in 1327 and in the accession of Henry IV in 1399.[65] Conventions were in these instances involved in the recognition of a new ruler because they were understood to be distinct from and, perhaps, more popular assemblies than Parliament. This association of Convention with some degree of popular sovereignty was widely recognized in 1688–9 as pamphleteers, theorists and politicians referred to the deliberate calling of a Convention, rather than Parliament, and the meaning of that term.[66] The fiction evolved that a Convention was a more immediate representative of the people or community than was Parliament, and so might exercise the authority of the whole people in establishing rulers or constituting government. This was another aspect of the definition of the Convention that emerged particularly after the Civil Wars, set forth, for example, by George Lawson and Henry Vane in the 1650s. These men viewed a Convention as an extraordinary gathering, akin to that body later assembled as America's constitutional Convention, capable of altering or creating the government anew.[67]

Whigs were not eager to be too closely associated with this definition and this legacy of the Civil Wars. Nor would they be likely to openly seek association with the Scottish example. The Scottish Convention of 1689 was a unicameral body dominated by Whigs and Presbyterians who set forth Revolution principles establishing constitutional and religious change; critics there attacked the unconstitutional means used to summon this Convention, and its continued meeting in violation of the constitution.[68] Since they were engaged in modifying, and at times repudiating, ideas of dissolution and real majesty, men like James Tyrrell found it to be much more prudent to associate the body of 1688–9 with the Convention Parliament of 1660 rather than with any kind of republican or Presbyterian Convention. For these and other reasons it has been posited that a popular Convention never came into use in England, and that a true revolutionary constituent assembly only came into being in eighteenth-century America.[69] Yet the image of a popular Convention was not simply dismissed in England, nor only entertained by commonwealthmen or those who subscribed to 'Rump Parliament doctrine'. The men who assembled in 1688–9 chose to call themselves a Convention not only because the events of November and December 1688 made a meeting of a regular Parliament impossible, but also because they hoped to avoid asserting the supremacy of Parliament and to claim authority and knowledge of the public good. To a certain degree Whigs accepted and promoted the idea of a Convention as a more popular and more representative body. They would not, however, acknowledge the consequences of such a view that would demand a real expansion of representation and would tend towards popular sovereignty. Many politicians and theorists wanted to utilize this fiction of the Convention as the body of the people, the nation assembled, but were hesitant to claim extraordinary powers and preferred to remain within the parameters of tradition.[70] Here then it was useful for the Whigs to associate Convention with Parliament rather than people. The Convention, like a regular Parliament, could be said to be 'the Nation assembled' or 'the body of the people', and thus benefited from the slow evolution of Parliament's identity as a representative institution.

The ways in which the people were thought to be present in the English Parliament had evolved with the growth of that institution from its beginnings as a body of informants or witnesses, called together by the king during the administrative expansion of the thirteenth century. Those men initially summoned to Parliament in the thirteenth century came as representatives of particular constituents and were endowed with complete power of attorney, *plena potestas*, in order to bind those individuals as if they had attended in person.[71] Over time, this 'body of the realm' came to be represented not so much by its magnates as by the parliamentary commons. This idea of proxies or representatives for individuals was extended to whole communities, and representation in the English Commons became a local and territorial matter that incorporated those who had not specifically authorized the representatives.[72] By the sixteenth century the image of Parliament as a representative body, containing and binding all persons in the realm, was essentially complete.[73]

Although the majority of people were excluded from choosing members of Parliament, the idea of representation remained viable. As the fiction of representation, of one man standing in for another, was expanded to include whole communities a system of virtual representation evolved, and the notion that Parliament represented the whole realm was increasingly articulated. Individuals, communities, the entire nation made up of participants and the excluded could be said to be virtually present and virtually represented by these men who stood for the whole realm. As parliamentary representation became more extensive, and complex, the paradox of representation emerged more clearly: representatives were not only seen as agents of their local communities but were also responsible for the whole nation, representatives of the interest of the whole realm, of the public good.[74] This is an essential aspect of all representative bodies, but it is a particularly important point with regard to seventeenth-century England because of its narrow base of political participants, and the broad conception of who was represented.

England's system of virtual representation, affirming that all members of the realm were present and consenting in Parliament, led to an emphasis on the representative's role as embodiment of the national interest. Parliament was described as the nation assembled, 'the body of the whole realm', but as G. R. Elton reminded us, this meant that 'the political nation was fully present – not the "people", a concept of neither ideological nor practical significance, but those interests powerful and concerned enough to engage in the activities which constituted the politics of the day'.[75] The myth of representation, of the people assembled in Parliament, masked the reality that the people assembled and represented were the political nation, Tyrrell's masters and freemen, the propertied and empowered. Parliament enhanced its legitimacy through this claim to be the embodiment of the nation. Moreover, it came to promote notions of popular sovereignty and to derive its authority from the original power of the people, in order to elevate its own power in the contest between king and Parliament during the Civil Wars.[76]

Although Tyrrell does not accept this history of Parliament's thirteenth-century foundations, he does recognize aspects of this evolution of parliamentary representation. The history and definition of Parliament and Convention in England, the traditional beliefs and accepted fictions which surrounded these institutions and identified them with 'the people', made Tyrrell's theory possible and believable. However the statement of these fictions made them subject to scrutiny and exposure made them more fragile. When the Convention sought to justify its actions through reference to the people it was easily attacked by critics like Sawyer. The Convention was, in fact, no more a popular or representative body than a regular Parliament. Lois Schwoerer has shown that the process of election to the Convention was only slightly different from elections to a regular Parliament, and that the composition of the Convention and Parliament were indistinguishable. The small changes made in the publishing of summons and length of time given for notice of elections are significant, asserts Schwoerer, 'for the care they reveal to preserve legal forms and at the same time protect partisan interests'.[77] The Whigs attempted to make the Convention more representative, but only in terms of Whig interests.

Whig ideas about contract and resistance posed too great a challenge to the ancient government and threatened to make change in the constitution and in the system of representation a real possibility. James Tyrrell's definition of the Convention as the people, and of the people as the 'Community of Masters of Families, and Freemen', was part of the Whig attempt to utilize a conceivable, but not literal, version of popular sovereignty. Tyrrell's immersion in natural law and theories of contract which attributed rationality and thus humanity to women and men, freeholders and copyholders, along with his defense of an early representative Parliament, led him towards an expansive definition of the people. The context within which his theory was elaborated, the system of virtual representation, and the recognition of property and gender as marks of rationality and inclusion, shaped and narrowed this definition. His conception of the people as masters, fathers and freemen, provided an ideologically sound response to Sawyer's challenge.

6
John Locke and Whig Theory

A review of Whig literature and a study of James Tyrrell's *Bibliotheca Politica* have shown that a defense of resistance was a central part of the Whig thesis of abdication and vacancy. In devising this theory of resistance, Whig authors employed a variety of political, legal and historical arguments in order to explain how abdication could entail resistance as well as vacancy. Most Whigs denied that abdication and resistance resulted in an entire dissolution of government. A few, like Tyrrell, openly confronted this essential question and the related issues of sovereignty in the people and the right or prospect of constitutional change. More than any other Whig theorist, however, it was James Tyrrell who fully explored the variety of possible arguments and ideas, and faced the challenges that were made to the Whig defense of resistance. In the breadth as well as detail of its arguments, Tyrrell's *Bibliotheca Politica* represents Whig ideology: in the frequent and real confrontations between Freeman and Meanwell, these dialogues reveal the political and ideological needs that shaped Whig theory; and in undertaking a critical approach to the justification of 1688 and offering a full explication of abdication and vacancy, Tyrrell's work demonstrates how the acceptance and success of Whig theory were possible.

Since other Whig tracts contain many of the arguments and ideas found in Tyrrell's work, it is *Bibliotheca Politica*, rather than John Locke's *Two Treatises of Government*, which constitutes the paradigm to which these works should, in the first instance, be compared. James Tyrrell, rather than John Locke, is the theorist of Whig Revolution. In defending resistance and Settlement, many Whigs shared

Tyrrell's ideas about the history and origins of the great council, and relied on a similar definition of the people. Some also conflated the tradition of this council with an image of the people who founded England's government. Still others pursued natural law arguments and conceded dissolution but also affirmed vacancy; they did not, however, conflate people and council and share Tyrrell's understanding of the identity of the Convention. This study of Whig theory, as it was articulated by these other Whigs and formulated by Tyrrell, enables us to understand how Revolution principles found acceptance through a reliance upon an Englishman's understanding of his law and his history, his self-perception as a man and an Englishman.

Finally, the understanding of Whig ideology not only illuminates the enduring impact of the Revolution of 1688-9, but it also has telling implications for the study of Locke's political theory and the analysis of his relationship to the Revolution Settlement. An appreciation of the Whig approach to dissolution, and a recognition of Whig theorists' confrontation with the ideas of Lawson and Locke, should provide an important context for any future reading of Locke's theory of resistance. This Whig context will shed light on the relationship of Locke's thought and actions to the Whig Revolution and regime, and will also provide some answers to historiographical and philosophical questions encountered in assessing Locke's intentions. In offering a few first steps in the reconsideration of the relationship between Locke and the Whigs, I hope also to problematize the traditional interpretation of Locke's role in the development of liberalism, and to offer some suggestions as to the history and transmission of the idea of popular sovereignty.

Entirely dissolved and merely vacant?

In considering the Whig context one important group of texts remains. There are a number of Whig authors who, like James Tyrrell, openly confronted the issue of dissolution in resistance. William Atwood, Matthew Tindal, Richard Kingston and the author of *A Friendly Debate between Dr. Kingsman, a Dissastisfied Clergy-man, and Gratianus Trimmer, a Neighbor Minister* provide different approaches to this question and should be read with an eye towards Tyrrell's *Bibliotheca Politica* as well as Locke's *Two Treatises of Government*. These Whig authors who did consider the consequences of abdication and resistance generally reflect the two sides of Tyrrell's analysis of dissolution. Some like Matthew Tindal and Richard Kingston admit that James II's tyranny and abdication resulted in the entire dissolution of government, but they also cling to the thesis of vacancy and endeavor to prove that the Convention need only fill the throne. These theorists share Tyrrell's goal of reconciling dissolution and vacancy but they differ in that they do not focus upon definitions of the Convention and the people as an explanation for the continuity of the ancient constitution. Others, like William Atwood, or the anonymous author of *A Discourse Concerning the... Present Conventions*, share Tyrrell's understanding of the Convention as the original people but never admit, along with Tyrrell and Locke, that violation, abdication and resistance would result in an entire dissolution of government.[1] Instead, they claim that only the kingship is dissolved and that there remains a constitutional solution for supplying the empty throne. Tyrrell's dialogues, and his conflation of council and people, suggest some connections across this apparent gap between dissolution and vacancy and between Locke and the Whigs.

One of the most pointed and public attacks on Lockean conclusions about dissolution and popular sovereignty was, in fact, made by the Whig lawyer, historian and polemicist, William Atwood. In his 1690 treatise, *The Fundamental Constitution of the English Government, Proving King William and Queen Mary are Lawful and Rightful King and Queen*, Atwood adheres to the Whig explanation of abdication and vacancy, and avoids dissolution by claiming a constitutional mechanism of self-preservation according to the acknowledged principle of *salus populi suprema lex*.[2] Atwood asserts that when the 'Contract between J.2 and his former Subjects' is destroyed by tyranny, the popular contract endures and power devolves 'to the People of Legal Interests in the Government, according to the Constitution'.[3] Atwood grounds this assertion upon the learned authority of Pufendorf, who explains:

> They who have once come together into a Civil Society, and subjected themselves to a King, since they have made that the Seat of their Fortunes, cannot be presumed to have been so slothful as to be willing to have their *new Civil Society* extinct upon the death of a King, and to return to their *Natural State* and *Anarchy*, to the hazarding of the Safety now settled. Wherefore when the Power

has not been *conferr'd* on a King by *Right of Inheritance*, or that he may dispose of the Succession at his pleasure, it is to be understood to be at *least tacitly agreed* amongst them, That presently upon the Death of a King, they shall meet together, and that in the place where the King fix'd his Dwelling. Nor can there well be wanting among any people, some Persons of Eminence, who for a while may keep the others in order, and cause them as soon as may be, to consult the Publick Good.[4]

Atwood insists that the assembly of people created by the initial social contract remains in existence. He chastises Locke for apparently ignoring the 'duplicity', or two stages, of contract:

> But there plainly was a farther Contract among themselves, to prevent *Anarchy* and Confusion, at any time when the *Throne* might be *vacant*; and by vertue of this *Contract* they have regularly made those Elections which are frequent in our Histories, and are authentick Presidents for our late Proceedings.[5]

Like the authors of *A Political Conference* and *A Discourse Concerning the...Present Conventions*, Atwood identifies the assembly of people, which is a part of the government, with the body of the original people who formed society and that government. This identification works to soften the implications of parliamentary sovereignty within the thesis of vacancy. Moreover, with this depiction of a popular assembly Atwood directly rejects any notion of dissolution. He shares Tyrrell's conflation of people and council, wherein the body of the people outside government becomes the assembly within, so that the devolution of power to the people does not entail the dissolution of government. In general, Atwood emphasizes the fact that the assembly meets and fills the vacancy according to established precedent, but he also insists that even if there were no such historical precedent, the vacancy would still be filled. 'But had there been no Warrant from former times for the late manner of proceeding,' he asks, 'the people of Legal Interests in the Government having been restor'd to their Original Right, Who can doubt, but that they had an absolute power over Forms?'[6] This admission of the potential for historical change does not mean that dissolution and constitutional change are possible, since method and form may change but the constitution does not fail. Atwood rejects dissolution not simply because he feared the possibility of 'the rabble' gaining power but also because he feared the loss of ancient rights and liberties entailed in the dissolution of the ancient constitution.[7]

According to William Atwood, abdication and vacancy reflect a proper comprehension of England's ancient constitution, and he charges Locke with misunderstanding that government and misrepresenting the Revolution. Atwood, like many others, believed that England's monarchy was originally elective, and that the tradition of hereditary succession that had evolved still entailed election and consent.[8] Thus he criticizes Locke for mistaking the English government for a strict hereditary monarchy, and insists that when the throne becomes vacant the original right of election returns to Parliament.[9] Atwood then tempers this admission of parliamentary sovereignty by identifying the two Houses with the body of the community. He appears to misread Locke's depiction of the government, and substitutes his own conception of the English constitution which rests on this conflation. Tyrrell shares Atwood's notion of England's monarchy as 'residually elective',[10] but differs in his admission of dissolution. For Tyrrell, the monarch's tyranny and abdication result in the dissolution of government: when government contradicts its very purpose it self-destructs.[11] This is an understanding of abdication and resistance which does not, however, follow the Lawsonian model of the dissolution of a mixed constitution once one part usurps the powers of another. Yet Tyrrell does assert both dissolution and vacancy and, like Atwood, he relies upon the conflation of Convention and people.

There were other theorists like Tyrrell who recognized and admitted resistance and dissolution and attempted to preserve arguments for vacancy. Matthew Tindal, that frequent critic of the Anglican clergy, wrote one such work, *An Essay Concerning Obedience to the Supreme Powers, and the Duty of Subjects in all Revolutions.*[12] In this essay Tindal does come to the thesis of dissolution through an understanding of an unbalanced, and thus destroyed, mixed government. Tindal observes that a king who assumes unlimited, tyrannical power not only abdicates government and destroys his own royal power, but also entirely destroys that government of which he formed a part. 'For no person can have at the same time a Will to rule according to Law, and Will to rule contrary to Law,' Tindal explains, '... and by making his Will the Law, he assumes the whole Legislative Power to himself, which wholly destroys the former Government; for a *new legislature is a new Form of Government*; and if the whole be destroyed, the share the King has in it must be so too, except a part can subsist, when the whole, by which and in which he enjoyed his part, is dissolved.'[13] In the tradition of Lawson and Locke, Tindal defends a right of resistance consistent with mixed monarchy, since the tyrant dissolves government and can no longer be obeyed. Indeed, Tindal was acquainted with Locke and the *Two Treatises*, and praises the 'late most Ingenious Author' who effectively criticized Sir Robert Filmer.[14] For Tindal, the tyrant's willful abdication entails dissolution, perhaps even a return to the state of nature, and Tindal addresses the question of who is qualified to ascertain when this tyranny and abdication have taken place. He posits that the people can judge the violation of their rights and can justifiably resist a tyrant but, unlike Locke and like Tyrrell, Tindal adheres to the claim that this is a 'declarative' and not authoritative power. He neither returns sovereign power to the people, nor asserts parliamentary supremacy.[15]

Tindal offers a variety of justifications of the Revolution Settlement and the authority of William and Mary, as he attempts to control dissolution and the question of where the power to settle government and to establish the constitution now resides. He considers conquest and *de facto* arguments, and reintegrates an element of consent and an emphasis upon the public good as the true test of the legitimacy of such rule.[16] Finally, Tindal reverts to ideas about vacancy, Convention, and a constitutional mechanism of self-preservation. He leans towards parliamentary supremacy, asserting that upon this vacancy in the throne, the 'Convention of States of the Kingdom' are the sole supreme judges who determine the succession. Yet he immediately turns away from this claim, towards an assertion of popular power:

> But supposing the King had no Legal Right, and that the Convention were not Legal Judges; yet if they were chosen by the Nation, to determine, upon the late King's leaving it, what was necessary to be done for the preservation of the Nation, it being necessary that somewhat should be resolved on; that necessity would give them a sufficient Right to do whatever they found necessary for the preservation of the Nation: Because no Nation can be brought

to that condition, but that it must have a Right to act for its own safety; which it cannot do, if it have not a Right to appoint Judges to determine what is to be done, and oblige particular persons to stand to their Determinations.[17]

Tindal relies upon an original mechanism of self-preservation, echoing the justification according to the principle of *salus populi* that was set forth in Atwood, *A Political Conference*, and other Whig tracts. However, Tindal differs in that he leaves open the possibility of constitutional change and the entire reformation of government by the appointed representatives of the nation. Tindal does not attempt to avoid parliamentary or popular sovereignty with the kind of conflation Tyrrell and Atwood offer, nor does he fully endorse either option. Although he posits a simple vacancy after dissolution, Tindal does not resolve the issue of real majesty nor – the fundamental problem of dissolution – the issue of justifiable and frequent constitutional change. It was this consequence, that the people could choose any new form of government by any means possible, that posed the real threat of dissolution. And the memory of the Civil Wars and the Commonwealth experiment exacerbated this fear of innovation.

Two other tracts provide good examples of this Whig attempt to address these threats of innovation and popular power while seeking to reconcile dissolution and vacancy. Both Richard Kingston, in *Tyranny Detected, and the Late Revolution Justify'd, by the Law of God, the Law of Nature, and the Practice of all Nations*, and the anonymous author of *A Friendly Debate* come to an admission of dissolution and the potential for constitutional change. Both texts rely upon claims to conscience and tradition in order to deny this outcome. Kingston, a chaplain to Charles II and minister with various preferments before the Revolution, was a writer for the government after 1688. In *Tyranny Detected* he presents a strong defense of abdication and resistance and an acknowledgment of dissolution.[18] Kingston claims that a tyrant's abrogation of the public safety, the very end of government, justifies resistance and even deposition,[19] and that the monarch's usurpation of unconstitutional powers results in dissolution.[20] He affirms both vacancy and dissolution: there is at once a power in the Convention to replace a king, and an end to government and constitution altogether, a return to 'the same Condition [the nation was] in when the *Original Contract* was first made'.[21] Kingston introduces further confusion with the idea that when the Convention met to fill the vacancy it had the right to act as if upon a dissolution, to re-form government and constitution. He states:

> ...and consequently, the *Convention* upon the *Vacancy* of the *Throne*, had Power to Model Things as the Present Circumstances of the Publick exacted, without being confin'd to the *Presidents* of former Ages; and yet so great was the Modesty of that Venerable Assembly, and their Care to prevent Innovations, that they did nothing but what had been already done upon the like Occasion many Hundred Years before.[22]

Kingston appears to extend the claim of simple parliamentary supremacy and endows the Convention with extraordinary constituent powers. He depicts it as a true constitutional convention. The Convention had the power to do what was necessary and to ignore historical precedent, but it acted out of care and respect for tradition and ancient forms as it filled the vacancy.

The author of *A Friendly Debate* also asserts that constitutional change was narrowly averted in 1689. The right to reform is here perceived to lie in the people who are embodied in an extraordinary Convention, and the author acknowledges their prudent exercise of restraint.[23] In this tract England's government is depicted as both a limited and a mixed monarchy, and dissolution is shown to result as much from the tyrant's violation of the public good as from his usurpation of the power and privileges of the other parts of government.[24] The people have a right to resist such destruction and the author has 'Trimmer', the defender of the Revolution, repeat George Lawson's authoritative statements about real majesty and the right of the people as citizens, not subjects. The community is seen to be 'one Person in Fiction of Law', and is composed of the whole people, defined as the greater and eminent part. This community is empowered to act and a Convention, rather than an ordinary Parliament, is entrusted to act for this people.[25] Thus, upon dissolution, power is shown to devolve to the Convention, 'and the Representatives of the Commons in it, have an extraordinary Trust, even that of forming us again, and settling us upon the best Foundation'. The author concludes that the result of this extraordinary occurrence is that 'the Constitution and Government is not changed, only the Persons of our Supreme

Governours'.[26] Although he acknowledges dissolution and real majesty, the author boldly claims that this is consistent with vacancy:

> That the Convention being called in an Extraordinary Case, for an Extraordinary Work, were trusted with an Extraordinary Great Power by the Community of *England*. The Real Majesty is in the Community of *England*. The Form of Government was dissolved. It is true, the Community was not reduced to the Original and pure state of Liberty, to frame a new Structure, new from the Foundation, because there were Heirs in pretence, in view and in expectation: And therefore, they were obliged in Conscience to do right to them that had the most undoubted Right. But the Settlement of the Government in the Person, or Persons, was in them.[27]

The result of dissolution is not depicted as a return to the state of nature, but rather the Convention of people reestablishes government in conscience to the next heirs and in conformity with immemorial custom.

> [T]hey did not exercise a Legislative Power, but they were put upon it how to reestablish the Government, as near as possibly they could, according to the Ancient Constitution. ... They were not advising how to draw up a new Form of Constitution; there were Ancient Land-marks to bound them, and the Model of the Building was in their Eye; and there were Ancient Laws and Custom, both Common and Statute, in Force. ... And they had the Authority of Laws, and Necessity both, for what they did. The Laws, by virtue of which they acted, were Customs immemorial, to meet and consult about the Publick Good, ... The Law of Nature was sufficient to call them together: And the urgent Law of Necessity laid upon them this Duty, which was not of their own making as was visible to all clear-sighted men.[28]

This Convention would have the power to remake government but would act only to reconstitute the ancient constitution; contract in the 'Law of Nature', and ancient constitution in the 'Model' 'Laws' and 'Customs', are once again forged together. The author's particular insistence upon conscience and tradition was similar to the emphasis placed by others, including Locke, upon the essential conservatism of the people, but it still allowed for uncertainty and could lead to more dramatic results.

James Tyrrell shared these authors' need to acknowledge dissolution and their desire to maintain a safe resolution in a simple vacancy in the throne. He too understands the significance of Lawson's distinction between real and personal majesty, and he too speaks in a language that depicts 'the people' as a group of respectable and eminent men. However, Tyrrell does not simply assure his readers that the Convention's conscience and respect for tradition were the safeguards that guaranteed the ancient constitution, and guaranteed that dissolution ended with vacancy. The conflation of the Convention with the people throughout Tyrrell's analysis of contract, in theory and in history, was the guard against constitutional change. The government might dissolve and authority might devolve to the people, but this people could not change England's ancient government because they were a part of that constitution. The focus upon the identity of the Convention and of the people comprises his justification for dissolution and vacancy.

John Locke's analysis of contract, government and tyranny also justifies resistance and admits dissolution. Much like the author of *A Friendly Debate*, Locke agrees with Lawson's conception of real majesty and the constituent authority of the people, and Locke contends that no ordinary representative can act for this people. Upon dissolution power is said to devolve to the whole people, who are now 'at liberty to provide for themselves, by erecting a new Legislative, differing from the other, by the change of Persons, or Form, or both as they shall find it most for their safety and good'.[29] He does not, however, go on to affirm that this people will simply fill the vacant throne because of their respect for tradition. Locke wholly admits dissolution and, like Matthew Tindal, wholly affirms the potential for real constitutional reform. The fears that this theory would arouse in his critics were apparent to Locke, and he insists that his principles would not open the door to frequent rebellion and constitutional change based on the slightest discontent. The conservative and phlegmatic character of the people is, according to Locke, the surest guard against change:

> People are not so easily got out of their old Forms, as some are apt to suggest. They are hardly to be prevailed with to amend the

acknowledg'd Faults, in the Frame they have been accustomed to. ... This slowness and aversion in the People to quit their old Constitutions, has, in the many Revolutions which have been seen in this Kingdom, in this and former Ages, still kept us to, or, after some interval of fruitless attempts, still brought us back again to our old Legislative of King, Lords and Commons: And whatever provocations have made the Crown be taken from some of our Princes Heads, they never carried the People so far, as to place it in another Line.[30]

Here Locke abandons abstraction and speaks directly to circumstances in England as he seeks to assure his contemporaries that the ancient constitution will be preserved because of the character of the English people.[31] Indeed, he insists that the people are less likely to foment chaos and rebellion than are rulers who are quick to act for private interest and personal gains.[32] This leads to the conclusion that popular sovereignty provides more stability than absolute monarchy since the people will be slow to seek fundamental change and rulers will be restrained by the possibility of popular action.[33] Yet this reassurance and moderation did not obscure the fact that Locke was defending a fundamental change in the constitution as legitimate. Unlike other Whigs, Locke could not offer constitutional assurances or reasons of conscience and tradition to explain why dissolution would simply result in a vacancy in the throne.[34] Even when Locke affirms that in practice, in England, there will be a replacement of a king and a reaffirmation of the Lords and Commons, according to his principles the people are still constituting anew a government of king-in-parliament. Locke maintains both the dissolution and the ultimate preservation of England's constitution, but he is not asserting vacancy.

Locke in the Revolution/the Revolution in Locke

The modern interpretation of John Locke's political thought has recognized this difference between Lockean theory and Whig Revolution principles, and it has shifted from an image of Locke as the Whig apologist for 1688 to an understanding of Locke as fundamentally different and more radical than his Whig contemporaries. Locke is considered to be more radical than his contemporaries not only because of his arguments for dissolution of government and for popular power, but also because his ideas about rights and equality are said to have opened up theoretical possibilities which have influenced positive change for traditionally disenfranchised groups. So, for example, Gordon Schochet has recently asserted that 'Lockean voluntarism in a radically different, modernized context opens up the concept "person" and makes possible political membership and significance beyond the narrow realm of white males.'[35] While appreciating this focus on difference, it is time, however, to reconsider some of the similarities between Lockean and Whig theory and the common ideological foundations they share. Some suggestions as to the degree to which Locke's thought differs from his contemporaries will contribute to the ongoing reassessment of Locke's originality and his impact, and the contested question of the development of liberalism. In particular, attention to some of the ideas Locke shared with the Whigs might illuminate the less radical implications of the Lockean notion of the constituent authority of the people.

With the notable exception of John Marshall's important study of Locke's heterodox religious beliefs, modern commentators generally focus upon the radicalism of Locke's social and political views.[36] And arguments for the radicalism of Locke's political thought rest, above all, upon the apparent novelty of his argument for dissolution, the possibility of an entire change in government and the image of this choice and power residing in a constituent people. Like many other Whig theorists Locke argued that the people are the source of governmental authority, and he based this claim on an understanding of natural law and a two-stage social contract. Locke posits that sovereign power is derived from free and equal individuals in a state of nature who transfer their individual power to execute the law of nature for the peace and preservation of mankind: 'Where-ever, therefore, any number of Men are so united into one Society, as to quit every one his Executive Power of the Law of Nature, and to resign it to the publick, there and there only is a *Political, or Civil Society*.'[37] Other Whigs similarly described this original liberty, necessity and the formation of a popular and a rectoral contract in a state of nature or in a Gothic or English history. Locke's additional emphasis upon a natural right of punishment as well as preservation was also posited by Tyrrell.[38]

The comparison with Tyrrell's theory of contract is instructive. As has been suggested, Locke's *Two Treatises* were likely aimed not only to refute Filmer's patriarchalism, but also to respond to *Patriarcha non Monarcha*, Tyrrell's earlier contribution to the attack on Filmer. This suggestion finds some support in Tyrrell's own interpretation of the objective of the *Two Treatises*. In two separate letters, Tyrrell pointedly noted to Locke the similarities between *Patriarcha non Monarcha* and the *Two Treatises*.[39] While urging Locke to write on the law of nature, and challenging him to improve upon Tyrrell's own essay on that subject, Tyrrell remarks: '[I] shall no more resent it then the publishing of the 2 Treatises of Government after Patriarcha non Monarcha; since if truth can be better represented, and improved: by a greater hand: I shall not value if my small performances, serve for a foyle to set it off.'[40] The question of Locke's intentions in the *Two Treatises* is interesting especially because it relates to an assessment of Tyrrell's intentions. Tyrrell's elaboration of a theory of resistance, offered in *Bibliotheca Politica*, was surely his response to Locke as well as his reaction to the changed circumstances of 1688 and a defense of Revolution and Settlement. In order to comprehend the relationship between Whig and Lockean theory it is clear that we must compare Locke not only with Whig Exclusion literature but also with the post-Revolution theory of resistance, and especially with those authors, like Tyrrell, who struggle with natural law, resistance, dissolution and vacancy.

In considering Locke's intentions David Wootton has made the strongest claim that Locke derived most of his ideas from Tyrrell's *Patriarcha non Monarcha*. Although Locke was acquainted with Tyrrell's main sources, such as Grotius, Pufendorf and Hunton, Wootton believes that Locke worked from Tyrrell's text and employed those arguments and elements that Tyrrell had already selected.[41] This contention that Locke was working directly from Tyrrell's text is not, however, essential to the overall point that Locke was responding to *Patriarcha non Monarcha*. It is fairly certain that Locke knew of Tyrrell's work before it was published, either through discussions while the two men were working on the response to Stillingfleet or by seeing the text itself. But Wootton also insists that Locke's theory was fundamentally different; for Wootton, Locke sought to 'detach' Tyrrell's arguments 'from a number of conservative assumptions to be found in Tyrrell', and in so doing Locke radicalized

Whig theory.[42] This conception of Locke's difference is in accord with the arguments of other scholars who point to Locke's expansion of ideas about natural equality, liberty, and an executive right which results in the right of judgment and resistance being placed in each individual. Thus, it is concluded that even if Locke starts from many of the same premises as Whig theorists, his theory is different because he pursues the progressive implications of these ideas.[43] Yet how far does Locke 'detach' these ideas from those 'conservative assumptions'?

First, Locke's theory of contract was also based upon common 'conservative' assumptions about gender and these assumptions color the possible implications of his theory. Locke's claims are still rooted, in many ways, in traditional assumptions about who is a person, which results in a narrow description of those individuals to whom power devolves. As some commentators have noted, although he emphasizes natural human freedom, equality and rationality, women are still excluded from Locke's polity.[44]

Here Locke shares the common Whig understanding of the relationship between biology, rationality and property, and these limiting ideas exist in conjunction with some of his more 'progressive' ideas about marriage and woman's part in the exercise of parental power. Locke is 'confused' and 'ambivalent' in his thinking about woman and about the family, Rachel Weil concurs, and he is inconsistent in the *Two Treatises* in the exposition of his core 'family–state distinction'. And Locke's ambivalence is similar, Weil notes, to those 'unresolved problems confronting Whig thinkers'.[45] Like Whig theorists, Locke does not resolve the tension inherent in his admission of a 'rational faculty' to women and his acceptance of the common assumption that women's reason, overall, is weaker and the demands of their biology stronger. For Locke, consciousness, intellect and reason are essential to the definition of a person and to the human capacity to adhere to natural law.[46] Yet woman is at once admitted and marginalized within this definition of a person. The notion of woman's identity as largely defined by her biology or sexuality is underscored even further in some of Locke's minor writings.[47] In his occasional writings and in his theoretical exposition of natural law and contract Locke does not simply provide the basis for an expansive and inclusive definition of the individual, but he also reaffirms standard, limiting, and exclusionary beliefs about exactly who is rational and has life, liberty and property to protect. The presence of these conservative assumptions and the impact of this Lockean and Whig ambivalence should not be ignored.[48]

More, perhaps, has been made of the progressive meaning of Locke's theory with regard to the inclusion of unpropertied men in the notion of the sovereign people, and the expansion of the political nation. The *Two Treatises* has been depicted as a 'democratic' and a 'communitarian' work.[49] It has also been argued, however, that Locke's insistence upon the equality and freedom of all men in the *Two Treatises* is developed along with some less egalitarian ideas about the exercise of reason and the development of private property.[50] For Locke, as for many Whig writers, assumptions about the natural and necessary development of family, inheritance, economy and society once again shape the definition of a person and a citizen, and affect the envisioned composition of the sovereign people. Locke, like Tyrrell, works within the natural law literature as he legitimates private property and founds government upon property rights in the *Second Treatise*. The fifth chapter, 'Of Property', is one of the most scrutinized sections of this work and there is an enormous literature surrounding Locke's theory of property, his treatment of the invention of money, the evolution of laws of inheritance, and issues of tacit versus express consent.[51] Within the property theory outlined there necessary inequalities can be seen to evolve according to Locke's understanding of human nature following its law and the divine plan in the development and distribution of property. Economic inequality is the fruit of a system of natural equality and freedom which precedes, and colors, political participation; scholars have noted that here too Locke excludes some people from membership in the political nation.[52] Even more, Locke's increasing scepticism about the ability of human reason adequately to establish the law of nature also serves to undermine his insistence upon natural law – and the natural rights that follow from that law and its sanctions. Locke's scepticism stemmed from a hedonic psychology which, David Wootton laments, was in persistent conflict with the democratic implications of his political theory.[53]

Although Locke adheres to notions of fundamental equality and freedom, he is not necessarily or only led from these natural law foundations to 'democratic' conclusions about political rights for the multitude. Locke does not specifically define the people as Tyrrell's 'masters and freemen', yet the qualities of rationality and freedom, prudence and virtue that he enumerates similarly lead to a definition of the people as adult males who possess some property.[54] Once again, there is an ambivalence in Locke's theory, and there are limitations on his democratic or egalitarian principles.[55]

Locke was, however, aware of these tensions and this ambivalence. Like other Whigs who referred to 'the people' he would have been challenged by his critics to admit that his definition must include the lower strata of English society, certainly those below the forty-shilling freehold. Would Locke have been more willing than most Whigs to contemplate such a conclusion? Arguments for the democratic or egalitarian intentions of the *Two Treatises* are bolstered by the claim that Locke actively sought some social change. Locke is said to have supported calls for an expanded franchise and a broadly representative Convention, and it is claimed that he would have been sympathetic to the kinds of criticism leveled at the Whig version of popular consent by the likes of Captain Thorogood and Sir Robert Sawyer. For some scholars Locke appears to be a radical egalitarian actor, mounting a defense of those Leveller principles enunciated at Putney years before.[56] Locke is also said to be allied with a fringe group of Whig radicals in the Convention who sought real constitutional reforms to be enacted by the authority of the people.[57]

One form of evidence for Locke's adherence to these radical political goals has been found in a comparison of his work with two contemporary polemical tracts addressed to the Convention, *A Letter to a Friend, Advising him in this Extraordinary Juncture how to Free the Nation For Ever* and *Good Advice before it be Too Late, being a Breviate for the Convention*.[58] The authors of these tracts, John Wildman and John Humfrey, expressed ideas similar to Locke's theory of dissolution and constituent authority. They went even further by making specific political demands regarding the elections to and the goals of the Convention, as they sought to make that body a true national assembly exercising extraordinary power.[59] Locke agreed with their notion that the Convention should act as a national constituent assembly and not as an ordinary Parliament, yet he did not join the call for an expanded suffrage.[60] Like the author of *A Friendly Debate*, Locke may have been content to attribute to the assembly of 1688–9 the powers of an extraordinary Convention, and quietly to accept the fiction of the Convention as the body of the people as long as it exercised those constituent powers. Although Locke's insistence upon dissolution and the constituent power of a popular assembly differed from the Whig view of the Convention there is some similarity in his apparent acceptance of the fiction of the Convention as 'the people'.[61]

A final question in considering the similarities and differences between Locke and the Whigs has to do with the absence of historical argument in the *Two Treatises*. Locke's unwillingness to speak in the language of the common law and the ancient constitution has been identified as a particularly novel characteristic of his work. Indeed, Locke's neglect of English history has been considered to be something of a mystery and scholars have proposed various solutions to the puzzle.[62] Many explanations rest on the premise that Locke's philosophical commitment precluded any recourse to history – that Locke denied that one could effectively argue from what is to what ought to be.[63] Again, this is part of that common belief that Locke was more logical, more coherent and had more philosophical goals than Whig theorists. According to this point of view Locke alone among his contemporaries wrote exclusively in the tradition of 'philosophical contractarianism', and did not participate in the Whig synthesis of ancient constitution and natural law.[64]

It is likely, however, that Locke's attitude towards history was more complex than that interpretation allows. Locke probably shared much of his contemporaries' view of history and their belief in the stability of England's ancient constitution. Letters and other occasional pieces provide evidence of Locke's historical sense and its effect on his political outlook; scholars have again looked to the complex interplay between the philosopher's ideas and his actions. For example, it has been noted that in *Some Thoughts Concerning Education* and *Some Thoughts Concerning Reading and Study for a Gentleman* Locke advises contemporary Englishmen that they should be well versed in the legal and political history of their own country. He recommends Tyrrell as well as Petyt, Atwood and Brady as valuable resources.[65] Locke, like other Whigs, was interested in the study and writing of history. Indeed Mark Glat claims that Locke went even further than Whig historians in his appreciation for the methodological challenges facing the historian. 'Locke probably rejected *English* historical thought and its attendant forms of political argument,' Glat asserts, 'because they ran counter to the more developed sense of history which ... he possessed.'[66] This sensitivity to historical context and method is, however, likely attributable again to Tyrrell's influence on Locke, since Tyrrell clearly grappled with these questions about language, context and meaning, and the methodological advances of Renaissance historians like Hotman, Baudouin and Bodin, in his *Bibliotheca Politica* and *General History*.[67]

Locke's familiarity with contemporary historical debate is also evident in a letter reflecting upon the work of the Convention which shows him urging the restoration of England's ancient constitution as the best possible course of action. '[T]he setlement of the nation upon sure grounds of peace and security is put into [the Convention's] hands,' Locke states, 'which can noe way soe well be don as by restoreing our ancient government, the best possibly that ever was if taken and put togeater all of a peice in its originall constitution. ... for that now they have an opportunity offerd to finde remedys and set up a constitution that may be lasting. For the security of civil rights and the liberty and property of all the subjects of the nation.'[68]

In a later letter, his 'call to the nation for unity', Locke echoes the Whig lawyer and MP Sir John Maynard in making a distinction between justifiable revolution and unlawful rebellion, and setting out the grounds for the end of allegiance to James II. Locke states:

> The miscarriages of the former reigns gave a rise and right to King William's comeing and ushered him into the throne.... If there were none [i.e. miscarriages] our complaints were mutiny and our redemtion rebellion and we ought to returne as fast as we can to our old obedience. They who thinke soe cannot doe otherwise and they who thinke there were miscarriages, such miscarriages as could have no other end but an abdication, have a very little care of his present Majestie if they will not joyn in a publique condemnation and abhorrence of them, since without they they [*sic*] can never justifie his ascent to the throne nor their mainteinance of him there.[69]

Locke here endorses the Whig view of abdication as resulting from James II's violations or 'miscarriages', asserting the end of James II's right and title and rejecting the image of William III as a usurper.[70] Locke's acceptance of an essentially unchanged form of government under William III, and his support for a 'restored' ancient constitution, have raised questions for some scholars regarding the possible conflict between Locke's idealistic vision of dissolution and individual resistance, and his pragmatic goals.[71]

The legacy of Revolution principles

There is, in the end, no real consensus on how to interpret Locke's theories and actions, and whether the 'democratic', 'communitarian' or 'egalitarian' impulses that lie therein were most important to him. Yet there is, I think, still some general consensus that Locke's ideas had these long-term egalitarian implications which in time were realized in expansive conceptions of equality and freedom. When we look at the similarities between Locke and the Whigs, however, we get a different picture. The comparison between Locke and the Whigs suggests two final conclusions.

First, the unsurprising fact that John Locke shared many Whig assumptions and confirmed many of the same ambiguities and contradictions leads to the more controversial claim that these aspects of his thought are just as important as any progressive implications his ideas may contain. Locke's theory of contract had conservative as well as radical or egalitarian implications, and could also provide support for a narrow interpretation of popular sovereignty. Certainly, Locke makes certain different philosophical and rhetorical choices from the Whigs, and his theory of resistance may pursue some more radical ideas, yet within that theory there are also pragmatic, conservative, 'Whiggish' elements. Further, when we look at these less egalitarian aspects of Locke's principles we find that there is not necessarily a conflict between the ideas espoused in the *Two Treatises* and his support for the Convention, the ancient constitution, and an understanding of the political nation defined as propertied freeholders.[72]

The essential notion of popular sovereignty within the theory articulated by Locke contains certain key ambiguities, such as those concerning political participation, economic and social equality, and their rational basis, that are a part of the liberal tradition.[73] When scholars primarily focus on the ways in which Locke's theory could be progressive they ignore the ways in which those same aspects of his theory could contribute to a reinforcement of inequality. Locke may, in many ways, be justly identified with liberalism, but there are also many ambiguities and illiberal notions that are codified, and thus endure, in this liberal theory.

Second, the comparison between Locke and the Whigs tells us something about the legacy of Whig Revolution principles and, of course, about the works of James Tyrrell. Whig theorists articulated many so-called 'Lockean' ideas in such a way as to suppress their egalitarian implications. Whigs talked about consent and equality in ways that made the applicability and range of these ideas contained. It was the Whigs who revived the theory of popular sovereignty in the 1680s, but their version of the argument was cautious, stressing adherence to the ancient constitution and identifying people with Parliament.[74] Because they did this, Whigs helped to make these ideas endure: it was because these ideas about consent and equality could not be extended that they were persuasive and accepted. Thus, such liberal ideas, and their democratic implications, rely not only on Locke's ability to open some theoretical doors but also, ironically, on Whig theorists' ability to close the door on those implications.

An understanding of the progressive implications of Whig Revolution principles, and the interrelationship between Whig and Lockean theory, helps to explain that seeming Whig paradox of 'non-revolutionary revolution', of revolution by degrees. An understanding of these intellectual and ideological contexts also helps to illuminate the transmission of ideas. It is clear that when we consider not only why but *how* a defense of resistance and ideas about equality and freedom survive, we must look to the legacy of Whig thought, and particularly to the work of James Tyrrell. Tyrrell's formulation of Whig principles highlights the modulation of these democratic or egalitarian implications. Through the manipulation of history and theory, and the conflation of Convention and people, ideas about consent, resistance, equality and freedom are at once acknowledged and their implications suppressed. Tyrrell and other Whigs provided an articulation of these concepts that was acceptable to the reason and beliefs of an earlier historical period, and their articulation had an impact upon the content and endurance of these ideas. A comparison, then, between James Tyrrell and John Locke or, more generally, between Locke and the Whigs, usefully complicates the history of liberal ideas. Familiar distinctions between the Burkean or conservative legacy of 1688 and the liberal legacy of John Locke can no longer easily be sustained.

Notes

Chapter One Introduction: The Question of Whig Resistance Theory

1. Gilbert Burnet, a Scottish Anglican cleric, was a well-traveled and highly-educated figure who was deeply engaged in English politics from the 1670s through the early 1700s. According to Tony Claydon, at the Revolution Burnet was 'a man very close to the heart of Williamite counsels, who was effectively acting as the prince's chief of propaganda during the invasion of England'. Tony Claydon, *William III and the Godly Revolution* (Cambridge: Cambridge University Press, 1996), p. 29. Burnet wrote a number of important treatises and sermons concerning the Revolution as well as two multivolume histories. William III installed Burnet as Bishop of Salisbury in 1689. For a view of Burnet as a crucial theorist of a providentialist as well as constitutionalist defense of the Revolution see Claydon, *William III and the Godly Revolution*, ch. 1.
2. Gilbert Burnet, *An Enquiry into Measures of Submission to the Supreme Authority: And of the Grounds upon which it may be Lawful or Necessary for Subjects, to Defend their Religion, Lives and Liberties*, in A Compleat Collection of Papers, in Twelve Parts (London, 1689), Collection II, pp. 11, 13.
3. Gilbert Burnet, *A Pastoral Letter Writ by the Right Reverend Father in God Gilbert, Lord Bishop of Sarum, to the Clergy of his Diocess, Concerning the Oaths of Allegiance and Supremacy to King William and Queen Mary* (London, 1689), pp. 19–20, 24–28.
4. Gilbert Burnet, *History of his Own Time*, rev. and abridged edn by Thomas Stackhouse (London: Everyman, 1906, reprint 1979), pp. 286, 293.
5. J. G. A. Pocock, 'The Fourth English Civil War: Dissolution, Desertion and Alternative Histories in the Glorious Revolution', *Government and Opposition*, 23, 2 (1988) 153.
6. Edmund Burke, *Reflections on the Revolution in France*, J. G. A. Pocock, ed. (Indianapolis: Hackett Publishing, 1987), p. 19; see also pp. 26–7.
7. William Blackstone, *Commentaries on the Laws of England*, vol. 1, bk 3, in *The Sovereignty of the Law: Selections from Blackstone's 'Commentaries on the Laws of England'*, Gareth Jones, ed. (Toronto: University of Toronto Press, 1973), pp. 82–4. See also Julian H. Franklin, *John Locke and the Theory of Sovereignty* (Cambridge: Cambridge University Press, 1978), p. 116.
8. Dates appear in this book according to England's Old Style calendar, and the year is taken to begin on 1 January.
9. See, for example, Robert Beddard, 'The Unexpected Revolution of 1688', in Robert Beddard, ed., *The Revolutions of 1688: The Andrew Browning Lectures*

(Oxford: Oxford University Press, 1991); J. R. Jones, *The Revolution of 1688 in England* (New York: W. W. Norton, 1972); idem., ed., *The Restored Monarchy 1660–1688* (Totowa, N. J.: Rowman & Littlefield, 1979); J. R. Western, *Monarchy and Revolution: The English State in the 1680s* (Totowa, NJ: Rowman and Littlefield, 1972); J. C. D. Clark, *English Society 1660–1832: Religion, Ideology and Politics during the Ancien Regime* (Cambridge: Cambridge University Press, 1985).

10. A variety of historians agree on this point. See, for example, Jones, *Revolution of 1688*; Western, *Monarchy and Revolution*; Christopher Hill, *The Century of Revolution, 1603–1714* (New York: W. W. Norton, 1961); W. A. Speck, *Reluctant Revolutionaries: Englishmen and the Revolution of 1688* (Oxford: Oxford University Press, 1989).

11. Mark Knights, 'A City Revolution: The Remodelling of the London Livery Companies in the 1680s', *English Historical Review*, 112 (1997) 1141–78.

12. John Miller, *Popery and Politics in England 1660–1688* (Cambridge: Cambridge University Press, 1973) pp. 203–13.

13. Jones, *Revolution of 1688*, pp. 107, 118–19, 262–7; Mark Goldie, 'The Political Thought of the Anglican Revolution', in Beddard, ed., *Revolutions of 1688*, pp. 108–11; Knights, 'City Revolution', 1157–72. But for some evidence of the success of James II's policy, and of Dissenters' enthusiastic collaboration with James, see also Mark Goldie, 'James II and the Dissenters' Revenge: the Commission of Enquiry of 1688', *Historical Research*, 66 (1993) 53–88, and Tim Harris, *Politics Under the Later Stuarts: Party Conflict in a Divided Society 1660–1715* (London: Longman, 1993), pp. 126–8.

14. Mark Goldie distinguishes between two revolutions, one 'Anglican' and one 'Williamite', and cogently argues that one was not a prelude for the other – indeed, that William III was disastrous for the Anglican goal of recapturing the monarchy. Goldie, 'Anglican Revolution', pp. 107–8. However, Anglicans' experience with James II, the existence of a Catholic heir, and James's final flight to France made arming on his behalf in a civil war more remote and the justification of his abdication and the accession of William and Mary more palatable.

15. Jones, *Revolution of 1688*, p. 190; J. G. A. Pocock, 'The Significance of 1688: Some Reflections on Whig History', in Beddard, ed., *Revolutions of 1688*, p. 272; Dale Hoak, 'The Anglo-Dutch Revolution of 1688–89', in Dale Hoak and Mordechai Feingold, eds, *The World of William and Mary: Anglo-Dutch Perspectives on the Revolution of 1688–89* (Stanford: Stanford University Press, 1996), pp. 1–26; Jonathan I. Israel, 'The Dutch Role in the Glorious Revolution', in Jonathan I. Israel ed., *The Anglo-Dutch Moment: Essays on the Glorious Revolution and Its World Impact* (Cambridge: Cambridge University Press, 1991), pp. 105–62. Robert Beddard notes two 'distinct, yet interlocking dimensions' to the Revolution, one internal and British, the other external and European. Beddard, 'Unexpected Revolution', in Beddard, ed., *Revolutions of 1688*, pp. 5–8, 10. Steven Pincus looks at the connections between these internal and

external dimensions, calling 1688 a 'nationalist revolution'. Steven Pincus, '"To Protect English Liberties": the English Nationalist Revolution of 1688–1689', in Tony Claydon and Ian McBride, eds, *Protestantism and National Identity: Britain and Ireland, c.1650–c.1850* (Cambridge: Cambridge University Press, 1998), pp. 75–104.
16. Robert Beddard, *A Kingdom without a King: The Journal of the Provisional Government in the Revolution of 1688* (Oxford: Phaidon Press, 1988), p. 13; Hoak, 'Anglo-Dutch Revolution', pp. 19–20.
17. Western, *Monarchy and Revolution*; Beddard, 'Unexpected Revolution', pp. 73–84; Hoak, 'Anglo-Dutch Revolution', pp. 23, 26.
18. Hoak, 'Anglo-Dutch Revolution', pp. 22–3; Howard Nenner, 'Sovereignty and the Succession in 1688–89', in Hoak and Feingold, eds, *World of William and Mary*, pp. 104–8. For insightful discussion of political argument and the warming pan scandal see Rachel J. Weil, 'The Politics of Legitimacy: Women and the Warming-pan Scandal', in Rachel J. Weil, *Political Passions: Gender, the Family and Political Argument in England 1680–1714* (Manchester: Manchester University Press, 1999), ch. 3.
19. These seven men were the Earls of Danby, Shrewsbury and Devonshire, Lord Lumley, Bishop Compton of London, Edward Russell and Henry Sidney. Beddard, *Kingdom without a King*, p. 17.
20. Tony Claydon, 'William III's *Declaration of Reasons* and the Glorious Revolution', *Historical Journal*, 39, 1 (1996) 89–90; Lois G. Schwoerer, *The Declaration of Rights, 1689* (Baltimore: Johns Hopkins Press, 1981) ch. 5; Jonathan I. Israel, 'Introduction', in Israel, ed. *Anglo-Dutch Moment*, pp. 1–43; Lois G. Schwoerer, 'Propaganda in the Revolution of 1688–9', *American Historical Review*, 82 (1977) 843–74.
21. Jones, *Revolution of 1688*, p. 262; Knights, 'City Revolution', 1169–72.
22. Beddard, *Kingdom without a King*, pp. 23–4; Paul Seaward, *The Restoration, 1660–1688* (London: Macmillan, 1991), p. 138. For a good description of the magnitude of William's forces see Hoak, 'Anglo-Dutch Revolution'.
23. Hilary Jenkinson, 'What happened to the Great Seal of James II?', *Antiquaries Journal*, 23, (1943) 1–13; E. S. De Beer, 'The Great Seal of James II: A Reply to Sir Hilary Jenkinson', *Antiquaries Journal*, 42 (1962) 81–90.
24. The proposed goals of the provisional government were to maintain law and order and to uphold James's kingship; Robert Beddard underscores the importance of this body with regard to peacekeeping, military supervision and effect on the political initiative. Beddard, *Kingdom without a King*, pp. 36, 41.
25. Claydon, 'William III's *Declaration*'; Beddard, *Kingdom without a King*, pp. 34–5.
26. Western, *Monarchy and Revolution*, p. 283. Beddard, 'Unexpected Revolution', p. 43. Note, too, the importance of the provisional government after James's first flight in preventing hostilities between the armies of the King and the Prince. Beddard, *Kingdom without a King*, p. 38. Mark Knights offers a different interpretation, arguing that chaos, confusion and the conflicts generated by the series of purges and policy reversals through the 1680s ended in paralysis in 1688. It is this 'paralysis', 'inertia' or

'listlessness', Knights concludes, that accounts for the lack of bloodshed, and avoidance of civil war, but also helps to account for the coming of revolution. Knights, 'City Revolution', 1177–8.
27. Pocock, 'The Fourth English Civil War', 159; idem., 'The Significance of 1688', p. 275.
28. Pocock, 'The Significance of 1688', pp. 278–9.
29. Robert Beddard surely goes too far in his claim that the actions of the Convention 'were of a secondary, not primary, political importance'. 'In the end,' Beddard continues, 'whatever the conflicting interests and opposed principles of its members, the Convention had to come to terms with dynastic and confessional realities over which it had little or no control.' Beddard, *Kingdom without a King*, p. 65; and cf. idem., 'Unexpected Revolution', pp. 73–4. In fact, given the events of the past six weeks, there *were* no certain 'realities', and the actions of the Convention, and of the Whigs within that body, were crucial in determining the political, social and religious settlement, and in establishing the enduring meaning of events.
30. William Cobbett, ed., *The Parliamentary History of England, from the Earliest Period to the Year 1803*, vol. 5 (London: T. C. Hansard, 1809; reprint, New York: AMS Press, 1966) p. 38.
31. As Tony Claydon notes, *de facto* arguments, for conquest or protection, were insufficient by the lights of William's own self-explanation. And, ironically, because of the great significance attached to the *Declaration of Reasons*, and because that document could *not* be used, effectively, to support his accession, William was forced 'to sit on the sidelines of crucial debates, in which his whole future hung in the balance'. Claydon, 'William III's *Declaration*', 99, 101; and cf. idem. *William III and the Godly Revolution*, pp. 24–8.
32. Beddard, 'Unexpected Revolution', p. 19.
33. Franklin, *John Locke*, pp. 89–90.
34. Ibid., p. 124.
35. Ibid., chs 3 and 4.
36. See below, Chapters 5 and 6. And for a discussion of the concept of 'real majesty', see Franklin, *John Locke*; Otto von Gierke, *Natural Law and the Theory of Society 1500 to 1800*, Ernest Baker, trans. and Introduction (Cambridge: Cambridge University Press, 1934); J. H. M. Salmon, *The French Religious Wars in English Political Thought* (Oxford: Oxford University Press, 1959); Brian Tierney, *Religion, Law and the Growth of Constitutional Thought, 1150–1650* (Cambridge: Cambridge University Press, 1982).
37. Cobbett, *Parliamentary History*, pp. 40–2.
38. Franklin, *John Locke*, p. 115; see also H. T. Dickinson, *Liberty and Property: Political Ideology in Eighteenth-Century Britain* (New York: Holmes & Meier, 1977), p. 82.
39. More recent work on William's role and on Dutch involvement persuasively contradicts Kenyon's verdict here. See, for example, Hoak, 'Anglo-Dutch Revolution'; Beddard, 'Unexpected Revolution'; Israel, ed., *Anglo-Dutch Moment*.

40. J. P. Kenyon, 'The Revolution of 1688: Resistance and Contract', in Neil McKendrick, ed., *Historical Perspectives: Studies in English Thought and Society in Honour of J. H. Plumb* (London: Europa, 1974), pp. 43–70; idem., *Revolution Principles: The Politics of Party 1689–1720*, reprint edn (Cambridge: Cambridge University Press, 1990). Kenyon's interpretation of 'abdication' prompted a number of responses, including Thomas Slaughter, '"Abdicate" and "Contract" in the Glorious Revolution', *Historical Journal*, 24, 2 (1981) 323–37; idem., '"Abdicate" and "Contract" Restored', *Historical Journal*, 28, 2 (1985) 399–403; John Miller, 'The Glorious Revolution: "Contract" and "Abdication" Reconsidered', *Historical Journal*, 25, 3 (1982) 541–55.
41. Conal Condren, *The Language of Politics in Seventeenth-Century England* (London: Macmillan, 1994), especially ch. 4.
42. While James Conniff has considered the persuasiveness of Whig theory, as articulated in Algernon Sidney's *Discourses Concerning Government*, he also perpetuates the assessment of the Whigs as confused, and as inferior to Locke. James Conniff, 'Reason and History in Early Whig Thought: The Case of Algernon Sidney', *Journal of the History of Ideas*, 43 (1992) 415–16.
43. Quentin Skinner, *The Foundations of Modern Political Thought*, vol. 1, (Cambridge: Cambridge University Press, 1978), p. xi.
44. Donald R. Kelley, *The Beginning of Ideology: Consciousness and Society in the French Reformation* (Cambridge: Cambridge University Press, 1983), pp. 1–10.
45. Quentin Skinner, 'A Reply to My Critics', in James Tully, ed., *Meaning and Context: Quentin Skinner and his Critics* (Princeton: Princeton University Press, 1988), p. 247.
46. Ibid., p. 240.
47. James Tyrrell, *Bibliotheca Politica: Or an Enquiry into the Ancient Constitution of the English Government; Both in Respect to the Just Extent of Regal Power, and the Rights and Liberties of the Subject. Wherein all the Chief Arguments, as well Against, as For the Late Revolution, are Impartially Represented, and Considered in Thirteen Dialogues* (London, 1694), Epistle Dedicatory. All subsequent references to *Bibliotheca Politica* will be to the modern facsimile edition, *Bibliotheca Politica: The First Complete Edition Containing the Fourteenth Dialogue of 1702*, 2 vols, Classics of Legal History in the Modern Era (New York: Garland, 1979). On the publishing history of *Bibliotheca Politica* see Chapter 3 below.
48. Ibid.
49. Ibid.; and note, too, the foregoing 'Advertisement to the Reader' in which Tyrrell expresses a willingness to allow other witnesses to step in.
50. Barbara Shapiro, 'The Concept "Fact": Legal Origins and Cultural Diffusion', *Albion*, 26, 1 (1994) 9–10, 13–26; idem., *A Culture of Fact: England 1550–1720* (Ithaca: Cornell University Press, 2000).
51. James Tyrrell, *Patriarcha non Monarcha. The Patriarch Unmonarch'd: Being Observations on a Late Treatise and Divers other Miscellanies, Published under the Name of Sir Robert Filmer Baronet. In Which the Falseness of those*

Opinions that would Make Monarchy Jure Divino are Laid Open: And the True Principles of Government and Property (especially in our Kingdom) Asserted (London, 1681).
52. Peter Laslett, 'Introduction', in John Locke, *Two Treatises of Government*, Peter Laslett, ed. (Cambridge: Cambridge University Press, 1963), p. 73; J. W. Gough, 'James Tyrrell, Whig Historian and Friend of John Locke', *Historical Journal*, 19, 3 (1976), 588.

Chapter Two Exclusion and the Evolution of Contract Theory in James Tyrrell's *Patriarcha non Monarcha*

1. See, for example, Julian H. Franklin, ed. and trans., *Constitutionalism and Resistance in the Sixteenth Century: Three Treatises by Hotman, Beza, and Mornay* (New York: Pegasus, 1969); J. H. M. Salmon, *French Religious Wars in English Political Thought*; Skinner, *Foundations of Modern Political Thought*, vol. 2; Gierke, *Natural Law and the Theory of Society*; J. W. Gough, *The Social Contract: A Critical Study of its Development* (Oxford: Oxford University Press, 1957); Johann P. Sommerville, *Politics and Ideology in England 1603–1640* (London: Longman, 1986).
2. Thus, J. G. A. Pocock refers to the 'dual nature of the Filmerian controversy', and illuminates the ways in which the debate over the antiquity of the Commons was related to the debate over the patriarchal theory of kingship. J. G. A. Pocock, *The Ancient Constitution and the Feudal Law: A Study of English Historical Thought in the Seventeenth Century, A Reissue with a Retrospect* (Cambridge: Cambridge University Press, 1987), pp. 187–8, 349–53.
3. B. Behrens, 'The Whig Theory of the Constitution in the Reign of Charles II', *The Cambridge Historical Journal*, 7, 1 (1941) 42–71; O. W. Furley, 'The Whig Exclusionists: Pamphlet Literature in the Exclusion Campaign, 1679–81', *Cambridge Historical Journal*, 13, 1 (1957) 19–36; J. R. Jones, *Country and Court, England 1658–1714* (Cambridge, Mass.: Harvard University Press, 1978); Richard Ashcraft, *Revolutionary Politics and Locke's 'Two Treatises of Government'* (Princeton: Princeton University Press, 1986).
4. Gary S. de Krey, 'The London Whigs and the Exclusion Crisis Reconsidered', in A. L. Beier, David Cannadine, and James M. Rosenheim, eds, *The First Modern Society: Essays in Honor of Lawrence Stone* (Cambridge: Cambridge University Press, 1988), pp. 457–82; Tim Harris, *London Crowds in the Reign of Charles II: Propaganda and Politics from the Restoration until the Exclusion Crisis* (Cambridge: Cambridge University Press, 1987); idem., *Politics Under the Later Stuarts*; Tim Harris, Paul Seaward and Mark Goldie, eds, *The Politics of Religion in Restoration England* (Oxford: Basil Blackwell, 1990); Mark Knights, *Politics and Opinion in Crisis, 1678–1681* (Cambridge: Cambridge University Press, 1994); Jonathan Scott, *Algernon Sidney and the English Republic, 1623–1677*

(Cambridge: Cambridge University Press, 1988); idem., *Algernon Sidney and the Restoration Crisis, 1677–1683* (Cambridge: Cambridge University Press, 1991); Richard L. Greaves *Secrets of the Kingdom: British Radicals from the Popish Plot to the Revolution of 1688* (Stanford: Stanford University Press, 1992); Melinda S. Zook, *Radical Whigs and Conspiratorial Politics in Late Stuart England* (University Park: Pennsylvania State University Press, 1999).
5. Thomas Hearne records a conversation with James Tyrrell from 29 August 1713 in which Tyrrell supposedly expressed such doubts: 'And a little while after [Tyrrell] added that if the Pretender were really the Son of King James then says he, he is King of England. Upon which said I, it hath not been proved that he is illegitimate. Concedimus says he, and then went away.' Thomas Hearne, *Remarks and Collections of Thomas Hearne*, vol. 4, D. W. Rannie, ed. (Oxford: Clarendon Press, 1898), pp. 231–2. I am grateful to J. G. A. Pocock for bringing this reference to my attention.
6. Tyrrell was at work against Filmer on two fronts: he and William Petyt were engaged to refute Filmer's *Freeholders Grand Inquest*, as he and Locke wrote against *Patriarcha*. Pocock, *Ancient Constitution*, pp. 345–8.
7. Knights, *Politics and Opinion in Crisis*. In dealing with problems of terminology Knights prefers 'succession crisis' to Exclusion, and 'loyalists' and 'oppositionists' to Tories and Whigs.
8. Harris, *Politics Under the Later Stuarts*, p. 80; idem., *London Crowds*; Mark Goldie, 'Danby, the Bishops and the Whigs', in Harris, Seaward and Goldie, eds, *Politics of Religion*, p. 78; Jones, *Country and Court*, pp. 209–13; Furley, 'Whig Exclusionists', 19.
9. Furley, 'Whig Exclusionists', 22; Harris, *Politics Under the Later Stuarts*, p. 83; Seaward, *The Restoration*, pp. 103–4.
10. Other suggestions included legitimating the Duke of Monmouth, Charles II's eldest, but illegitimate, son; creating a regency, with the Prince of Orange ruling in James's stead; and remarrying Charles to a new, Protestant wife in order to bear a new heir to the throne. Harris, *Politics Under the Later Stuarts*, p. 83; Jones, *Country and Court*, p. 208; Knights, *Politics and Opinion in Crisis*, pp. 31–6.
11. The Earl of Shaftesbury, quoted in Maurice Cranston, *John Locke: A Biography* (Oxford: Oxford University Press, 1985), p. 186.
12. Harris, *Politics Under the Later Stuarts*, pp. 87–8; Western, *Monarchy and Revolution*, pp. 35–45.
13. Harris, *Politics Under the Later Stuarts*, p. 83; J. R. Jones, *The First Whigs: The Politics of the Exclusion Crisis, 1678–1683* (Oxford: Oxford University Press, 1961), pp. 9–19, 214; Western, *Monarchy and Revolution*, p. 36. For the debate more generally see Scott, *Algernon Sidney and the Restoration Crisis*; Knights, *Politics and Opinion in Crisis*; and the contributors to the issue devoted to 'Order and Authority: Creating Party in Restoration England', *Albion*, 25, 4 (1993) 565–651.
14. Robert Willman, 'The Origins of "Whig" and "Tory" in English Political Language', *Historical Journal*, 17, 2 (1974) 247–64.

15. Harris, *Politics Under the Later Stuarts*, p. 82; Zook, *Radical Whigs*, p. xvii. Knights, 'City Revolution', offers a corrective to the exclusive focus on religious explanation for party, and emphasizes economic and social issues in his study of the remodeling of London livery companies. Weil, *Political Passions*, looks at the role of gender in the development of party divisions and political argument.
16. The 'Critical Notes' on Stillingfleet have usually been identified as a collaborative work, written by Tyrrell and Locke. However John Marshall has provided evidence to show that Tyrrell acted as Locke's amanuensis for much of the composition of this work, and suggests that Locke was 'sole author'. John Marshall, 'John Locke and Latitudinarianism', in Richard Kroll, Richard Ashcraft and Perez Zagorin, eds, *Philosophy, Science and Religion in England 1640–1700* (Cambridge: Cambridge University Press, 1992), p. 277. Cf. Laslett, 'Introduction', in *Two Treatises*, p. 73. The sermons written by Edward Stillingfleet were *The Mischief of Separation. A Sermon Preached at Guild-Hall Chappel, May ii MDCLXXX* (London, 1680), and *The Unreasonableness of Separation: Or, An Impartial Account of the History, Nature, and Pleas of the Present Separation from the Communion of the Church of England* (London, 1681). Also in contrast to Laslett, J. W. Gough asserts that during these years Locke often visited Tyrrell at his manor in Oakley, in Buckinghamshire. There are indications, however, that Tyrrell divided his time between Shotover and Oakley, and his letters to Locke often refer to news and to visits in Oxford. See Gough, 'James Tyrrell', 581; cf. E. S. De Beer, ed., *The Correspondence of John Locke*, vol. 2 (Oxford: Clarendon Press, 1976), pp. 210–12, 289–90, 523–5, 569–71.
17. Cranston, *John Locke*, p. 38.
18. As the eldest son of Elizabeth and of Sir Timothy Tyrrell, Baronet, of Shotover near Oxford, James inherited the family estate at Oakley, in Buckinghamshire. Cranston, *John Locke*, pp. 38, 66 ; Leslie Stephen, ed., *Dictionary of National Biography* (London: Smith, Elder, 1885–1904) (hereafter cited as *DNB*), s.v. 'Tyrrell, James' and 'Ussher, James'; Gough, 'James Tyrrell', 582. In addition to *The Power Communicated by God to the Prince* Ussher's publications include, for example, *An Answer to a Challenge Made by a Jesuite in Ireland* (London, 1621), *A Body of Divinitie, or The Summe and Substance of Christian Religion, Catechistically Propounded, and Explained, by way of Question and Answer* (London, 1645), *A Discourse of the Religion Anciently Professed by the Irish and British* (London, 1631), and *Episcopal and Presbyterial Government Conjoyned, Proposed as an Expedient for the Compremising of the Differences and Preventing of those Troubles about the Matter of Church-government* (London, 1679).
19. Locke became Ashley's personal physician, and moved to Exeter House in 1667. Cranston, *John Locke*, pp. 103–4.
20. Ibid., pp. 27–28, 92, 117.
21. Locke and his closest friends used a set of 'fanciful names' to address one another, following a French practice and mostly taken from Charles Sorel, *The Extravagant Shepherd: or, the History of the Shepherd Lysis*. An

Anti-romance, trans. John Davies (London, 1653; 2nd edn 1660). The editor of Locke's correspondence explains that while Tyrrell's nickname 'Musidore' was the name of a dog in *The Extravagant Shepherd* 'the source is more likely to be Sorel, *The Comical History of Francion* (1655), bk. v, where Musidorus is a threadbare poet'. De Beer, ed., *Correspondence of Locke*, vol. 1, pp. xviii–ix, 324, n. 1.

22. See the letter of 15 October 1691 for a catalogue of various possessions being returned to Locke after almost a decade at Oakley. Ibid., vol. 3, pp. 313–17.
23. Ibid., vol. 2, p. 766.
24. All the letters dated from March 1691 to August 1692 are concerned with logistics and lists. For example a letter from 19 March 1691 indicates that Locke was looking for some of his gilt spoons; another from 29 June 1691 has Tyrrell engaged in cataloguing Locke's books at Oakley. Tyrrell remains busy in the fall of 1691 and the winter of 1692 sending packages to Locke and tracking down various books and trunks, cupboards and carpets that were misplaced or that he and his family had used over the years. Ibid., vol. 4, pp. 242–4, 284–7, 313–17, 323–4, 330–1, 380–3, 385–7, 408–10, 493–6.
25. Ibid, vol. 2, p. 767.
26. John Locke, *An Essay Concerning Human Understanding*, Peter Nidditch ed. (Oxford: Clarendon Press, 1975), bk 1, ch. 3, sect. 13, pp. 74–5 and bk 2, ch. 27, sects 9–12, pp. 335–7. David Wootton, 'John Locke: Socinian or Natural Law Theorist?', in James Crimmins ed., *Religion, Secularization and Political Thought* (London: Routledge, 1989), pp. 40–2; John Marshall, *John Locke: Resistance, Religion and Responsibility* (Cambridge: Cambridge University Press, 1994), pp. 386–7; John Dunn, *The Political Thought of John Locke: An Historical Account of the Argument of the 'Two Treatises of Government'* (Cambridge: Cambridge University Press, 1988), pp. 81–2.
27. Tyrrell refers to his *Patriarcha non Monarcha* in letters of 30 August 1690 and 9 August 1692. Tyrrell also refers to his *A Brief Disquistion of the Law of Nature, according to the Principles and Method laid down in the Reverend Dr Cumberland's Latin treatise on that Subject* (London, 1692) in letters of 27 July 1690 and 19 March 1691. In a letter of 22 October 1691 Tyrrell asks Locke to look over and comment upon this *Disquisition*: 'if you doe not designe to publish any thing your self upon the same subject; . . . I would allso the rather have you see it because I have quoted divers things in it out of your booke.' De Beer, ed., *Correspondence of Locke*, vol. 4, pp. 108–9, 117, 243–4, 323–4, 495.
28. Ibid., pp. 108–9.
29. Ibid., letter of 30 August 1690, pp. 117–18. Questions about Locke's authorship of the *Two Treatises* also appear in an earlier letter of 18 March 1690, p. 36.
30. Ibid., vol. 2, pp. 210–12, 289–90, 417–19, 523–5, 569–71, 596–7.
31. Ashcraft, *Revolutionary Politics*, pp. 387–8. Melinda Zook's recent work on the 'conspiratorial politics' of the 1680s affirms that during these years Tyrrell was living 'a sedate existence at Oakley'. Zook, *Radical Whigs*,

p. 177. Philip Milton's challenge to the narrative of Locke's involvement in the Rye House Plot also exonerates Tyrrell. Philip Milton 'John Locke and the Rye House Plot', *Historical Journal*, 43, 3 (2000) 662–3, 666.
32. Laslett, 'Introduction', in *Two Treatises*, pp. 73–4. Gough, 'James Tyrrell', 585–6. Richard Tuck argues that there was, in fact, collaboration, and that Locke's influence on Tyrrell resulted in the addition of a late, 'Lockean' section to Tyrrell's book. In this way Tuck also explains the faulty composition and pagination of the work. Richard Tuck, *Natural Rights Theories: Their Origin and Development* (Cambridge: Cambridge University Press, 1979), pp. 169–70. Similarly David Wootton sees this faulty composition as evidence that Tyrrell changed his mind some time during the printing process, but Wootton argues that the change was to modify the 'dangerous' aspects of the text, and that in fact Tyrrell's *Patriarcha non Monarcha* influenced Locke's book. Wootton, 'Introduction', in *Political Writings of John Locke*, David Wootton ed. (New York: Mentor Books, 1993), pp. 58–60.
33. It has often been noted that there are some broad areas of agreement as well as some striking common images and examples that appear in both Tyrrell's and Locke's political treatises. Wootton, 'Introduction', in *Political Writings*, pp. 57–61, 78–89; Marshall, *John Locke*, pp. 234–5; Richard Ashcraft, 'Revolutionary Politics and Locke's *Two Treatises of Government*', *Political Theory*, 8 (1980) 444. Tyrrell himself noted, in a letter to Locke in 1690, that the author of the *Two Treatises* 'agreed perfectly with my conceptions in Patriarch non Mon: (which he had quoted)', as he expressed his suspicion that Locke was, in fact, that author. In his research among Locke's papers, John Marshall discovered a page from the manuscript of Tyrrell's *Patriarcha non Monarcha* interleaved with the commentary on Stillingfleet's sermons; Marshall, like Wootton, suggests that Locke's *Two Treatises* were written in response to *Patriarcha non Monarcha*. Marshall, *John Locke*, pp. 234–7; Wootton, 'Introduction', in *Political Writings*, pp. 77–89.
34. Mark Goldie, 'John Locke and Anglican Royalism', *Political Studies*, 31 (1983) 66; Gordon J. Schochet, 'Sir Robert Filmer: Some New Bibliographical Discoveries', *The Library*, fifth series, 26 (1971) 154–60.
35. Goldie, 'Locke and Anglican Royalism', 67.
36. Salmon, *French Religious Wars in English Political Thought*, chs 5–6.
37. Salmon, *French Religious Wars in English Political Thought*, ch. 3, pp. 39–57; Franklin, *John Locke*; Harro Hopfl and Martyn P. Thompson, 'The History of Contract as a Motif in Political Thought', *American Historical Review*, 84, 4 (1979) 919–44. And note, for example, Mark Goldie's exemplary Tory, Francis Turner, cites Arnisaeus and Grotius rather than Bodin and Hobbes. Mark Goldie, 'Restoration Political Thought', in Lionel K. J. Glassey, ed., *The Reigns of Charles II and James VII & II* (New York: St Martin's Press, 1997), p. 20.
38. Evidence, uncovered by Richard Tuck and by Johann Sommerville, has substantially altered Laslett's and Daly's original arguments for dating Patriarcha to the 1630s or 1640s. See James Daly, *Sir Robert Filmer and*

English Political Thought (Toronto: University of Toronto Press, 1979), p. 4; Peter Laslett, 'Sir Robert Filmer: The Man versus the Whig Myth', *William and Mary Quarterly*, 5, 4 (1948) 531; Johann P. Sommerville, 'Introduction', in Sir Robert Filmer, *Patriarcha and other Writings*, Johann P. Sommerville, ed., (Cambridge: Cambridge University Press, 1991), pp. viii, xxxii–xxxiv; Richard Tuck, 'A new date for Filmer's *Patriarcha'*, *Historical Journal*, 29 (1986) 183–6.
39. Sir Robert Filmer, *The Anarchy of a Limited or Mixed Monarchy*, (London, 1648); *The Free-holders Grand Inquest Touching our Soveraigne Lord the King and his Parliament* (London, 1648).
40. Daly, *Filmer and Political Thought*, p. 14.
41. Locke, *Two Treatises*, I, par. 2, p. 176.
42. Glenn Burgess has challenged the notion that there was such an established and broad absolutist theory in the early part of the seventeenth century in England. Yet his definition of absolutism, and his recognition of those few he terms absolutists, would be in accord with my delineation of these basic tenets. Glenn Burgess, *Absolute Monarchy and the Stuart Constitution* (New Haven: Yale University Press, 1996), pp. 209–10, 218.
43. Johann P. Sommerville, 'Absolutism and Royalism', in J. H. Burns with Mark Goldie, eds, *The Cambridge History of Political Thought, 1400–1800* (Cambridge: Cambridge University Press, 1991), pp. 350–8.
44. Dickinson, *Liberty and Property*, p. 14.
45. Harris, *Politics Under the Later Stuarts*, p. 58; Goldie, 'Locke and Anglican Royalism'; Sommerville, *Politics and Ideology*, pp. 27–34.
46. Mark Goldie, a well-known authority on Tory ideology, cites the work of William Falkner, Thomas Goddard, George Hickes, Nathaniel Johnston, John Nalson, William Sherlock, Edmund Bohun, Sir George Mackenzie and Francis Turner alongside Filmer's treatises as examples of Tory absolutism. Goldie summarizes the fundamentals of Tory absolutist ideology as '[a] juristic theory of sovereignty, a natural law theory of patriarchalism, a scriptural doctrine of non-resistance and an historical theory about parliament'. Goldie, 'Restoration Political Thought', pp. 19–25. Finally, even Burgess comes to acknowledge Tory acceptance of 'Filmer's' absolutist principles. Burgess *Absolute Monarchy*, pp. 216–17,
47. Goldie, 'Restoration Political Thought', pp. 25–7.
48. Goldie, 'Locke and Anglican Royalism', 61. Here I agree with Goldie and Sommerville, and disagree with Daly, on the representative nature of Filmer's work. See Sommerville, *Politics and Ideology*, ch. 1; idem., 'Introduction' in *Patriarcha and Other Writings*, p. xviii; and idem., 'Absolutism and Royalism', p. 359.
49. Other prominent critics of Filmer included Algernon Sidney, *Discourses Concerning Government* (London, 1698); Thomas Hunt, *The Great and Weighty Considerations Relating to the Duke of York or, Successor of the Crown. Offered to the King, and both Houses of Parliament: Considered* (London, 1680); idem., *Mr. Hunt's Postscript for Rectifying Some Mistakes in some of the Inferior Clergy, Mischievous to our Government and Religion*

Notes 179

(London, 1682). For a thorough discussion of Hunt see Zook, *Radical Whigs*; for Sidney see Scott, *Algernon Sidney and the English Republic* and *Algernon Sidney and the Restoration Crisis*.
50. Tyrrell, *Patriarcha non Monarcha*, Preface.
51. On Whig and Tory uses of arguments from 'liberty' see Tim Harris, '"Lives, Liberties and Estates"': Rhetorics of Liberty in the Reign of Charles II', in Harris, Seaward, Goldie, eds, *Politics of Religion*, pp. 217–42.
52. Tyrrell, *Patriarcha non Monarcha*, Preface. Tyrrell might be said to be recognizing that conceptual shift that Burgess argues for, and to be reading Filmer without the lens of the 'parliamentary hermeneutic'.
53. Ibid.
54. Gordon J. Schochet, *Patriarchalism in Political Thought: The Authoritarian Family and Political Speculation and Attitudes Especially in Seventeenth-Century England* (New York: Basic Books, 1975), p. 194. Weil, *Political Passions*, Part I.
55. Tyrrell, *Patriarcha non Monarcha*, p. 44.
56. Ibid., p. 8; Locke, *Two Treatises*, I, par. 6, p. 180, pars 61–3, pp. 222–3.
57. Tyrrell, *Patriarcha non Monarcha*, p. 10.
58. Ibid., pp. 18–19.
59. Ibid., p. 17.
60. Ibid., pp. 17, 30.
61. Ibid., pp. 24, 104–5, 111.
62. Ibid., p. 104, and p. 98 second pagination. Compare Filmer's defense of Scripture, and his attack on the authority of the 'heathen authors', in his *Observations upon Aristotles Politiques* in Filmer, *Patriarcha and Other Writings*, p. 236.
63. Tyrrell, *Patriarcha non Monarcha*, p. 117.
64. These men are 'supernatural' in that they act by virtue of divinely implanted reason and the law of nature, and in creation become more than men. Moreover, the image of this original people remains larger-than-life even when connected to the 'real history' of the Patriarchs, or the legendary founders of Rome and Venice.
65. Laurence Coupe, *Myth* (New York: Routledge, 1997), pp. 5–6, 57–62; Mircea Eliade, *Myth and Reality* (New York: Harper & Row, 1963; Harper Colophon, 1975), pp. 5–11; Christopher G. Flood, *Political Myth, A Theoretical Introduction* (New York: Garland, 1996), pp. 27–44.
66. Locke, *Two Treatises*, II, pars 110–11, pp. 386–7; Tyrrell, *Patriarcha non Monarcha*, p. 37.
67. Goldie, 'Restoration Political Thought'; Sommerville, 'Absolutism and Royalism'. Locke cites Filmer's objections, *Two Treatises*, II, par. 100, pp. 377–8.
68. Tyrrell, *Patriarcha non Monarcha*, p. 98 second pagination; Locke, *Two Treatises*, II, par. 104, p. 380.
69. Samuel Pufendorf, *De Jure Naturae et Gentium, Libri Octo*, vol. 2, C. H. Oldfather and W. A. Oldfather trans., Carnegie Endowment for International Peace, Division of International Law, Classics of International Law, no. 17 (Oxford: Clarendon Press, 1934), p. 977.

180 Notes

70. Tyrrell, *Patriarcha non Monarcha*, p. 85; Locke, *Two Treatises*, II, par. 102, p. 379; Salmon, *French Religious Wars in English Political Thought*, p. 168.
71. Tyrrell, *Patriarcha non Monarcha*, pp. 37, 47; Locke, *Two Treatises*, II, pars 105–12, pp. 380–9; cf Pufendorf, *De Jure Naturae et Gentium*, vol. 2, p. 1007. This passage provides evidence for Rachel Weil's contention that Tyrrell 'plays into the very family-state analogy he claims to reject'. Weil, *Political Passions*, p. 59.
72. Tyrrell, *Patriarcha non Monarcha*, pp. 83–4.
73. Ibid., pp. 84, 93.
74. Filmer, *Patriarcha*, in *Patriarcha and Other Writings*, pp. 10–11; idem., *Anarchy of a Mixed or Limited Monarchy*, in *Patriarcha and Other Writings*, p. 143.
75. Weil, *Political Passions*, pp. 23, 35.
76. There is a growing literature analyzing the role of women in contract theory which includes, for example: Teresa Brennan and Carole Pateman, '"Mere Auxiliaries to the Commonwealth": Women and the Origins of Liberalism', *Political Studies*, 27 (1979) 183–200; Susan Moller Okin, *Women in Western Political Thought* (Princeton: Princeton University Press, 1979); L. M. G. Clark, 'Women and John Locke: Or, Who Owns the Apples in the Garden of Eden?', *Canadian Journal of Philosophy*, 7, 4 (1977) 699–724; Carole Pateman, *The Sexual Contract: Aspects of Patriarchal Liberalism* (Stanford: Stanford University Press, 1988); Carole Pateman and Mary L. Shanley, eds, *Feminist Interpretations and Political Theory* (University Park: Pennsylvania State University Press, 1991); Julia Rudolph, 'Rape and Resistance: Women and Consent in Seventeenth-Century English Legal and Political Thought', *Journal of British Studies*, 39, 2 (2000), 157–84; Mary L. Shanley, 'Marriage Contract and Social Contract in Seventeenth-Century English Political Thought', *Western Political Quarterly*, 32 (1979) 79–91; Margaret R. Sommerville, *Sex and Subjection: Attitudes to Women in Early-Modern Society* (London: Arnold, 1995); Hilda L. Smith, *Reason's Disciples: Seventeenth-century English Feminists* (Urbana: University of Illinois Press, 1982); idem., ed., *Women Writers and the Early Modern British Political Tradition* (Cambridge: Cambridge University Press, 1998); Weil, *Political Passions*. Weil is surely right in her insight that it is this ambivalence or instability of both Whig and Lockean theory that has led to such 'radically divergent interpretations' of these theories and their significance. Weil, *Political Passions* p. 78.
77. Tyrrell, *Patriarcha non Monarcha*, pp. 110–11; see also p. 52 on the authority of Eve/wife in the state of nature. Tyrrell's later reaffirmation of these, and subsequent points, can be found in *Bibliotheca Politica*, Dialogue 1.
78. Ibid., p. 109.
79. Ibid., pp. 111, 113. Locke, *Two Treatises*, II, par. 80, p. 363, simply states that 'the Father . . . is bound to take care for those he hath begot'. Rachel Weil notes the frequency of Tyrrell's discussion of violence in the family, and emphasizes its importance. Weil, *Political Passions*, pp. 62–6. And cf.

Tyrrell's vision not only of violent husbands but also of murderous wives, sons and brothers in Tyrrell, *Bibliotheca Politica*, Dialogue 1, pp. 32–4.
80. Weil, *Political Passions*, p. 51.
81. Locke, *Two Treatises*, II, pars 82–3, pp. 364–5; Melissa A. Butler, 'Early Liberal Roots of Feminism: John Locke and the Attack on Patriarchy', in Carole Pateman and Mary L. Shanley, eds, *Feminist Interpretations and Political Theory*, p. 85; Weil, *Political Passions*, pp. 74–7. On Locke see Chapter 6 below.
82. Pateman, *Sexual Contract*, p. 42.
83. Ibid., pp. 83–4.
84. Mary Astell, *Reflections Upon Marriage*, in *Political Writings*, Patricia Springborg, ed. (Cambridge: Cambridge University Press, 1996), p. 18; Pateman, *Sexual Contract*, p. 41; Weil *Political Passions*, pp. 42–3.
85. Margaret Sommerville does acknowledge that some contradiction remains – although she often frames it as a contradiction between theory and practice. Sommerville, *Sex and Subjection*, p. 250. Rachel Weil depicts the ambivalence or contradiction as 'unresolved questions in whig political thought', and argues that the 'family–state distinction' employed by theorists was a fundamentally unstable strategy. Weil, *Political Passions*, pp. 42–3, 79.
86. Pufendorf, *De Jure Naturae et Gentium*, vol. 2, p. 845. Cf. Locke on the 'first Society' between 'Man and Wife'. Locke, *Two Treatises*, II, par. 77, p. 362.
87. Tyrrell, Weil later adds, was 'ambivalent about the power wives might have if they did not contract to give it away'. Weil, *Political Passions*, pp. 44, 66.
88. Pufendorf, *De Jure Naturae et Gentium*, vol. 2, pp. 845, 855–7.
89. Tyrrell, *Patriarcha non Monarcha*, pp. 84, 110–11; Pufendorf, *De Jure Naturae et Gentium*, vol. 2, pp. 853, 859–60, 862, 916. Locke agrees only with the third reason, the 'natural' explanation. Locke, *Two Treatises*, I, par. 47, p. 210, II, par. 82, p. 364. Others, like Gilbert Burnet for example, also acknowledged the scriptural authority for female subordination. Gilbert Burnet, *Enquiry into the Measures of Submission*, sect. 14; Sommerville, *Sex and Subjection*, ch. 2; Weil, *Political Passions*, p. 73.
90. Tyrrell, *Patriarcha non Monarcha*, p. 14; Locke, *Two Treatises*, II, pars 78–80, pp. 362–3.
91. Tyrrell, *Patriarcha non Monarcha*, p. 112; cf. Pufendorf, *De Jure Naturae et Gentium*, vol. 2, p. 860. Tyrrell often nearly transcribes Pufendorf without citing him.
92. Cf. other Whig theorists who later make this same argument: White Kennett, *A Dialogue Between Two Friends, Occasioned by the late Revolution of Affairs, and the Oath of Allegiance* (London, 1689), p. 17; Richard Kingston, *Tyranny Detected and the Late Revolution Justify'd by the Law of God, the Law of Nature, and the Practice of all Nations* (London, 1699), pp. 50–1; *A Political Conference Between Aulicus, a Courtier, Demas, a Country-man, and*

Civicus, a Citizen: Clearing the Original of Civil Government, the Powers and Duties of Soveraigns and Subjects (London, 1689), p. 30.
93. Tyrrell, *Patriarcha non Monarcha*, p. 109.
94. Pufendorf, *De Jure Naturae et Gentium*, vol. 2, p. 863.
95. Pateman, *Sexual Contract*, p. 53.
96. Tyrrell, *Patriarcha non Monarcha*, pp. 111–12; Pufendorf, *De Jure Naturae et Gentium*, vol. 2, p. 859.
97. Pufendorf, like other theorists, recognizes the Amazons as an example of women creating a state, and establishing a female ruler; but he explains that this only takes place in a female world, where women may be equal to other women. For the discussion of political authority in a queen see, for example, Locke, *Two Treatises*, I, par. 47, p. 210; Tyrrell, *Patriarcha non Monarcha*, p. 15; idem., *Bibliotheca Politica*, Dialogue 5, p. 366; Sommerville, *Sex and Subjection*, pp. 51–60; Weil, *Political Passions*, pp. 65–6.
98. Locke, *Two Treatises*, II, par. 54, p. 346; Butler, 'Early Liberal Roots of Feminism', p. 89. See also Chapter 6 below.
99. Here is where I question Sommerville's argument against Pateman. The subordination of women was *qualitatively* different from the subordination of 'weak and stupid' men since women's inequality was not a matter of degrees (of intelligence, strength, talent) but was a fundamental, inescapable disability. The assumptions or claims about women's natural inferiority in reason, in body/womb, meant that women could not – even abstractly – enjoy equal political rights. See Sommerville, ch. 8, esp. n. 41.
100. Pufendorf, *De Jure Naturae et Gentium*, vol. 2, p. 845.
101. Tyrrell, *Patriarcha non Monarcha*, p. 116.
102. Ibid., pp. 83–4.
103. Stephen Buckle, *Natural Law and the Theory of Property, Grotius to Hume* (Oxford: Oxford University Press, 1991); Thomas A. Horne, *Property Rights and Poverty: Political Argument in Britain, 1605–1834* (Chapel Hill: University of North Carolina Press, 1990), p. 10; David McNally, 'Locke, Levellers and Liberty: Property and Democracy in the Thought of the First Whigs', *History of Political Thought*, X, 1 (1989) 34.
104. Horne, *Property Rights and Poverty*, p. 20.
105. Ibid., pp. 99–100; Hugo Grotius, *De Jure Belli ac Pacis, Libri Tres*, vol. 2, F. W. Kelsey trans., Carnegie Endowment for International Peace, Division of International Law, Classics of International Law, no. 3 (Oxford: Clarendon Press, 1925), pp. 186–7; R. B. Schlatter, *Private Property: The History of an Idea* (New Brunswick: Rutgers University Press, 1951), pp. 48–9; Istvan Hont and Michael Ignatieff, 'Needs and Justice in the *Wealth of Nations*; An Introductory Essay', in Istvan Hont and Michael Ignatieff, eds, *Wealth and Virtue: The Shaping of Political Economy in the Scottish Enlightenment* (Cambridge: Cambridge University Press, 1983), p. 27.
106. Tyrrell, *Patriarcha non Monarcha*, p. 110.
107. Tuck, *Natural Rights Theories*, pp. 72–3.

108. *An Agreement of the People for a Firm and Present Peace upon Grounds of Common Right and Freedom*, in Andrew Sharp, ed., *The English Levellers* (Cambridge: Cambridge University Press, 1998), pp. 92–101. David Wootton, 'Leveller Democracy and the Puritan Revolution', in Burns with Goldie, eds, *Cambridge History of Political Thought*, pp. 412–13.
109. Filmer, *Observations Concerning the Originall of Government* in Filmer, *Patriarcha and other Writings*, p. 218.
110. Pufendorf, *De Jure Naturae et Gentium*, vol. 2, pp. 523–32. Pufendorf was, in turn, drawing upon Suarez's distinction between 'preceptive' and 'permissive' natural law.
111. Tyrrell, *Patriarcha non Monarcha*, p. 109; cf. Pufendorf, *De Jure Naturae et Gentium*, vol. 2, p. 537.
112. Tyrrell, *Patriarcha non Monarcha*, pp. 102–3. Thomas Horne notes that Pufendorf 'envisioned a wide variety of property systems, with many combinations of private and communal rights, as falling under the legitimacy conferred by natural law'. Horne, *Property Rights and Poverty*, p. 35.
113. Tyrrell, *Patriarcha non Monarcha*, pp. 111–12; Horne, *Property Rights and Poverty*, p. 9.
114. Tyrrell, *Patriarcha non Monarcha*, pp. 113–14 second pagination; Pufendorf, *De Jure Naturae et Gentium*, vol. 2, p. 539.
115. Grotius, *De Jure Belli ac Pacis*, vol. 2, pp. 189–90, 206; Filmer, *Observations Concerning the Originall of Government*, in Filmer, *Patriarcha and Other Writings*, p. 234.
116. Locke, *Two Treatises*, II, pars 25–51, pp. 327–44; Tyrrell, *Patriarcha non Monarcha*, pp. 112–15 second pagination; Horne, *Property Rights and Poverty* pp. 44, 49.
117. Tyrrell, *Patriarcha non Monarcha*, pp. 112–13; Locke, *Two Treatises*, II, par. 31, p. 332; Grotius, *De Jure Belli ac Pacis*, vol. 2, p. 193.
118. Tyrrell, *Patriarcha non Monarcha*, pp. 107–8 second pagination.
119. Horne, *Property Rights and Poverty*, p. 29.
120. Ibid.
121. As Thomas Horne notes, with reference to Cumberland and Pufendorf, '[a] defense of the existing distribution of property, a concern that economic desires be moderate, and a recognition of the right of necessity were all characteristic of seventeenth-century attitudes towards property'. Ibid., p. 32.
122. Ibid., p. 86.
123. Ibid., p. 87.
124. See Chapter 6 below.
125. Locke, *Two Treatises*, II, par. 73, p. 358, par. 119, p. 392.
126. Ibid., par. 119, p. 392.
127. Tyrrell, *Patriarcha non Monarcha*, pp. 87–8; Locke, *Two Treatises*, II, par. 122, p. 394.
128. Tyrrell, *Patriarcha non Monarcha*, p. 88.
129. Ibid., pp. 128–9, 136–8 second pagination, 209ff. especially 255–6.

184 Notes

130. Philip Hunton, *A Treatise of Monarchy, Containing Two Parts: I. Concerning Monarchy in General. II. Concerning this Particular Monarchy. Wherein All the Maine Questions Occurrent in Both, are Stated, Disputed, and Determined* (London, 1643).
131. Tyrrell, *Patriarcha non Monarcha*, p. 212.
132. Ibid., 216–17; Hunton, *Treatise of Monarchy*, pp. 17–18.
133. David Wootton, 'Introduction', in David Wootton, ed., *Divine Right and Democracy: An Anthology of Political Writing in Stuart England* (New York: Penguin Books, 1986), pp. 37, 48; Franklin, *John Locke* pp. 39–48. It was, perhaps, this tendency that led to the burning of Hunton's *Treatise of Monarchy* at Oxford University in 1683.
134. Tyrrell, *Patriarcha non Monarcha*, pp. 218–19.
135. Tyrrell, *Patriarcha non Monarcha*, pp. 129–30; Ashcraft, *Revolution Politics*, ch. 7.
136. Tyrrell, *Patriarcha non Monarcha*, p. 231.
137. Note, however, that Tyrrell does defend Hunton's idea of the people's ability to render a 'natural and moral judgment', although he does not attribute to them an authoritative and civil power over the king. Tyrrell, *Patriarcha non Monarcha*, pp. 234ff. Compare this to Tyrrell's later defense of the Convention's 'declarative' power in *Bibliotheca Politica*.
138. Tyrrell, *Patriarcha non Monarcha*, p. 77.
139. Ibid.
140. Aristotle, *The Politics*, bk 3, ch. 3 (1276a34), T. A. Sinclair, trans. and Trevor J. Saunders, ed., revised edn (New York: Penguin Books, 1981), pp. 175–6.
141. Pocock, *Ancient Constitution*, p. 338.
142. Filmer, *Anarchy of a Mixed or Limited Monarchy*, in Filmer, *Patriarcha and Other Writings*, p. 142.
143. Tyrrell, *Patriarcha non Monarcha*, pp. 50–1, 227–8.
144. Ibid., p. 126.
145. Ibid., p. 73; Filmer, *Patriarcha*, in Filmer, *Patriarcha and Other Writings*, pp. 10–11; idem., *Anarchy of a Mixed or Limited Monarchy*, in Filmer, *Patriarcha and Other Writings*, p. 143.
146. Ashcraft, *Revolutionary Politics*, pp. 298–302.
147. Tyrrell, *Patriarcha non Monarcha*, p. 74.
148. Ibid., pp. 51, 60.
149. Ashcraft, *Revolutionary Politics*, pp. 298–302; Harris, *Politics Under the Later Stuarts*, p. 101; Wootton, 'Introduction', in *Divine Right and Democracy*, pp. 46–50.
150. *Captain Thorogood His Opinion of the Point of Succession, To a Brother of the Blade in Scotland* (n.p., 1679), p. 3.
151. Ibid.
152. Ibid., p. 5.
153. Ibid.
154. Wootton, 'Introduction', in *Divine Right and Democracy*, pp. 45–50.
155. Harris, *Politics Under the Later Stuarts*, p. 101; Knights, *Politics and Opinion*, pp. 306–11.

Chapter Three 'To preserve the Original Constitution of Parliaments': Revolution and Preservation in James Tyrrell's Whig History

1. Tyrrell, *Bibliotheca Politica*, Dialogue 8, p. 613.
2. Pocock, *Ancient Constitution*, pp. 187–8, 347–8.
3. *DNB*, s.v. 'Atwood, William'; Zook, *Radical Whigs*, pp. 66–86, 159–64. William Petyt, *The Antient Right of the Commons of England Asserted; Or a Discourse Proving by Records and the Best Historians that the Commons of England were ever an Essential Part of Parliament* (London, 1680); William Atwood, *Jani Anglorum Facies Nova: Or, Several Monuments of Antiquity Touching the Great Councils of the Kingdom and the Court of the Kings Immediate Tenants and Officers, from the first of William the First, to the forty ninth of Henry the Third, Reviv'd and Clear'd* (London, 1680); Robert Brady, *A Full and Clear Answer to a Book Written by William Petit; Printed in the Year 1680 . . . With a True Historical Account of the Famous Colloquim or Parliament, 49 Hen III. And a Glossary Expounding Some Few Words Used Frequently in Our Antient Records, Laws and Historians. Together with Some Animadversions Upon a Book Called Jani Anglorum Facies Nova* (London, 1681). Pocock, *Ancient Constitution*, pp. 188–93, 345–8; idem., 'The Varieties of Whiggism from Exclusion to Reform: A History of Ideology and Discourse', in *Virtue, Commerce and History. Essays on Political Thought and History, Chiefly in the Eighteenth Century* (Cambridge: Cambridge University Press, 1985), pp. 221–2; Corinne Comstock Weston and Janelle Greenberg, *Subjects and Sovereigns: The Grand Controversy over Legal Sovereignty in Stuart England* (Cambridge: Cambridge University Press, 1981), p. 184.
4. *DNB*, s.v. 'Brady, Robert'; Pocock, *Ancient Constitution*, pp.194–5.
5. Robert Brady, 'Epistle to the Candid Reader', in *An Introduction to The Old English History. Comprehended in Three Several Tracts. The First, an Answer to Mr Petyt's Rights of the Commons Asserted; and to a Book Entitled Jani Anglorum Facies Nova; the Second Edition, very much Inlarged. The Second, an Answer to a Book Intituled Argumentum Antinormannicum. . . . The Third, the Exact History of the Succession of the Crown of England . . .* (London, 1684), p. 3.
6. Ibid., p. 4.
7. Ibid., p. 5.
8. Tyrrell, *Patriarcha non Monarcha*, Preface; Tyrrell to William Petyt, 1681, Inner Temple, London, Petyt MS. 538, 65, fol. 302.
9. James Tyrrell, *A Brief Enquiry into the Ancient Constitution and Government of England, As well in Respect of the Administration as Succession Thereof* (London, 1695); idem., *The General History of England, Both Ecclesiastical and Civil; From the Earliest Accounts of Time, To the Reign of His Present Majesty, King William III*, 3 vols (London, 1704). Tyrrell completed three volumes of this work, reaching only to the reign of Richard II.
10. Tyrrell, *Bibliotheca Politica*, Epistle Dedicatory.
11. Ibid.

12. Ibid. Tyrrell claimed similar intentions and concern for the public good in the dedication to his edition of Bishop Cumberland's work on natural law. James Tyrrell, *A Brief Disquisition of the Law of Nature*, 2nd edn (London, 1701; reprint, Littleton, Colo.: Fred B. Rothman and Company, 1987), Epistle Dedicatory.
13. Wilfrid R. Prest, *The Rise of the Barristers: a Social History of the English Bar 1590–1640* (Oxford: Clarendon Press, 1991); Brian P. Levack, *The Civil Lawyers in England 1603–1641: a Political Study* (Oxford: Clarendon Press, 1973).
14. Tyrrell, *Bibliotheca Politica*, Epistle Dedicatory. Note the difference from the imagined participants in Tyrrell's *A Brief Enquiry*, where 'an understanding Freeholder' seeks the opinion of a Justice of the Peace.
15. Kenyon, *Revolution Principles*, 36–7, n. 8.
16. Note, for example, the disputes raised by William Sherlock's publications which included not only the highly contested *The Case of Allegiance due to Sovereign Powers Stated and Resolved, according to Scripture and Reason, and the Principles of the Church of England, with a More Particular Respect to the Oath Lately Enjoyed, of Allegiance to their Present Majesties, K. William and Q. Mary* (London 1691) but also a first and second *Letter to a Friend, concerning a French Invasion, to Restore the Late King James to His Throne* (London, 1692). See the bibliography in Mark Goldie, 'The Revolution of 1689 and the Structure of Political Argument: An Essay and an Annotated Bibliography of Pamphlets on the Allegiance Controversy', *Bulletin of Research in the Humanities*, 83, 4 (1980) 557–8.
17. The first dialogue in the collected edition of 1694 is misdated: it is dated 1694, while dialogues two through five are dated 1692 and their title pages refer to the first dialogue as already having been published. There are surviving separate copies of this first dialogue bearing the publication date of 1691/2.
18. Kenyon, *Revolution Principles*, pp. 66–9; Zook, *Radical Whigs*, p. 184.
19. Tyrrell, *Bibiliotheca Politica*, Dialogue 9, Preface.
20. See, for example, Meanwell's criticism. Ibid., Dialogue 5, p. 338.
21. Ibid., p. 317. Some confusion remains, and Freeman does, at times, come closer to a theory of coordination, for example in Dialogue 5, pp. 341–5. On the balance of the ancient constitution see Glenn Burgess, *The Politics of the Ancient Constitution: An Introduction to English Political Thought, 1603–1642* (University Park, PA: Pennsylvania State University Press, 1993), pp. 5–6; Pocock, *Ancient Constitution*, pt II, chs 1–2; Weston and Greenberg, *Subjects and Sovereigns*. For other Whigs on England's limited and mixed government see Chapter 4 below, especially n. 69.
22. Tyrrell, *Bibliotheca Politica*, Dialogue 5, pp. 347–8.
23. Ibid.
24. Ibid., p. 349.
25. Hunton, *Treatise of Monarchy*, 35–6; Samuel Kliger, *The Goths in England, A Study in Seventeenth and Eighteenth Century Thought* (Cambridge, Mass.: Harvard University Press, 1952), p. 131; cf. Tyrrell, *Bibliotheca Politica*, Dialogue 5, p. 365 and idem., *General History*, vol. 1, bks 3, 5.

Notes 187

26. Kliger, *Goths in England*, p. 131.
27. Ibid., pp. 12–13. Tyrrell, *Bibliotheca Politica* Dialogue 5, pp. 356–9, cites Tacitus' *Germania* and explains that the Angli and the Saxons 'were either all one and the same Nation, or very little different'. Even the pre-Saxon inhabitants, the Britons, were sometimes seen as 'Gothic' or 'Gallic' or as sharing in the freedoms of the 'Gothic constitution'. See Tyrrell, *General History*, vol. 1, bk 1, pp. 4–7, 17–18; Nathaniel Bacon, *An Historical and Political Discourse of the Laws and Government of England, From the First Times to the End of the Reign of Queen Elizabeth. With a Vindication of the Ancient Way of Parliaments in England. Collected from some Manuscript Notes of John Selden Esq.* (London, 1689); R. J. Smith, *The Gothic Bequest: Medieval Institutions in British Thought 1688–1863* (Cambridge: Cambridge University Press, 1987), p. 41.
28. A. T. Bradford, 'Stuart Absolutism and the "Utility" of Tacitus', *Huntington Library Quarterly*, 46 (1983) 127–55; Ronald Mellor, 'Introduction', in Ronald Mellor, ed., *Tacitus, The Classical Heritage* (New York: Garland, 1995).
29. Donald R. Kelley, '*Tacitus Noster*: The *Germania* in the Renaissance and Reformation', in T. J. Luce and A. J. Woodman, eds, *Tacitus and the Tacitean Tradition* (Princeton: Princeton University Press, 1993). Mellor, 'Introduction', in *Tacitus*, pp. xxxii–xxxvii. Tyrell cites both Tacitus' *Germania* and Hotman's *Francogallia* in *Bibliotheca Politica*, Dialogue 5, p. 365, and in *Patriarcha non Monarcha*, pp. 221–2, 250; William Atwood also cites Hotman's *Francogallia* in Atwood, *The Fundamental Constitution of the English Government, Proving King William and Queen Mary are Lawful and Rightful King and Queen* (London, 1690), ch. 7. Tacitean history could be seen as a kind of Reformation history: Germanic liberty was religious as well as political, linked with freedom from Rome, and this was another important element of English national history.
30. Tyrrell, *Bibliotheca Politica*, Dialogue 5, pp. 356–60, 365, Dialogue 8, pp. 606–7.
31. Kelley, '*Tacitus Noster*', p. 163. Kelley argues, with regard to the influence of Tacitus in sixteenth-century Germany and Italy: 'In general, however, what Tacitus inspired posthumously was not *historia*, as Andrea Alciato wrote in the preface to his annotations on Tacitus, but rather *eruditio* – not narrative history but the more profound and perhaps mystical search for the founding fathers (*Vorfahrer, vorfordern*) and the difficult and myth-ridden questions of national spirit and origins.' Ibid., p. 162.
32. Tyrrell, *Bibliotheca Politica*, Dialogue 5, pp. 349–50, 365. Robert Atkyns, *The Power, Jurisdiction and Priviledge of Parliament; and the Antiquity of the House of Commons Asserted: Occasioned by an Information in the Kings Bench, by the Attorney General, Against the Speaker of the House of Commons* (London, 1689), p. 34; Atwood, *Fundamental Constitution*.
33. Tyrrell, *Bibliotheca Politica*, Dialogue 5, p. 367, Dialogue 10, p. 704.
34. Ibid., Dialogue 5, pp. 349–50.
35. Ibid., p. 350.

36. Brady builds upon the historical researches of earlier scholars such as Henry Spelman and William Dugdale. For the development of English historiography and antiquarian scholarship see Pocock, *Ancient Constitution*; D. C. Douglas, *English Scholars 1660–1730* (London: Eyre & Spottiswoode, 1951); Arthur B. Ferguson, *Clio Unbound: Perception of the Social and Cultural Past in Renaissance England* (Durham: Duke University Press, 1979); F. Smith Fussner, *The Historical Revolution: English Historical Writing and Thought 1580–1640* (London: Routledge & Paul, 1962); Joseph M. Levine, *Humanism and History: Origins of Modern English Historiography* (Ithaca: Cornell University Press, 1987); Smith, *The Gothic Bequest*; Daniel R. Woolf, *The Idea of History in Early Stuart England: Erudition, Ideology, and 'The Light of Truth' from the Accession of James I to the Civil War* (Toronto: University of Toronto Press, 1990).
37. Pocock, *Ancient Constitution*, pp. 197–8.
38. Ibid., pp. 196–209, 351–3; D. C. Douglas, *English Scholars*, pp. 130–1; Meanwell's position in Tyrrell, *Bibliotheca Politica*, Dialogues 6 and 7; Brady, *Introduction to English History*, pp. 14, 18–19.
39. Tyrrell, *Bibliotheca Politica*, Dialogue 10, p. 712.
40. D. W. L. Earl, 'Procrustean Feudalism: An Interpretative Dilemma in English Historical Narration, 1700–25', *Historical Journal*, 19, 1 (1976) 37.
41. Earl, 'Procrustean Feudalism', 38; Philip Hicks, *Neoclassical History and English Culture: From Clarendon to Hume* (New York: St. Martin's Press, 1996), pp. 86–7, 93–4.
42. Tyrrell, *Bibliotheca Politica*, Dialogue 6, p. 375.
43. See for example, Tyrrell, *Bibliotheca Politica*, Dialogue 6, p. 419.
44. Ibid., Dialogue 6, p. 374, Dialogue 8, pp. 608–10, Dialogue 10, p. 707. These passages seem to suggest that comparative law and history did influence the English understanding of their own constitution. On the question of English 'insularity' see: Christopher Brooks and Kevin Sharpe, 'Debate: History, English Law and the Renaissance', *Past and Present*, 72 (1976) 133–42; Donald R. Kelley, 'History, English Law and the Renaissance', *Past and Present*, 65 (1974) 24–51; idem., 'History, English Law and the Renaissance: a Rejoinder', *Past and Present*, 72 (1976) 143–6; R. H. Helmholz, 'Continental Law and Common Law: Historical Strangers or Companions?', in David Sugarman, ed., *Law in History: Histories of Law and Society*, vol. 2 (New York: New York University Press, 1996), pp. 19–40; Pocock, *Ancient Constitution*; Burgess, *Politics of the Ancient Constitution*.
45. Kelley, '*Tacitus Noster*', pp. 162–3, 167.
46. Tyrrell, *Bibliotheca Politica*, Dialogue 6, pp. 377, 419, 428, Dialogue 7, p. 490.
47. Ibid., Dialogue 6, p. 374. See also Tyrrell, *General History*, vol. 1, Preface; Atkyns, *Power, Jurisdiction and Priviledge*, p. 29.
48. Tyrrell, *Bibliotheca Politica*, Dialogue 6, pp. 383–5, 395, 423, Dialogue 8, pp. 545–61.
49. Ibid., Dialogue 6, p. 419.
50. Pocock, *Ancient Constitution*, pp. 197–8.

51. Tyrrell, *Bibliotheca Politica*, Dialogue 6, pp. 380–1; Earl, 'Procrustean Feudalism', 40–41.
52. Tyrrell, *Bibliotheca Politica*, Dialogue 6, p. 381.
53. Ibid., Dialogue 6, pp. 375, 381–2, Dialogue 8; Petyt, *Antient Right*, Proofs #1, 2, 5.
54. Tyrrell, *Bibliotheca Politica*, Dialogue 6, p. 387.
55. Ibid., pp. 425, 428; idem., *General History*, vol. 1, Preface, pp. lxxii–cxxv.
56. Brady, *Introduction to English History*, p. 4, cited above.
57. Ibid., pp. 4–5.
58. Tyrrell, *Bibliotheca Politica*, Dialogue 7, p. 509.
59. Ibid., Dialogue 6, pp. 419–21.
60. Ibid., p. 428.
61. Ibid., Dialogue 7, pp. 442–3, Dialogue 10, pp. 729–35. Petyt, *Antient Right*, p. 20; Edward Cooke, *Argumentum Anti-Normannicum: Or an Argument Proving, from Ancient Histories and Records, that William, Duke of Normandy, Made No Absolute Conquest of England by the Sword; in the Sense of our Modern Writers* (London, 1682), ch. 3; Pocock, *Ancient Constitution*, p. 198; Earl, 'Procrustean Feudalism', 44. See Brady, *Introduction to English History*, Appendix, for his catalogue of landholdings in the Domesday Book.
62. Christopher Hill, 'The Norman Yoke', in *Puritanism and Revolution: Studies in Interpretation of the English Revolution of the Seventeenth Century* (London: Secker & Warburg, 1958; New York: reprint edn Schocken Books, 1964) pp. 50–122; Quentin Skinner 'History and Ideology in the English Revolution', *Historical Journal*, 8, 2 (1965) 151–78; Mark Goldie, 'Edmund Bohun and *Jus Gentium* in the Revolution Debate, 1689–1693', *Historical Journal*, 20, 3 (1977) 569–86; Sommerville, *Politics and Ideology*, pp. 86–114.
63. Tyrrell, *Bibliotheca Politica*, Dialogue 5, p. 322, Dialogue 7, p. 455, Dialogue 10, p. 715; Cooke, *Argumentum Anti-Normannicum*, especially the 'Explanation of the Frontispiece', and pts I-II; Bacon, *Historical and Political Discourse*, part I, chs 45–6 and Conclusion; Petyt, *Antient Right*, pp. 29–31, 104–5; Daniel Whitby, *An Historical Account of Some Things Relating to the Nature of the English Government, and the Conceptions Which Our Forefathers Had of It. With Some Inferences Thence Made for the Satisfaction of Those Who Scruple the Oath of Allegiance to King William and Queen Mary* (London, 1689), pp. 13–14, 55–60; Sir Herbert Butterfield, *Magna Carta in the Historiography of the Sixteenth and Seventeenth Centuries* (Reading: University of Reading Press, 1969); Janelle Greenberg, 'The Confessor's Laws and the Radical Face of the Ancient Constitution', *English Historical Review*, (1989) 611–37.
64. Petyt, *Antient Right*, p. 25; Tyrrell, *Bibliotheca Politica*, Dialogue 10, pp. 715, 722; Earl, 'Procrustean Feudalism', 43.
65. Smith, *Gothic Bequest*, p. 18.
66. Tyrrell, *Bibliotheca Politica*, Dialogue 5, p. 321.
67. Ibid., Dialogue 6, p. 425, Dialogue 7, p. 453; Bacon, *Historical and Political Discourse*, pp. 36–8.
68. Tyrrell, *Bibliotheca Politica*, Dialogue 6, p. 383.

69. Ibid., Dialogue 8, pp. 576, 585.
70. Ibid., Dialogue 5, pp. 349–50, Dialogue 6, p. 513.
71. Ibid., Dialogue 6, p. 402; see also Dialogue 7, pp. 469, 491. And cf. the remarks made by Sir Robert Sawyer recorded in Anchitel Grey, ed., *Debates of the House of Commons from the Year 1667 to the Year 1694*, vol. 9, p. 22, and in Lois G. Schwoerer, ed., '"A Jornall of the Convention at Westminster Begun the 22 of January 1688/9"', *Bulletin of the Institute of Historical Research*, 49 (1976) 252–3.
72. Tyrrell, *Bibliotheca Politica*, Dialogue 6, p. 403, Dialogue 7, p. 513.
73. Tyrrell adheres to this image of the ancient council as a meeting of all freemen in his later *General History*. See, for example, Tyrrell, *General History*, vol. 1, pp. civ–cv.
74. Tyrrell, *Bibliotheca Politica*, Dialogue 7, p. 513.
75. Ibid.
76. Ibid., Dialogue 6, p. 391. Compare Atwood, *Jani Anglorum Facies Nova*, p. 264.
77. Tyrrell, *Bibliotheca Politica*, Dialogue 7, p. 513.
78. Ibid., pp. 454, 465.
79. Ibid., pp. 513–14.
80. Burgess, *Politics of the Ancient Constitution*, pp. 7, 10–11, 14.
81. Thus, I disagree with Glenn Burgess's contention that the very idea of original contract 'was the direct opposite of immemoriality'. Burgess, *Politics of the Ancient Constitution*, p. 231.
82. Cf. Woolf, *Idea of History in Early Stuart England*, ch. 1; Pocock, *The Machiavellian Moment: Florentine Political Thought and the Atlantic Republican Tradition* (Princeton: Princeton University Press, 1975), pt I; idem., *Politics, Language and Time*, especially chs 5 and 7.
83. Tyrrell, *Bibliotheca Politica*, Dialogue 7, pp. 487–8, Dialogue 8, pp. 570–1.
84. For specific historical examples cited by Tyrrell see Chapter 5 below.
85. Burgess, *Politics of the Ancient Constitution*, p. 102; see also pp. 17–19 and Pocock, *Ancient Constitution*, pp. 271–6.
86. Burgess, *Politics of the Ancient Constitution*, pp. 34, 41; Sommerville, *Politics and Ideology*, pp. 92–5.
87. Tyrrell, *General History*, vol. 2, bk 1, pp. 17–18, bk 3, p. 141.
88. Some Whig historians suggested that the government of the Britons included a public assembly and enshrined fundamental laws and liberties. Bacon, *Historical and Political Discourse*, ch. 1; Petyt, *Antient Right*, p. 3; see also Burgess, *Politics of the Ancient Constitution*, p. 64, for John Selden's recognition of this point.
89. Burgess, *Politics of the Ancient Constitution*, p. 17.
90. Ibid., pp. 99–105, 225–31.
91. Tyrrell, *Bibliotheca Politica*, Dialogue 8, p. 583; Brady, *Introduction to English History*, p. 86.
92. Ibid., pp. 576, 585.
93. Ibid., p. 585.
94. The Whigs certainly cannot be said to be reviving the kind of 'pacified' and 'constitutionalized' politics of Jacobean consensus described by Burgess

in *Absolute Monarchy and the Stuart Constitution*. For Burgess's analysis of the Whigs' difference see especially ch. 7.
95. By the late seventeenth century the ancient constitution had not degenerated, as Burgess and Pocock at times contend, from a mentalité into a 'move' made by Whigs to further a particular political cause. If we employ Burgess's own definition of mentalite as that which 'shaped men's assumptions and thinking, that told them what moves to make' there may still be good cause for viewing ancient constitutionalism as a mentalite that helped to shape Whig theory and the Revolution Settlement. Cf. Burgess, *Politics of the Ancient Constitution*, pp. 4–5, 114, 224.
96. Tyrrell, *Bibliotheca Politica*, Dialogue 5, pp. 339, 341, Dialogue 6, pp. 433–4. Freeman lodged a similar complaint with Meanwell with regard to his anachronistic definition of 'noble', Dialogue 6, p. 374.
97. Ibid., Dialogue 5, p. 355, Dialogue 8, p. 546.
98. Compare Brady's similar reliance on these different techniques. Pocock, *Ancient Constitution*, pp. 225–6.
99. Tyrrell, *Bibliotheca Politica*, Dialogue 6, pp. 385, 393, Dialogue 7, p. 443, Dialogue 10, p. 709.
100. Note Tyrrell's claim to be 'so fair a Representer, as not to curtail the Doctor's Arguments, but rather to enlarge them when he thought he had a just occasion'. Ibid., Dialogue 7, p. 542.
101. Ibid., Epistle Dedicatory.
102. Ibid.
103. Ibid., Dialogue 6, Preface.
104. Jean Bodin, *Method for the Easy Comprehension of History*, Beatrice Reynolds, trans. (New York: Columbia University Press, 1945) chs 4–5; Julian H. Franklin, *Jean Bodin and the Sixteenth Century Revolution in the Methodology of Law and History* (New York: Columbia University Press, 1963), pp. 149–50.
105. Tyrrell, *Bibliotheca Politica*, Epistle Dedicatory.
106. Pocock, *Ancient Constitution*, pp. 197–8; Smith, *Gothic Bequest*, pp. 7–8.
107. Smith, *Gothic Bequest*, p. 8.
108. Ibid., pp. 16–17, provides an example of Brady's distorted use of sources in the writing of his history.
109. Edmund S. Morgan, *Inventing the People: The Rise of Popular Sovereignty in England and America* (New York: W. W. Norton, 1988), pp. 48–50.
110. Skinner, 'History and Ideology', 178.

Chapter Four   Whig Theories and Theorists after 1688: the Case for Resistance

1. For collections of literature see *State Tracts: A Collection of Several Treatises Relating to the Government* (London, 1689); *State Tracts: Being a Further Collection of Several Choice Treatises Relating to the Government* (London, 1692); *Somers Tracts, A Collection of Scarce and Valuable Tracts, on the Most Interesting and Entertaining Subjects: But Chiefly Such as Relate to*

the *History and Constitution of these Kingdoms, selected from Libraries; ...Particularly that of the Late Lord Somers*, 13 vols, Walter Scott, ed., 2nd edn (London, 1809–15); and Mark Goldie's comprehensive bibliography in 'Revolution of 1689 and Structure of Political Argument'.
2. Mark Goldie calculates that 49 percent of Whig authors employed 'contractual resistance' arguments, and 10 percent offered the idea of 'resistance in extremis'. Goldie, 'Revolution of 1689 and Structure of Political Argument', 490. On Sacheverell and Whig resistance theory in the eighteenth century see *The Bishop of Salisbury's and the Bishop of Oxford's Speeches in the House of Lords on the First Article of Impeachment of Dr Henry Sacheverell; and also, the Bishop of Lincoln's and Bishop of Norwich's Speeches at the Opening of the Second Article of the Said Impeachment* (London: 1710); Kenyon *Revolution Principles*, p. 5; Caroline Robbins, *The Eighteenth-Century Commonwealthman: Studies in the Transmission, Development and Circumstance of English Liberal Thought from the Restoration of Charles II until the War with the Thirteen Colonies* (Cambridge, Mass.: Harvard University Press, 1959); Lois G. Schwoerer 'The Right to Resist: Whig Resistance Theory, 1688 to 1694' in Nicholas Phillipson and Quentin Skinner, eds, *Political Discourse in Early Modern Britain* (Cambridge: Cambridge University Press, 1993), pp. 251–2.
3. George L. Cherry, 'The Role of the Convention Parliament (1688–1689) in Parliamentary Supremacy', *Journal of the History of Ideas*, 17 (1956) 390–406; idem., *The Convention Parliament of 1689: A Biographical Study of its Members* (New York: Bookman Associates, 1966); Eveline Cruickshanks, John Ferris and David Hayton, 'The House of Commons Vote on the Transfer of the Crown, 5 February 1689', *Bulletin of the Institute of Historical Research*, 52, 125 (1979) 37–47; Eveline Cruickshanks, David Hayton and Clive Jones, 'Divisions in the House of Lords on the Transfer of the Crown and Other Issues, 1689–94: Ten New Lists', *Bulletin of the Institute of Historical Research*, 53, 127 (1980) 56–87; Henry Horwitz, 'Parliament and the Glorious Revolution', *Bulletin of the Institute of Historical Research*, 47 (1974) 36–52; Jones, *Revolution of 1688*, ch. 11; Kenyon, *Revolution Principles*, ch. 1; Schwoerer, *Declaration of Rights*; idem., 'Jornall', 242–63.
4. Horwitz, 'Parliament and Glorious Revolution', 38; Schwoerer, *Declaration of Rights*, p. 128.
5. Beddard, *Kingdom without a King*, p. 63; Goldie, 'Revolution of 1689 and Structure of Political Argument', 510.
6. Goldie, 'Revolution of 1689 and Structure of Political Argument', 487, citing the 'De Facto Act', 11 Hen. 7, c.1 (1495).
7. The first group, of 29 peers, met on 11 December, called together by letters under Archbishop Sancroft's signature; on 21 December more than sixty met the Prince at St James, and on 25 December approximately ninety peers advised William on how to summon a convention. Cobbett, *Parliamentary History*, vol. 5, pp. 19–23; Henry Horwitz, *Parliament, Policy and Politics in the Reign of William III* (Newark: University of Delaware Press, 1977) pp. 6–8.
8. Horwitz, 'Parliament and Glorious Revolution', 38–9.

9. Ibid., 39; Schwoerer, *Declaration of Rights*, p. 136.
10. Herbert, like most Convention members, both Tory and Whig, was affected by various personal, professional and political influences. He was the son-in-law of the Tory Sir Robert Sawyer, president of the Royal Society in 1689–90, and the recipient of John Locke's dedication to the *Essay Concerning Human Understanding*. *DNB*, s.v. 'Herbert, Thomas'; Schwoerer, *Declaration of Rights*, p. 135.
11. Cobbett, *Parliamentary History*, vol. 5, pp. 24–5; Horwitz, 'Parliament and Glorious Revolution', 39; Harris, *Politics Under the Later Stuarts*, p. 132.
12. Schwoerer, *Declaration of Rights*, pp. 134–5, 171–2.
13. Horwitz, 'Parliament and the Glorious Revolution', 42.
14. Overall, fairly even numbers of Whig and Tory members were returned: there were 174 'known Whigs', 156 'known Tories', and 183 'new members'. Harris, *Politics Under the Later Stuarts*, pp. 132–3; Schwoerer, *Declaration of Rights*, p. 172.
15. Schwoerer, *Declaration of Rights*, pp. 171–2.
16. Beddard, *Kingdom without a King*, pp. 51–2, 55–6 ; *DNB*, s.v. 'Powle, Henry', and 'Savile, Sir George'; Harris, *Politics Under the Later Stuarts*, p. 133.
17. Horwitz, 'Parliament and Glorious Revolution', 42; Schwoerer, *Declaration of Rights*, pp. 173–4; Cruickshanks et al., 'Divisions in the House of Lords', 59.
18. *DNB*, s.v. 'Hampden, Richard'; Horwitz, *Parliament, Politics and Policy*, p. 9. Richard Hampden's son John practiced more radical politics than his father: he was tried for his involvement in the Rye House Plot, and served as spokesman for the radical Whigs in the Convention. *DNB*, s.v. 'Hampden, John, the younger'; Mark Goldie, 'The Roots of True Whiggism', *History of Political Thought*, 1, 2 (1980) 195–236; Zook, *Radical Whigs*, pp. 112–15.
19. Schwoerer, *Declaration of Rights*, p. 174; idem., 'Jornall', 245–6.
20. Schwoerer, *Declaration of Rights*, pp. 172–4. The debate is recorded in Cobbett, *Parliamentary History*, vol. 5, pp. 36–50; Schwoerer, 'Jornall'; Grey, *Debates*, vol. 9, pp. 6–25. A comparison of all three accounts allows for a more accurate reconstruction of the flow of argument and yields a more comprehensive record of the proceedings.
21. Cobbett, *Parliamentary History*, vol. 5, pp. 36–8.
22. Gilbert Dolben was part of a distinguished family: he was the eldest son of John Dolben, late Archbishop of York, and the nephew of William Dolben. In this speech, Gilbert Dolben demonstrated his learning by citing Grotius, Hotman and others in his speech; he is also mentioned by Dryden for having presented the poet with an important collection of Virgil's works. *DNB*, s.v. 'Dolben, Sir Gilbert', and 'Dolben, Sir William'; Schwoerer, *Declaration of Rights*, p. 174, n. 27; idem., 'Jornall', 246, n. 1.
23. Richard Temple sat in Cromwell's Parliaments, and at the Restoration became an active and important member of the Cavalier Parliament. Throughout the 1670s and 1680s he was both a critic of the Crown and its beneficiary. Temple moved decisively over to the Williamite side after

James II's first flight, and he was a prominent figure in William's House of Commons. *DNB*, s.v. 'Temple, Sir Richard'; Schwoerer, *Declaration of Rights*, pp. 50–2.
24. Schwoerer, 'Jornall', 249–51.
25. Beddard, *Kingdom without a King*, p. 51. Howard, like so many others, had a long political career in which he adhered to many different governments and groups. A former royalist who supported Charles II, he was labelled 'vile' by Shaftesbury; among the facts recorded concerning his personal life it is interesting to note that Howard was married to Dryden's sister, and had a daughter who became a Roman Catholic abbess. *DNB*, s.v. 'Howard, Sir Robert'; Schwoerer, *Declaration of Rights*, pp. 304–5; H. J. Oliver, *Sir Robert Howard, 1626–1698: a Critical Biography* (Durham: Duke University Press, 1963).
26. Grey, *Debates*, p. 20. Cf. Howard in Schwoerer, 'Jornall', 250: 'The Originall of Power was by Pact by Agreement from the People, & sure none ever intended perfectly to enslave themselves and their Posterity: but wee have seen Violences offerd to our very Constitution.'
27. Sir Henry Capel, Sir William Pulteney, Sir John Maynard in Schwoerer, 'Jornall', 252, 255, 258.
28. Howard in Schwoerer, 'Jornall', 251. Pulteney points to the deposition of Richard II, and Somers refers to the deposition of King Sigismond of Sweden. Ibid., 255, 257. Howard, who had written a history of Richard II (published 1681, expanded and reissued 1689), also referred to that monarch as an example during the debates. Schwoerer, *Declaration of Rights*, p. 177.
29. Schwoerer, 'Jornall', 258. Cf. others, such as Pulteney and Treby on resistance. Ibid., 255, 260. And cf. Locke's letter, discussed in Chapter 6 below.
30. John Maynard was an elderly and distinguished member of the Convention. He was an active MP, officeholder, and lawyer long before as well as after the Restoration, and he had been associated with Shaftesbury and the first Whigs. A respected legal authority, Maynard was a part of the defense, along with Treby and Pollexfen, in the Fitzharris case. *DNB*, s.v. 'Maynard, Sir John'; Schwoerer, *Declaration of Rights*, pp. 36–7.
31. Schwoerer, 'Jornall', 251.
32. Grey, *Debates*, vol. 9, p. 20.
33. Schwoerer, 'Jornall', 252.
34. Ibid., 258.
35. Ibid., 258; Grey, *Debates*, vol. 9, p. 18. Sawyer and Finch equate abdication and demise, demonstrating how these terms could be manipulated and the ways in which the Convention resolution would allow for deliberate ambiguity.
36. *DNB*, s.v. 'Sawyer, Sir Robert', and 'Finch, Heneage'; Jones, *Revolution of 1688*, p. 125; Schwoerer, *Declaration of Rights*, p. 36; J. P. Kenyon, ed., *The Stuart Constitution 1603–1688: Documents and Commentary* (Cambridge: Cambridge University Press, 1966), pp. 420–4
37. Grey, *Debates*, vol. 9, p. 22.

38. *DNB*, s.v. 'Treby, Sir George'; Schwoerer, *Declaration of Rights*, chs 2–3; Greaves, *Secrets of the Kingdom*, pp. 22–4.
39. Schwoerer, 'Jornall', 254–5.
40. Cobbett, *Parliamentary History*, vol. 5, p. 50. See also Treby. Ibid., p. 40; Grey, *Debates*, vol. 9, p. 13.
41. Schwoerer, 'Jornall', 262.
42. Cobbett, *Parliamentary History*, vol. 5, p. 50.
43. Robert Atkyns came from family of eminent lawyers and judges. In 1661 Atkyns became Recorder of Bristol, and in 1672 he became a judge of the Court of Common Pleas. He was purged from that court in 1679, and forced to resign the recordership, because of his political views. Subsequently, Atkyns became involved in the defense of Lord Russell, and the defense of William Williams and the privilege of Parliament. After the Revolution Atkyns was appointed Chief Baron of the Exchequer (a position recently held by his brother Edward, and by his father Edward some decades earlier) and he succeeded Halifax as Speaker of the House of Lords. *DNB*, s.v. 'Atkyns, Sir Robert'; Schwoerer, *Declaration of Rights*, p. 164; Cobbett, *Parliamentary History*, vol. 5, pp. 58–9.
44. Cherry, 'Role of the Convention Parliament', 394–5; Kenyon, *Revolution Principles*, p. 12. Legal counsellors to the Lords were Atkyns, Petyt, Sir Edward Nevill, Sir John Holt, Sir William Whitlocke, George Bradbury, and Sir Cresswell Levinz.
45. Cherry, 'Role of the Convention Parliament', 395; Cobbett, *Parliamentary History*, vol. 5, p. 59.
46. Cobbett, *Parliamentary History*, vol. 5, pp. 65–6; Kenyon, *Revolution Principles*, p. 12.
47. Cobbett, *Parliamentary History*, vol. 5, pp. 69–72. John Somers was an established Whig lawyer as well as author, having associated with some of the first Whigs and contributed to various Whig tracts in 1680–81. He served as a member of the defense counsel in the trial of the Seven Bishops, and was chairman of the second committee engaged in drafting Declaration of Rights. John Holt acted as legal counsel for the Crown in a number of cases in the 1680s and served as Recorder of London in 1685–6. Soon after the Revolution Holt was appointed legal advisor to the Lords, and by the fall of 1689 he had become Lord Chief Justice of the King's Bench, and a member of the privy council. *DNB*, s.v. 'Somers, John', 'Holt, Sir John'; Schwoerer, *Declaration of Rights*, pp. 34–6, 47–50.
48. Cobbett, *Parliamentary History*, vol. 5, p. 84.
49. Ibid. p. 103.
50. The Lord Bishop of Ely, the Earl of Rochester and the Earl of Nottingham, in ibid., pp. 75, 94, 105.
51. Ibid. p. 96.
52. Ibid. p. 100.
53. Ibid., p. 94; Horwitz, *Parliament, Policy and Politics*, p. 11.
54. *DNB*, s.v. 'Pollexfen, Sir Henry'; Schwoerer, *Declaration of Rights*, pp. 55–6.
55. Cobbett, *Parliamentary History*, vol. 5, p. 88.
56. Goldie, 'Roots of Whiggism', 217.

57. Horwitz, *Parliament, Policy and Politics*, p. 11. Cruickshanks', et al., work on the voting records in the Lords and Commons corrects Horwitz's picture of the fundamental role of Maryites led by Danby, and reveals the crucial role of loyalist deserters. Cruickshanks, et al., 'Divisions in the House of Lords', 59–63.
58. Franklin, *John Locke*, pp. 98–9. Cf. the radical Whig understanding in Goldie, 'Roots of Whiggism', 212–14.
59. Goldie, 'Roots of Whiggism', 220.
60. Howard Nenner, 'Pretense and Pragmatism: The Response to Uncertainty in the Succession Crisis of 1689', in Lois G. Schwoerer, ed., *The Revolution of 1688–1689: Changing Perspectives* (Cambridge: Cambridge University Press, 1992), p. 84.
61. Cobbett, *Parliamentary History*, vol. 5, p. 32.
62. Grey, *Debates*, vol. 10, pp. 103ff.
63. Goldie, 'Roots of Whiggism', 195, 230–4; John Brewer, *The Sinews of Power: War, Money and the English State, 1688–1783* (Cambridge, Mass.: Harvard University Press, 1988), ch. 5.
64. See Tyrrell's references to his exchanges with other scholars in his letters to Locke, De Beer, ed., *Correspondence of Locke*, vol. 4, pp. 10–12, 35–7, 100–2, 107–9, 116–19, 619–20. Also note Tyrrell's other correspondence: Tyrrell to William Petyt, 1681, Inner Temple, London, Petyt MS 538, 65, fol. 302; Tyrrell to Roger Gale, April, 170?, BL, Stowe Collection 748, fol. 123; and Thomas Hearne to Tyrrell, 26 July 1709, Bodl., Rawlinson MS 110, fol. 15.
65. *DNB*, s.v. 'Tyrrell, James'; Goldie, 'Roots of Whiggism', 202.
66. Goldie, 'Roots of Whiggism', Ashcraft, *Revolutionary Politics*, and Zook, *Radical Whigs*, have traced the various connections among the radical Whigs.
67. Goldie, 'Revolution of 1689 and Structure of Political Argument', 518–19; Claydon, *William III and the Godly Revolution*, ch. 5; Lois G. Schwoerer, 'Press and Parliament in the Revolution of 1689', *Historical Journal*, 20, 3 (1977) 545–67.
68. William Atwood, *Fundamental Constitution*, p. ix; cf. Cobbett, *Parliamentary History*, vol. 5, pp. 38–9.
69. Some Whig authors depict the English government as both mixed and limited, the king ruling in council and limited by fundamental law. See, for example, Thomas Comber, *A Letter to a Bishop Concerning the Present Settlement and the New Oaths* (London, 1689), pp. 4–5; *The New Oath of Allegiance Justified, from the Original Constitution of the English Monarchy* (London 1689) pp. 6–7, 9–14; Tyrrell, *Bibliotheca Politica*, Dialogue 5, p. 317. Others view it as a simple limited monarchy; see, for example, Whitby, *An Historical Account*, sect. 6.
70. *The Anatomy of a Jacobite-Tory: in a Dialogue between Whig and Tory, Occasioned by the Act for Recognizing King William and Queen Mary* (London, 1690); Atwood, *Fundamental Constitution*; Richard Claridge, *A Second Defence of the Present Government under K. Wm, and Q. Mary, Delivered in a Sermon, Preached October the 6th 1689* (London, 1689); *A Friendly Debate Between Dr. Kingsman, A Dissatisfied Clergy-man, and Gratianus Trimmer,*

a Neighbor Minister, Concerning The late Thanksgiving-Day; the Prince's Descent into England; the Nobility and Gentries joining with him; the Acts of the Honourable Convention; the Nature of our English Government; the Secret League with France; the Oaths of Allegiance and Supremacy, &c (London, 1689); Kennett, *A Dialogue Between Two Friends; The New Oath of Allegiance*; Whitby, *An Historical Account*. G. V. Bennett, the author of a biography of White Kennett, questions whether this *Dialogue Between Two Friends* was in fact written by Kennett since it was written at a time when he was not yet fully reconciled to the Revolution and allegiance to William and Mary. Bennett does not, however, provide conclusive evidence that Kennett was not the author, and so I am following the traditional ascription of this work. G. V. Bennett, *White Kennett, 1660–1728, Bishop of Peterborough: A Study in the Political and Ecclesiastical History of the Early Eighteenth Century* (London: SPCK, 1957), p. 12, n. 4; Goldie, 'Revolution of 1689 and Structure of Political Argument', 495–9, 545.

71. Pierre Allix, *An Examination of the Scruples of Those who Refuse to Take the Oath of Allegiance* (London, 1689); *The Anatomy*, p. 16; Atwood, *Fundamental Constitution*, p. iv, and ch. 8; Claridge, *A Second Defence*, p. 28; Kennett, *A Dialogue Between Two Friends*, p. 13; *The New Oath*, p. 12; Whitby, *An Historical Account*, pp. 13–14, 29, 60. Cf. the Lords' debate above; and cf. Tyrrell, Chapter 3 above.
72. Daniel Whitby was a graduate of Trinity College, Oxford, and held the position of prebend of Taunton Regis. He was a prolific commentator, publishing sermons and discourses on controversial topics such as allegiance, comprehension, and the debate over the doctrine of the Trinity. *DNB*, s.v. 'Whitby, Daniel'.
73. Whitby, *An Historical Account*, pp. 13–14.
74. Ibid., pp. 5–6; *The Anatomy*, p. 16; Greenberg, 'Confessor's Laws', 611–37.
75. *The New Oath*, p. 12.
76. Ibid., p. 7.
77. They depict ancient rights and liberties enjoyed by Gothic ancestors, both leaders and followers in conquest, and extended to conquered Britons by their constitution. Atwood, *Fundamental Constitution*; *The New Oath*, p. 7. See Chapter 3 above.
78. Whitby, *An Historical Account*, p. 5.
79. Ibid., pp. 1–2; *The Anatomy*, pp. 7–9; *The New Oath*, p. 6.
80. *The Anatomy*, pp. 7–8.
81. *A Discourse Concerning the Nature, Power, and Proper Effects of the Present Conventions in Both Kingdoms called by the Prince of Orange* (London, 1689), pp. 6–7; Whitby, *An Historical Account*, pp. 36–7.
82. Kennett, *A Dialogue Between Two Friends*, p. 4; Sir P. Georgeson, *The Defence of the Parliament of England in the Case of James the II: Or a Treatise of Regal Power and of the Right of the People Drawn from Ancient Councils, the Determination of Wise-men, and more Especially from the Ordinances of the Doctors of the Church of Rome, as also from Reasons fecht from the Law of Nature and of Nations* (London, 1692), p. 16. In addition to publishing on matters of doctrine, and performing his clerical duties, Kennett was an

accomplished antiquarian who wrote works of history and collected important historical manuscripts. *DNB*, s.v. 'Kennett, White D. D.'; Bennett, *White Kennett*.
83. Kennett, *A Dialogue Between Two Friends*, p. 4.
84. Cf. Locke, *Two Treatises*, II, pars 6–8, pp. 311–12; also Matthew Tindal, *An Essay Concerning Obedience to the Supreme Powers, and the Duty of Subjects in all Revolutions. With Some Considerations Touching the Present Juncture of Affairs* (London, 1694), p. 6.
85. Kennett, *A Dialogue Between Two Friends*, pp. 10–11; Georgeson, *A Defence of the Parliament*, p. 18. Note that Georgeson reminds us this is still no argument for natural subjection and absolute sovereignty since human nature is subjected to sin but not to other men.
86. Kennett, *A Dialogue Between Two Friends*, p. 10.
87. Georgeson, *A Defence of the Parliament*, p. 18; Kennett, *A Dialogue Between Two Friends*, p. 11; *A Political Conference*, pp. 16–17, 24.
88. *A Discourse Concerning the ... Present Conventions*, pp. 1–2.
89. Ibid., p. 2.
90. Ibid., p. 12.
91. Ibid., p. 4. Cf. Locke, *Two Treatises*, II, pars 95–8, pp. 374–7.
92. Tindal, *An Essay Concerning Obedience*, p. 2. Matthew Tindal was for a time a Catholic, during the reign of James II, and a former student of the nonjuror George Hickes. But by the spring of 1688 he was publicly taking the Anglican sacrament, and he went on to publish treatises expressing Whig and low-church views which generated a wide number of responses. Tindal and Locke became acquainted in the later 1690s. *DNB*, s.v. 'Tindal, Matthew'; Marshall, *John Locke*, pp. xxi, 409, 454.
93. Tindal, *An Essay Concerning Obedience*, pp. 2–3; cf. Kennett, *A Dialogue Between Two Friends*, p. 11.
94. Tindal, *An Essay Concerning Obedience*, p. 16.
95. Georgeson, *The Defence of the Parliament*, p. 22.
96. Whitby, *An Historical Account*, pp. 17–18; Kingston, *Tyranny Detected*, pp. 242–6.
97. Schwoerer, 'The Right to Resist', pp. 242–3.
98. Kennett, *A Dialogue Between Two Friends*, p. 17; Kingston, *Tyranny Detected*, pp. 50–1; *A Political Conference*, p. 30.
99. See, for example, Georgeson, *The Defence of the Parliament*, ch. 2.
100. Claridge, *A Second Defence*, p. 25; Burnet, *A Pastoral Letter*, p. 28; *The New Oath*, pp. 15–16; Whitby, *An Historical Account*, sects 2, 3, 6.
101. On the publication, translation and popularity of Grotius see Goldie, 'Edmund Bohun', 577. And note other aspects of the dissemination of Grotius's thought in Filmer's discussion of *De Jure Belli ac Pacis* in his *Observations Concerning the Originall of Government* (1652, 1679), and in the Whig response to Filmer.
102. Claridge, *A Second Defence*, pp. 26–7; cf. Georgeson, *The Defence of the Parliament*, pp. 19–20; Goldie, 'Edmund Bohun', 578. Richard Claridge was rector of Peopleton in Worcester from 1673 until 1691; an increasing sympathy with nonconformity led Claridge to resign his living, and by

Notes 199

1696 he had joined the Society of Friends, becoming a Quaker minister in 1697. Claridge spent the rest of his life engaged in the defense of dissent – involved in law suits and active in print. *DNB*, s.v. 'Claridge, Richard'.
103. Kennett, *A Dialogue Between Two Friends*, p. 29. Matthew Tindal also calls upon the example of the Maccabees. Tindal, *An Essay Concerning Obedience*, pp. 63–4. Cf. Grotius, *De Jure Belli ac Pacis*, bk. 1, ch. 4, sect. 5.
104. Kennett, *A Dialogue Between Two Friends*, p. 24.
105. *The Anatomy*, pp. 17–18. Cf. Locke's and Tyrrell's use of Barclay: Locke, *Two Treatises*, II, pars 232–9, pp. 467–76; Tyrrell, *Bibliotheca Politica*, Dialogue 3, pp. 148–52. With regard to the tradition of citing Barclay, Grotius, Bilson and Falkner for allowable exceptions to the doctrine of non-resistance see Salmon, *French Religious Wars in English Political Thought*, pp. 85, 137–8, 154; Goldie, 'Edmund Bohun', 578; idem., 'Revolution of 1689 and Structure of Political Argument'.
106. Kennett, *A Dialogue Between Two Friends*, pp. 33–8; Claridge, *A Second Defence*, pp. 24–8; Kingston, *Tyranny Detected*, pp. 50–78.
107. *The Anatomy*, p. 26.
108. *The New Oath*, pp. 17–18.
109. Ibid. pp. 25–6.
110. *A Discourse Concerning the . . . Present Conventions*, pp. 6–7.
111. *A Political Conference*, p. 31; cf. Pufendorf and Atwood, discussed in Chapter 6 below.
112. *A Political Conference*, pp. 33–4.
113. Ibid. p. 38.
114. Ibid. pp. 39–40.
115. *A Discourse Concerning the . . . Present Conventions*, pp. 14–17; *A Political Conference*, p. 32.
116. Comber, *A Letter to a Bishop*. Mark Goldie suggests that Comber's authorship of this tract is 'slightly doubtful'. Goldie, 'Revolution of 1689 and Structure of Political Argument', 536.
117. Goldie, 'Edmund Bohun', 570, 574–5.
118. Thomas Comber held various clerical positions – for example, he was Precentor of York, and chaplain to Princess Anne – in the 1670s and 1680s, and was a close friend of John Dolben, Archbishop of York and father of the Convention MP, Gilbert Dolben. Upon taking the oaths to William and Mary, Comber was installed as Dean of Durham in 1691. Although he was enthusiastic about the new regime, he was less certain about its plans for toleration and comprehension. *DNB*, s.v. 'Comber, Thomas D. D.'; Craig Rose, *England in the 1690s: Revolution, Religion and War* (Oxford: Blackwell, 1999), pp. 106–8, 167–8.
119. Comber, *A Letter to a Bishop*, p. 7.
120. Ibid. p. 5.
121. Ibid. p. 21; Goldie, 'Edmund Bohun', 580–1.
122. Mark Goldie identifies three types of conquest argument: *de facto*, historical-legal, and *jus gentium*. Goldie, 'Edmund Bohun', 570. On the use of *de facto* theory see also Kenyon, *Revolution Principles*, ch. 3.

200 Notes

123. Comber, *A Letter to a Bishop*, p. 22. The idea that the conquest applied only to the king was a common misconstruction and, as Mark Goldie points out, a strained interpretation of Grotius. Goldie, 'Edmund Bohun', 582.
124. Comber, *A Letter to a Bishop*, p. 22.
125. Some examples of Whig theorists' rejection of just war and *de facto* versions of conquest argument appear in *An Account of Mr Blunts late Book, Entituled, King William and Queen Mary Conquerors, Ordered by the H of C, to be Burnt by the hand of the Common Hangman on Wednesday Morning Next, at Ten of the Clock, in the Palace Yard, Westminster* (London, 1693); *The Anatomy*; Samuel Johnson, *An Argument Proving, That the Abrogation of King James by the People of England from the Regal Throne, and the Promotion of the Prince of Orange, one of the Royal Family, to the Throne of the Kingdom in his Stead, was according to the Constitution of the English Government, and Prescribed by it* (London, 1692); James Parkinson, *An Examination of Dr Sherlock's Book, Entituled, The Case of Allegiance due to Sovereign Powers, Stated and Resolved, &c.* (London, 1691); Tindal, *An Essay Concerning Obedience*; and Tyrrell, *Bibliotheca Politica*, Dialogue 13. Mark Goldie adds that Jacobites, Whig-Jacobites and radical Whigs offered explicit arguments against *de facto* and conquest; the burning of Burnet's *Pastoral Letter* and Parliament's repudiation of conquest theory would be a triumph for the Country Party and a defeat for the Court in 1693. Goldie, 'Revolution of 1689 and Structure of Political Argument', 516–17.
126. *DNB*, s.v. 'Comber, Thomas D. D'; Goldie, 'Revolution of 1689 and Structure of Political Argument', 504.
127. Goldie, 'Edmund Bohun', 581–2.

Chapter Five   Resistance in Tyrrell's *Bibliotheca Politica*: the People and the Convention

1. Even those scholars who consider themselves at odds concur on the presence, if not prevalence, of contract theory. See, for example, Miller, '"Contract" and "Abdication" Reconsidered', 544; Slaughter, '"Abdicate" and "Contract"', 325; Hopfl and Thompson, 'History of Contract', 919–44; Kenyon, *Revolution Principles*, ch. 2; Cherry, 'The Role of the Convention Parliament'; Goldie, 'Revolution of 1689 and Structure of Political Argument', 486–7, 508–9; Schwoerer, *Declaration of Rights*, p. 160; Dickinson, *Liberty and Property*, pp. 75–6.
2. Hopfl and Thompson, 'History of Contract', 941–3.
3. Thomas Slaughter recognizes the presence of resistance in the meaning of abdication, although he exaggerates – resistance does not necessarily denote deposition. Slaughter, '"Abdicate and Contract,"' 329, 331.
4. Schwoerer, 'Jornall', 252–253. Compare Grey's account cited in Chapter 4 above.
5. Tyrrell, *Bibliotheca Politica*, Dialogue 3, pp. 146–7, 154, Dialogue 9, pp. 649, 678.

6. Cf. Kennett, *A Dialogue Between Two Friends*; Georgeson, *A Defence of the Parliament*; Tindal, *An Essay Concerning Obedience*; *A Discourse Concerning the... Present Conventions*; *A Political Conference*.
7. Tyrrell, *Bibliotheca Politica*, Dialogue 11, p. 777. Tyrrell cites Samuel Pufendorf, *De Jure Naturae et Gentium*, bk 3, ch. 7; this reference is transposed, see Pufendorf, bk 7, ch. 3.
8. Tyrrell, *Bibliotheca Politica*, Dialogue 11, p. 776; Franklin, *John Locke*, p. 34; idem., *Constitutionalism and Resistance*. Compare Chapter 2 above.
9. Tyrrell, *Bibliotheca Politica*, Dialogue 11, p. 778.
10. Pufendorf, *De Jure Naturae et Gentium*, pp. 162–4.
11. Tyrrell, *Bibliotheca Politica*, Dialogue 11, p. 778; cf. Pufendorf, *De Jure Naturae et Gentium*, pp. 949–66; Locke, *Two Treatises*, II, pars 105–7, pp. 380–2; *A Discourse Concerning the... Present Conventions*, pp. 1–2.
12. Dickinson is right to stress this conflation of contract and ancient constitution but in so doing he tends to diminish the role of contract theory. His assertion, for example, that Tyrrell never seriously discusses 'Locke's contract theory based on reason and natural right' is not borne out by a thorough reading of *Bibliotheca Politica* or *Patriarcha non Monarcha*. Dickinson, *Liberty and Property*, pp. 71–2.
13. Tyrrell, *Bibliotheca Politica*, Dialogue 11, p. 814.
14. Ibid., Dialogue 9, pp. 666–70.
15. Ibid., p. 649.
16. Ibid., Dialogue 9, p. 678, Dialogue 11, p. 828.
17. Ibid., Dialogue 9, pp. 654–5, 684–6.
18. Ibid., Dialogue 3, p. 151; cf. Locke, *Two Treatises*, II, pars 232–9, pp. 467–76; *The Anatomy*, pp. 17–18. On Barclay's, and others', exceptions to non-resistance see Chapter 4 above.
19. Tyrrell, *Bibliotheca Politica*, Dialogue 9, p. 689, Dialogue 10, pp. 698–9, 703; Kenyon, *Revolution Principles*, p. 10; Grey, *Debates*, vol. 9, pp. 11–13.
20. Tyrrell, *Bibliotheca Politica*, Dialogue 11, p. 805. See also Dialogue 9, p. 638.
21. Ibid., Dialogue 9, p. 645.
22. Ibid., Dialogue 3, p. 151, Dialogue 10, p. 702.
23. Ibid., Dialogue 3, p. 174.
24. Ibid., Dialogue 3, p. 155; see also Dialogue 4, pp. 267, 274, 296.
25. Ibid., Dialogue 3, p. 177.
26. George Lawson, *Politica Sacra et Civilis: Or, A Model of Civil and Ecclesiastical Government* (London, 1660; 2nd edn London, 1689), pp. 381–4; Franklin, *John Locke*, pp. 64–80; Conal Condren, *George Lawson's 'Politica' and the English Revolution* (Cambridge: Cambridge University Press, 1989), pp. 52–4.
27. See the dispute between Julian Franklin and Conal Condren over the interpretation of Lawson's *Politica Sacra et Civilis*, and its tendencies towards resistance or settlement, in Franklin, *John Locke*; idem., Review of Condren's *George Lawson's 'Politica'*, *History of Political Thought*, 11, 3 (1990) 536–40; Condren, *George Lawson's 'Politica'*; idem., 'J. H. Franklin on "George Lawson, Politics and the English Revolution"', *History of Political Thought*, 12, 3 (1991) 560–4. Against Franklin's assertion that

Lawson's is the work from which Locke draws his solution to the problem of resistance in a mixed monarchy, Condren has argued that George Lawson offered no such clear-cut solution. For Condren Lawson was, in fact, seeking to avoid a theory of resistance by offering a theory of dissolution. And yet James Tyrrell, like other Whig contemporaries, did not make this sharp separation between dissolution and resistance; indeed dissolution could be seen as the key to the distinction between justifiable resistance and abhorrent rebellion. See Tyrrell, *Bibliotheca Politica*, Dialogue 3, pp. 176–7. Condren would argue that this later use of Lawson's concepts was a collapsing of Lawson's distinction between resistance and dissolution. Condren, *George Lawson's 'Politica'*, pp. 154, 165.
28. Tyrrell, *Bibliotheca Politica*, Dialogue 11, pp. 778–9.
29. Pufendorf, *De Jure Naturae et Gentium*, p. 1058. See Tyrrell, *Patriarcha non Monarcha*, p. 239.
30. The difficulties arising from reference to 'the people' are clearly articulated in Tyrrell's frequent prefatory attempts to qualify and control this phrase. Tyrrell, *Bibliotheca Politica*, Prefaces to Dialogues 1, 9, 10; see also Kenyon, *Revolution Principles*, pp. 47–50; Zook, *Radical Whigs*, pp. 180–1.
31. Tyrrell, *Bibliotheca Politica*, Dialogue 3, pp. 182–3, Dialogue 9, pp. 657, 665, Dialogue 11, p. 781.
32. Ibid., Dialogue 3, p. 183, Dialogue 11, p. 808.
33. Tierney, *Religion, Law, and Constitutional Thought*; Wootton, 'Introduction', *Divine Right and Democracy*, pp. 47–50. Similar assurances are found in the work of George Lawson, who states: 'When I mention the people of England as the primary subjects of Power, and the heir of real Majesty, I mean the rational judicious party; for no consent of people, that is not rational and agreeable to the Laws of God, is of any force, And I exclude not only such as are barely Members virtually, but all Rebels, Traytors, and malignant persons . . . .And when many Members of a Community are insufficient of themselves to judge, what is just and good, & many of them perverted, the power remains in *parte saniore, aut in parte hujus partis valentiore*; and in those, who upon right information shall consent with them.' Lawson, *Politica Sacra et Civilis*, p. 383. Lawson's community may be divided into *cives* and *virtualiter*, and even *eminenter cives*. Tierney, *Religion, Law, and Constitutional Thought*, p. 100; Franklin, *John Locke*, p. 70; Condren, *George Lawson's 'Politica'*, pp. 88–9.
34. Tyrrell, *Bibliotheca Politica*, Dialogue 11, p. 808.
35. Ibid., Dialogue 9, pp. 617–28, Dialogue 12, pp. 840–1, 855–62.
36. Ibid., Dialogue 3, p. 158.
37. Ibid., Dialogue 9, p. 658, Dialogue 10, p. 703.
38. Ibid., Dialogue 9, pp. 615–17.
39. Ibid., Dialogue 11, p. 772.
40. Ibid., pp. 772–3 and, previously cited, 778–9.
41. Ibid., p. 773.
42. Ibid., pp. 774–6.
43. Ibid., Dialogue 10, p. 704, Dialogue 11, p. 772.
44. Ibid., Dialogue 11, p. 779.

45. Ibid., Dialogue 12, p. 879.
46. Franklin, *John Locke*, pp. 67, 73.
47. Tyrrell, *Bibliotheca Politica*, Dialogue 10, pp. 704, 706, Dialogue 11, p. 773. The insistent definition of the people as clergy, nobles and commons facilitates this conflation of people and council, for example in Dialogue 12, pp. 840–1. Although Tyrrell's exploration of the composition of the *populus* in England's ancient constitution starts out broadly because of his desire to assert the presence of the commons and the antiquity of Parliament, he also affirms the equation of the people with the propertied. Tyrrell, *Bibliotheca Politica*, Dialogue 6, especially pp. 385, 387.
48. Ibid., Dialogue 12, pp. 855, 859–60, 889.
49. Ibid., p. 885.
50. Ibid., Dialogue 11, p. 779.
51. Ibid., Dialogue 12, p. 891; see Chapter 3, 'Immemorial, original, ancient', above.
52. Tyrrell, *Bibliotheca Politica*, Dialogue 12, p. 890.
53. Ibid., p. 891.
54. Ibid. Cf. Atwood, *Fundamental Constitution*, pp. 100, 102; and Pufendorf, *De Jure Naturae et Gentium*, pp. 1091–2.
55. See also Tyrrell, *Bibliotheca Politica*, Dialogue 12, pp. 895–6 for the merging of the terms convention/great council/Parliament.
56. Ibid., Dialogue 9, p. 657.
57. J. Franklin Jameson, 'The Early Political Uses of the Word Convention', *American Historical Review*, 3 (1897–98) 480, 484; W. J. Jones, *Politics and the Bench: The Judges and the Origins of the English Civil War* (London: George Allen & Unwin, 1971), pp. 81, 157–8.
58. Jameson, 'Early Uses of Convention', 481; Bruce Ackerman, *We the People: Foundations* (Cambridge, Mass.: Harvard University Press, 1991), p. 174; Gordon S. Wood, *The Creation of the American Republic, 1776–1787* (New York: W. W. Norton, 1972), p. 311.
59. Jameson, 'Early Uses of Convention', 485.
60. Robert Sangster Rait, *The Parliaments of Scotland* (Glasgow: Maclehose, 1924), pp. 145–6; Rosalind Mitchison, *A History of Scotland* (New York: Methuen, 1982), pp. 63, 168.
61. Rait, *Parliaments of Scotland*, pp. 139–47, 156; J. D. Mackie, *A History of Scotland*, rev. edn, Bruce Lenman and Geoffrey Parker, eds (London: Penguin Books, 1978), pp. 211–13.
62. Rait, *Parliaments of Scotland*, pp. 151–3; Jameson, 'Early Uses of Convention', 485; Colin Kidd, *Subverting Scotland's Past: Scottish Whig Historians and the Creation of an Anglo-British Identity, 1689–c.1830* (Cambridge: Cambridge University Press, 1993), pp. 132–3.
63. Rait, *Parliaments of Scotland*, pp. 155–8; Mackie, *A History of Scotland*, p. 180.
64. Rait, *Parliaments of Scotland*, pp. 160–2.
65. May McKisack, *The Fourteenth Century, 1307–99* (Oxford: Clarendon Press, 1959), pp. 91–2, 494–6.

66. Jameson, 'Early Uses of Convention', 479; Morgan, *Inventing the People*, p. 108; Sawyer, Howard in Grey, *Debates*, vol. 9, pp. 20–2; Kingston, *Tyranny Detected*, pp. 241–2, discussed in Chapter 6 below.
67. Morgan, *Inventing the People*, pp. 88–91, 108; Franklin, *John Locke*, pp. 73–4; Jameson, 'Early Uses of Convention', 484.
68. Tim Harris, 'The People, the Law, and the Constitution in Scotland and England: A Comparative Approach to the Glorious Revolution', *Journal of British Studies*, 38 (1999) 28–58; Kidd, *Subverting Scotland's Past*, pp. 132–4.
69. Ackerman, *We the People*, p. 175; Morgan, *Inventing the People*, p. 91; Wood, *Creation of the American Republic*, ch. 8.
70. Morgan, *Inventing the People*, pp. 112–14.
71. G. R. Elton, '"The Body of the Whole Realm": Parliament and Representation in Medieval and Tudor England', in *Studies in Tudor and Stuart Politics and Government: Papers and Reviews 1946–72*, vol. 2 (Cambridge: Cambridge University Press, 1974), p. 48; Morgan, *Inventing the People*, p. 39.
72. Elton, '"Body of the Realm"', p. 40; Morgan, *Inventing the People*, p. 41; J. R. Maddicott, 'Parliament and the Constituencies, 1272–1377', and A. L. Brown, 'Parliament 1377–1422', in R. G. Davies and J. H. Denton, eds, *The English Parliament in the Middle Ages* (Philadelphia: University of Pennsylvania Press, 1981), pp. 61–87, 109–40.
73. Elton, '"Body of the Realm"', pp. 26, 36–7, 57; G. L. Harriss, 'The Formation of Parliament, 1272–1377', and A. R. Myers, 'Parliament 1422–1509', in Davies and Denton, *The English Parliament in the Middle Ages*, R. G. Davies and J. H. Denton, eds (Philadelphia: University of Pennsylvania Press, 1981) pp. 29–60, 141–84.
74. Morgan, *Inventing the People*, pp. 46–7; Hanna Fenichel Pitkin, *The Concept of Representation* (Berkeley: University of California Press, 1969).
75. Elton, '"Body of the Whole Realm"', p. 47.
76. Morgan, *Inventing the People*, p. 58; Pocock, *Ancient Constitution*, pp. 124–5.
77. Schwoerer, *Declaration of Rights*, p. 137.

Chapter Six John Locke and Whig Theory

1. Atwood, *Fundamental Constitution*; see also *A Discourse Concerning the... Present Conventions*, and *A Political Conference*, discussed in Chapter 4 above.
2. Atwood, *Fundamental Constitution*, pp. 98, 100–2 (p. 101 mispaginated as p. 97). Cf. *The New Oath*, pp. 17–18, 25–6; *A Political Conference*, pp. 33–4, cited in Chapter 4 above.
3. Atwood, *Fundamental Constitution*, p. 98.
4. Ibid., p. 100. Atwood is citing Samuel Pufendorf, *De Jure Naturae et Gentium*, bk 7, ch. 7, sects 8–9. Cf. Tyrrell, *Bibliotheca Politica*, Dialogue 12, p. 891.
5. Atwood, *Fundamental Constitution*, p. 102.

6. Ibid., 110. Here I think Atwood does try to follow Pufendorf in the idea of a new election by some version of the general community; Atwood may, as Julian Franklin argues, distort the English constitution, but not Pufendorf's meaning. Cf. Franklin, *John Locke*, p. 106.
7. Zook, *Radical Whigs*, pp. 162–3.
8. Atwood, *Fundamental Constitution*, chs 4 and 8.
9. Ibid., p. 101 (mispaginated as p. 97); Franklin, *John Locke*, p. 114.
10. Franklin, *John Locke*, p. 114.
11. Tyrrell, *Bibliotheca Politica*, Dialogue 3, p. 157.
12. On Tindal, see above, Chapter 4, n. 92.
13. Tindal, *An Essay Concerning Obedience*, pp. 9–10.
14. Ibid., pp. 5–6.
15. Ibid., pp. 10–11.
16. Ibid., pp. 15–22, 36–9, 42.
17. Ibid., p. 65.
18. Kingston, *Tyranny Detected*, pp. 45, 47, 57–8, 60–5. *DNB*, s.v. 'Kingston, Richard'.
19. Kingston, *Tyranny Detected*, pp. 63, 252–3.
20. Ibid., p. 257.
21. Ibid., p. 241. Kingston uses the terms Convention, Convention of Estates, and Conventional Parliament.
22. Ibid., pp. 241–2.
23. *A Friendly Debate*, p. 28.
24. Ibid., pp. 17, 23–4, 42, 50.
25. Ibid., pp. 38–9.
26. Ibid., p. 39.
27. Ibid., pp. 67–8.
28. Ibid., pp. 68–9.
29. Locke, *Two Treatises*, II, para. 220, p. 459.
30. Ibid., par. 223, pp. 462–3.
31. Franklin, *John Locke*, p. 112.
32. Locke, *Two Treatises*, II, par. 226, p. 464, and para. 230, pp. 466–7.
33. James Tully, *An Approach to Political Philosophy: Locke in Contexts* (Cambridge: Cambridge University Press, 1993), p. 45. Cf. Richard Ashcraft's idea that Locke is being 'ironic' and 'bitter' when he points to the disinclination of the people to engage in resistance and revolution. Ashcraft, *Revolutionary Politics*, p. 309.
34. Franklin, *John Locke*, p. 112.
35. Gordon J. Schochet, 'The Significant Sounds of Silence: the Absence of Women from the Political Thought of Sir Robert Filmer and John Locke (or, "Why can't a woman be more like a man?")', in Smith, ed., *Women Writers and the Early Modern British Political Tradition*, p. 221. Ruth W. Grant argues that Locke presents 'a coherent defense of the liberal state'. Grant analyzes the ways in which Locke provided 'adequate solutions' to problems that face all liberal theories, and implies that in so doing Locke preserved 'the premise of liberal theory – human freedom'. Ruth W. Grant, *John Locke's Liberalism* (Chicago: University of Chicago Press, 1987), pp. 6, 11.

206   Notes

36. My work has followed this trend and will, in what follows, look at the impact of the analysis of Whig literature for these views – only touching occasionally on the relationship between Locke's religious and political ideas. Marshall's *John Locke* does build upon the examination of the religious foundations of Locke's political thought offered by Dunn, *The Political Thought of John Locke*.
37. Locke, *Two Treatises*, II, par. 89, p. 368, see also paras 6–7, pp. 311–12.
38. Tyrrell, *Patriarcha non Monarcha*, p. 11; idem., *Bibliotheca Politica*, Dialogue 12, pp. 32–3, 35, 39–40; Wootton, 'Introduction', in *Political Writings*, p. 80.
39. Tyrrell to Locke, in De Beer, ed., *Correspondence of Locke*, vol. 4, letter of 30 August 1690, pp. 116–19, and letter of 9 August 1692, pp. 493–6.
40. Ibid., p. 495. Tyrrell's *A Brief Disquisition of the Law of Nature* was first published in 1692.
41. Wootton, 'Introduction', in *Political Writings*, p. 83. For evidence of Locke's exposure to Tyrrell's manuscript see Marshall, *John Locke*, pp. 234–7, and Chapter 2 above.
42. Wootton, 'Introduction', in *Political Writings*, pp. 77–83, 88.
43. See also Franklin, *John Locke*; Gordon J. Schochet, 'Why Should History Matter? Political Theory and the History of Discourse', in J. G. A. Pocock, with the assistance of Gordon J. Schochet and Lois G. Schwoerer, eds, *The Varieties of British Political Thought, 1500–1800* (Cambridge: Cambridge University Press, 1993), pp. 321–57; Lois G. Schwoerer, 'Locke, Lockean Ideas, and the Glorious Revolution', *Journal of the History of Ideas*, 51, 4 (1990) 531–48; Martyn P. Thompson, 'Significant Silences in Locke's *Two Treatises of Government*: Constitutional History, Contract and Law', *Historical Journal*, 31, 2 (1987) 275–94.
44. Schochet, 'Significant Sounds of Silence'; Nancy Tuana, *Women and the History of Philosophy* (New York: Paragon House, 1992), pp. 86–97; and see Chapter 2, n. 76 above.
45. Weil, *Political Passions*, pp. 75, 78–9.
46. Locke, *An Essay Concerning Human Understanding*, pp. 335, 672; Marshall, *John Locke*, pp. 398–402.
47. For example in an essay on 'Virtue' (1681) Locke acknowledges the conventional basis for virtue and vice for men and women yet he also asserts, regarding women, that 'the chief end of her being [is] the propagation of mankind'. See also the discussion of adultery and bigamy in 'Atlantis' (1678). John Locke, *Political Essays*, Mark Goldie, ed. (Cambridge: Cambridge University Press, 1997) pp. 256, 288.
48. Compare Pateman, *Sexual Contract*, and Schochet's response in 'Significant Sounds of Silence', pp. 223, 241. See also Jacqueline Stevens, 'The Reasonableness of John Locke's Majority, Property Rights, Consent, and Resistance in the *Second Treatise*', *Political Theory*, 24, 3 (1996) n. 22.
49. See, for example, Ashcraft, *Revolutionary Politics*; Franklin, *John Locke*; Judith Richards, Lotte Mulligan, and John K. Graham, '"Property" and "People": Political Usages of Locke and Some Contemporaries', *Journal of the History of Ideas*, 42 (1981), 29–51; James Tully, *A Discourse on*

Property: John Locke and his Adversaries (Cambridge: Cambridge University Press, 1980); Matthew H. Kramer, *John Locke and the Origins of Private Property: Philosophical Explorations of Individualism, Community, and Equality* (Cambridge: Cambridge University Press, 1997).

50. The less egalitarian, 'accumulative', 'bourgeois', and 'agrarian capitalist' Locke has been analyzed most notably by C. B. Macpherson, *The Political Theory of Possessive Individualism: Hobbes to Locke* (Oxford: Oxford University Press, 1962), and Neal Wood, *John Locke and Agrarian Capitalism* (Berkeley: University of California Press, 1984).

51. Locke, *Two Treatises*, II, pars 25–51, pp. 327–44. Matthew Kramer offers a fairly extensive list of this literature in Kramer, *John Locke and the Origins of Property*, p. 93, n. 1, and 'Citational Appendix' pp. 319–45.

52. Gordon J. Schochet, 'Radical Politics and Ashcraft's Treatise on Locke', *Journal of the History of Ideas*, 50 (1989) 502–3; Wootton, 'Introduction', in *Political Writings*, pp. 117–19; McNally, 'Locke, Levellers and Liberty'. Not only are many people excluded from Locke's social contract but, some have argued, the rights of membership in that community are themselves restricted. See Ellen Meiksins Wood, 'Radicalism, Capitalism and Historical Contexts: Not Only a Reply to Richard Ashcraft on John Locke', *History of Political Thought*, 15, 3 (1994) 324.

53. Wootton, 'John Locke: Socinian or Natural Law Theorist?', pp. 62–3.

54. Schochet, 'Radical Politics', 502–4; Schwoerer, 'Lockean Ideas', 535; Tuana, *Women and Philosophy*, pp. 93–7; Christopher Anderson, '"Safe Enough in His Honesty and Prudence": The Ordinary Conduct of Government in the Thought of John Locke', *History of Political Thought*, 13, 4 (1992) 605–30.

55. Marshall, *John Locke*, pp. 275–7. For further discussion of imprecision and ambiguity in Locke's notions of trust, virtue and prudence see Anderson, '"Safe Enough in His Honesty and Prudence"'.

56. Franklin, *John Locke*, p. 117; J. L. Rahe, 'John Locke's Philosophical Partisanship', *The Political Science Reviewer*, 20 (1991) 1–44; Stevens, 'Reasonableness of John Locke's Majority'; Tully, *Discourse on Property*. Ashcraft champions the view that Locke's people included the 'lowest social classes'. Ashcraft, *Revolutionary Politics*, pp. 303–12. For responses see Mark Goldie, 'John Locke's Circle and James II', *Historical Journal*, 35, 3 (1992) 557–86; Schochet, 'Radical Politics'; Schwoerer, 'Lockean Ideas'; Wootton, 'Introduction', in *Political Writings*; idem., 'John Locke and Richard Ashcraft's *Revolutionary Politics*', *Political Studies*, 40 (1992) 79–98; Milton, 'John Locke and the Rye House Plot'; Ellen Meiksins Wood, 'Locke Against Democracy: Consent, Representation and Suffrage in the *Two Treatises*', *History of Political Thought*, 13, 4 (1992) 657–89; idem., 'Radicalism, Capitalism and Historical Contexts'.

57. Franklin, *John Locke*, pp. 118–22; Ashcraft, *Revolutionary Politics*, ch. 11, associates Locke with radicals and political subversives outside the Convention.

58. [John Wildman], *A Letter to a Friend, Advising him in this Extraordinary Juncture how to Free the Nation For Ever* (London, 1689), in *Somers Tracts*,

vol. 10, pp. 196–8; [John Humfrey], *Good Advice Before it be Too Late, being a Breviate for the Convention* (London, 1689) in *Somers Tracts*, vol. 10, pp. 198–202.
59. Ibid., pp. 195–196, 199–202.
60. Schwoerer, 'Lockean Ideas', 536. Further evidence of Locke's attitude towards the Convention is found in a letter he wrote criticizing the Convention for transforming itself into an ordinary Parliament. Locke to Clarke, 8 Feb. 1689, quoted in Franklin, *John Locke*, p. 121.
61. Cf. Marshall, *John Locke*, pp. 275–6.
62. For some of these explanations see, for example, Franklin, *John Locke*; Pocock, *Ancient Constitution*; Schwoerer, 'Lockean Ideas'; Charles D. Tarlton, '"The Rulers Now on Earth": Locke's *Two Treatises* and the Revolution of 1688', *Historical Journal*, 28, 2 (1985) 279–98.
63. Mark Glat, 'John Locke's Historical Sense', *Review of Politics*, 43, 1 (1981) 3, 6.
64. Thompson, 'Significant Silences', 277, 280, 285. Cf. Tarlton, 'Rulers Now on Earth'.
65. *Some Thoughts Concerning Reading and Study for a Gentleman* in Locke, *Political Essays*, pp. 349, 358; Marshall, *John Locke*, p. 278.
66. Glat, 'Locke's Historical Sense', 5.
67. Ibid., 5–8; see Chapter 3 above.
68. Locke to Edward Clarke, 8 February 1689, quoted in Tarlton, 'Rulers Now on Earth', 294.
69. James Farr and Clayton Roberts, 'John Locke on the Glorious Revolution: A Rediscovered Document', *Historical Journal*, 28, 2 (1985) 396–7; compare Maynard, Chapter 4 above.
70. Farr and Roberts, 'Locke on the Glorious Revolution', 397; Schwoerer, 'Lockean Ideas', 538; Marshall, *John Locke*, pp. 278–80.
71. Thompson, 'Significant Silences', 290–1; Schwoerer, 'Lockean Ideas', 540–2. Cf. John Dunn, 'The Politics of Locke in England and America in the Eighteenth Century', in *John Locke: Problems and Perspectives*, John Yolton, ed. (Cambridge: Cambridge University Press, 1969), p. 50; Ron Becker, 'The Ideological Commitment of Locke: Freemen and Servants in the *Two Treatises of Government*', *History of Political Thought*, 13, 4 (1992) 631–56. And cf. Ruth W. Grant on the tensions between theory and practice in Locke: Grant, *John Locke's Liberalism*, pp. 202–5.
72. David Wootton does not seek to emphasize the idea of coherence, but he does offer support for my reading of the non-egalitarian implications of Locke's theory. Wootton, 'Introduction', in *Political Writings*, 117–19.
73. Ibid., 119.
74. Morgan, *Inventing the People*, 120–1.

Select Bibliography

Manuscript Sources

Bodleian Library, Oxford.
  Locke MS.c22
  Smith MS.54
  Rawlinson MS.110
British Library, London.
  Stowe MS.748.
Inner Temple Library, London.
  Petyt MS.538

Primary Published Sources

An Account of Mr Blunts late Book, Entituled, King William and Queen Mary Conquerors, Ordered by the H of C, to be Burnt by the Hand of the Common Hangman on Wednesday Morning Next, at Ten of the Clock, in the Palace Yard, Westminster (London, 1693).

An Agreement of the People for a Firm and Present Peace upon Grounds of Common Right and Freedom. The English Levellers. Andrew Sharp, ed. (Cambridge: Cambridge University Press, 1998), pp. 92–101.

Allix, Pierre. *An Examination of the Scruples of Those who Refuse to Take the Oath of Allegiance* (London, 1689).

The Anatomy of a Jacobite-Tory: in a Dialogue between Whig and Tory, Occasioned by the Act for Recognizing King William and Queen Mary (London, 1690).

An Answer to Two Papers, Called, A Lords Speech Without-Doors and a Commoners Speech. Wherein the Objections Against the Present Management of Affairs, are Dissolved (London, 1689).

Astell, Mary. *Reflections Upon Marriage. Political Writings.* Patricia Springborg ed. (Cambridge: Cambridge University Press, 1996).

Atkyns, Robert. *An Enquiry into the Power of Dispensing with Penal Statutes.* 2nd edn (London, 1689).

———. *The Power, Jurisdiction and Privilege of Parliament; and the Antiquity of the House of Commons Asserted: Occasioned by an Information in the Kings Bench, by the Attorney General, Against the Speaker of the House of Commons* (London, 1689).

Atwood, William. *The Fundamental Constitution of the English Government, Proving King William and Queen Mary are Lawful and Rightful King and Queen* (London, 1690).

———. *Jani Anglorum Facies Nova: Or, Several Monuments of Antiquity Touching the Great Councils of the Kingdom and the Court of the Kings Immediate Tenants and Officers, from the first of William the First, to the forty ninth of Henry the Third, Reviv'd and Clear'd* (London, 1680).

——. *Reflections Upon a Treasonable Opinion, Industriously Promoted, Against Signing the National Association: And the Entring into it Prov'd to be the Duty of All the Subjects of this Kingdom* (London, 1696).

Bacon, Nathaniel. *An Historical and Political Discourse of the Laws and Government of England, From the First Times to the End of the Reign of Queen Elizabeth. With a Vindication of the Ancient Way of Parliaments in England. Collected from some Manuscript Notes of John Selden Esq.* Reprint edn (London, 1689).

The Bishop of Salisbury's and the Bishop of Oxford's Speeches in the House of Lords on the First Article of Impeachment of Dr Henry Sacheverell; and also, the Bishop of Lincoln's and Bishop of Norwich's Speeches at the Opening of the Second Article of the Said Impeachment (London: 1710).

Blackstone, William. *The Sovereignty of the Law: Selections from Blackstone's 'Commentaries on the Laws of England'.* Gareth Jones ed. (Toronto: University of Toronto Press, 1973).

Blount, Charles. *An Appeal from the Country to the City for the Preservation of his Majesties Person, Liberty, Property and the Protestant Religion* (London, 1679).

——. *A Dialogue Between K. W. and the late K. J. on the Banks of the Boyn, the Day before the Battel* (n.p., n.d.).

——. *The Sale of Esau's Birth-right; Or, the New Buckingham Ballad, to the Tun of the London Gentlewoman, or Little Peggy Ramsey* (n.p., 1679).

Bohun, Edmund. *A Defence of Sir Robert Filmer, Against the Mistakes and Misrepresentations of Algernon Sidney, Esq; In a Paper Delivered by him to the Sheriffs upon the Scaffold on Tower-Hill, on Fryday December the 7th 1683 before his Execution there* (London, 1684).

——. *Patriarcha: or the Natural Power of Kings. By the Learned Sir Robert Filmer Baronet. The Second Edition. Corrected According to the Original Manuscript of the Author, Out of Which in Several Places Many Large Additions are Made Amounting in the Whole to Ten Pages, and Many Mistakes Rectified. To Which is Added, A Preface to the Reader in which this Piece is Vindicated from the Cavils and Misconstructions of the Author of a Book Stiled Patriarcha non Monarcha* (London, 1685).

Brady, Sir Robert. *A Full and Clear Answer to a Book Written by William Petit; Printed in the Year 1680 . . . With a True Historical Account of the Famous Colloquim or Parliament, 49 Hen III. And a Glossary Expounding Some Few Words Used Frequently in Our Antient Records, Laws and Historians. Together with Some Animadversions Upon a Book Called Jani Anglorum Facies Nova* (London, 1681).

——. *An Introduction to The Old English History. Comprehended in Three Several Tracts. The First, an Answer to Mr Petyt's Rights of the Commons Asserted; and to a Book Entitled Jani Anglorum Facies Nova; the Second Edition, very much Inlarged. The Second, an Answer to a Book Intituled Argumentum Antinormannicum. . . . The Third, the Exact History of the Succession of the Crown of England. . . .* (London, 1684).

A Brief Collection of Some Memorandums: Or Things Humbly Offerd to the Consideration of the Members of the Great Convention, and of the Succeeding Parliament (London, 1689).

Buchanan, George. *De Jure Regni Apud Scotos*. Duncan H. MacNeill, trans. and commentary. Edinburgh: William Maclellan, 1964.
Burke, Edmund. *Reflections on the Revolution in France*. J. G. A. Pocock ed. (Indianapolis: Hackett Publishing, 1987).
Burnet, Gilbert. *A Compleat Collection of Papers, in Twelve Parts: Relating to the Great Revolutions in England and Scotland, from the Time of the Seven Bishops Petitioning . . . to the Coronation of King William and Queen Mary*. (London, 1689).
———. *History of his Own Time*. 6 vols. Oxford, 1883. Thomas Stackhouse, rev. and abridged edn (London: Everyman, 1906; reprint, 1979).
———. *A Memorial Offered to Her Royal Highness, the Princess Sophia, Electoress and Dutchess Dowager of Hanover. Containing a Delineation of the Constitution and Policy of England* (London, 1815).
———. *A Pastoral Letter Writ by the Right Reverend Father in God Gilbert, Lord Bishop of Sarum, to the Clergy of his Diocess, Concerning the Oaths of Allegiance and Supremacy to King William and Queen Mary* (London, 1689).
———. *A Sermon Preached before the House of Peers in the Abbey of Westminster, on the 5th of November 1689. Being Gun-Powder Treason Day, As Likewise The Day of his Majesties Landing in England*. London, 1689.
———. *A Sermon Preached before the Right-Honourable The Lord Mayor and Alderman of the City of London at Bow-Church, September 2, 1680* London, 1680.
———. *A Sermon Preached in the Chappel of St. James's, Before His Highness the Prince of Orange, the 23rd of December, 1688*. London, 1689.
———. *Six Papers by Gilbert Burnet, D. D. To which is Added, 'An Apology for the Church of England', &c, And 'An Enquiry into the Measures of Submission to the Supream Authority', &c* (London, 1689).
Captain Thorogood His Opinion of the Point of Succession, To a Brother of the Blade in Scotland (n.p., 1679).
Claridge, Richard. *A Second Defence of the Present Government under K. Wm, and Q. Mary, Delivered in a Sermon, Preached October the 6th 1689* (London, 1689).
Cobbett, William, ed. *The Parliamentary History of England, from the Earliest Period to the year 1803*. 36 vols (London: T. C. Hansard, 1806–1820; reprint New York: AMS Press, 1966).
Comber, Thomas. *A Letter to a Bishop Concerning the Present Settlement and the New Oaths* (London, 1689).
Cooke, Edward. *Argumentum Anti-Normannicum: Or an Argument Proving, from Ancient Histories and Records, that William, Duke of Normandy, Made No Absolute Conquest of England by the Sword; in the Sense of our Modern Writers* (London, 1682).
The Debates in Deposing Kings; And of the Royal Succession of Great Britain (London, 1688).
Delamer, Henry. *The Works of the Right Honourable Henry late Lord Delamer, and Earl of Warrington*. London, 1694.
A Discourse Concerning the Nature, Power, and Proper Effects of the Present Conventions in Both Kingdoms called by the Prince of Orange (London, 1689).
Filmer, Sir Robert. *Patriarcha and other Writings*. Johann P. Sommerville, ed. (Cambridge: Cambridge University Press, 1991).

212 Select Bibliography

Fortescue, Sir John. *De Laudibus Legum Anglie*. S. B. Chrimes, ed. and trans. (Cambridge: Cambridge University Press, 1949).

A Friendly Debate Between Dr. Kingsman, A Dissatisfied Clergy-man, and Gratianus Trimmer, a Neighbor Minister, Concerning The late Thanksgiving-Day; the Prince's Descent into England; the Nobility and Gentries Joining with Him; the Acts of the Honourable Convention; the Nature of our English Government; the Secret League with France; the Oaths of Allegiance and Supremacy, &c (London, 1689).

Georgeson, Sir P. *The Defence of the Parliament of England in the Case of James the II: Or a Treatise of Regal Power and of the Right of the People Drawn from Ancient Councils, the Determination of Wise-men, and more Especially from the Ordinances of the Doctors of the Church of Rome, as also from Reasons fecht from the Law of Nature and of Nations* (London, 1692).

Grey, Anchitel. *Debates of the House of Commons from the Year 1667 to the Year 1694*. 10 vols (London, 1769).

Grotius, Hugo. *De Jure Belli ac Pacis, Libri Tres*. 2 vols. F. W. Kelsey, trans. Carnegie Endowment for International Peace, Division of International Law, Classics of International Law, no.3 (Oxford: Clarendon Press, 1925).

Hearne, Thomas. *Remarks and Collections of Thomas Hearne*. 11 vols. C. E. Doble, D. W. Rannie and H. E. Salter, eds (Oxford: Clarendon Press, 1885–1921).

Hickes, George. *A Discourse of the Soveraign Power, in a Sermon Preached at St Mary Le Bow, Nov. 28, 1682. Before the Artillery Company of London* (London, 1682).

——. *A Sermon Preached before the Lord Mayor, Aldermen, and Citizens of London, at Bow-Church, on the 30th of January 1681/2* (London, 1682).

[Humfrey, John.] *Good Advice Before it be Too Late, being a Breviate for the Convention* (London, 1689).

Hunton, Philip. *A Treatise of Monarchy, Containing Two Parts: I. Concerning Monarchy in General. II. Concerning this Particular Monarchy. Wherein All the Maine Questions Occurrent in Both, are Stated, Disputed, and Determined* (London, 1643).

Johnson, Samuel. *An Argument Proving, That the Abrogation of King James by the People of England from the Regal Throne, and the Promotion of the Prince of Orange, one of the Royal family, to the Throne of the Kingdom in his Stead, was according to the Constitution of the English Government, and Prescribed by it* (London, 1692).

Kennett, White. *A Dialogue Between Two Friends, Occasioned by the Late Revolution of Affairs, and the Oath of Allegiance* (London, 1689).

K. William, or K. Lewis, Wherein is Set Forth the Inevitable Necessity These Nations Lye Under, of Submitting Wholly to One or Another of These Kings (London, 1689).

Kingston, Richard. *Tyranny Detected and the Late Revolution Justify'd by the Law of God, the Law of Nature, and the Practice of all Nations* (London, 1699).

Lawson, George. *Politica Sacra et Civilis: Or, A Model of Civil and Ecclesiastical Government* (London, 1660; 2nd edn London, 1689).

LeVassor, Michel. *Les Soupirs de la France Esclave, Qui Aspire Apres la Liberte* (Amsterdam: n.p., 1689).

———. *Letters Written by a French Gentlemen, Giving a Faithful and Particular Account of the Transactions at the Court of France, Relating to the Publick Interest of Europe* (London, 1695).
Locke, John. *The Correspondence of John Locke.* 8 vols. E. S. De Beer, ed. (Oxford: Clarendon Press, 1976).
———. *An Essay Concerning Human Understanding.* Peter Nidditch, ed. (Oxford: Clarendon Press, 1975).
———. *Political Essays.* Mark Goldie, ed. (Cambridge: Cambridge University Press, 1997).
———. *Political Writings of John Locke.* David Wootton, ed. (New York: Mentor Books, 1993).
———. *Two Treatises of Government.* Peter Laslett, ed. (Cambridge: Cambridge University Press, 1963).
Long, Thomas. *A Resolution of Certain Queries Concerning Submission to the Present Government* (London, 1689).
The New Oath of Allegiance Justified, from the Original Constitution of the English Monarchy (London 1689).
Parker, Henry. *Jus Populi. Or a Discourse Wherein Clear Satisfaction is Given, as Well Concerning the Right of Subjects, as the Right of Princes* (London, 1644).
Parkinson, James. *An Examination of Dr Sherlock's Book, Entituled, The Case of Allegiance due to Sovereign Powers, Stated and Resolved, &c.* (London, 1691).
Parsons, Robert. *A Conference about the Next Succession* (London, 1594).
Petyt, William. *The Antient Right of the Commons of England Asserted; Or a Discourse Proving by Records and the Best Historians that the Commons of England were ever an Essential Part of Parliament* (London, 1680).
A Political Conference Between Aulicus, a Courtier, Demas, a Country-man, and Civicus, a Citizen: Clearing the Original of Civil Government, the Powers and Duties of Soveraigns and Subjects (London, 1689).
Ponet, John. *A Short Treatise of Politique Power, And of the True Obedience which Subjects Owe to Kings, and other Civill Governours* (n.p., 1556; reprint, London: n.p., 1642).
The Proceedings of the Present Parliament Justified by the Opinion of the Most Judicious and Learned Hugo Grotius (London, 1689).
Pufendorf, Samuel. *De Jure Naturae et Gentium, Libri Octo.* 2 vols. C. H. Oldfather and W. A. Oldfather, trans. Carnegie Endowment for International Peace, Division of International Law, Classics of International Law, no. 17 (Oxford: Clarendon Press, 1934).
Schwoerer, Lois G., ed. '"A Jornall of the Convention at Westminster Begun the 22 of January 1688/9"'. *Bulletin of the Institute of Historical Research*, 49 — —(1976), 242–63.
Sherlock, William. *The Case of Allegiance due to Sovereign Powers Stated and Resolved, according to Scripture and reason, and the Principles of the Church of England, with a More Particular Respect to the Oath Lately Enjoyed, of Allegiance to their Present Majesties, K. William and Q. Mary* (London, 1691).
———. *A Letter to a Friend, concerning a French Invasion, to Restore the Late King James to His Throne* (London, 1692).
———. *A Second Letter to a Friend, concerning the French Invasion* (London, 1692).

Sidney, Algernon. *Discourses Concerning Government* (London, 1698).
Somers Tracts, A Collection of Scarce and Valuable Tracts, on the Most Interesting and Entertaining Subjects: But Chiefly Such as Relate to the History and Constitution of these Kingdoms, selected from Libraries; . . . Particularly that of the Late Lord Somers. 13 vols. Walter Scott, ed. 2nd edn (London, 1809–15).
The State of Parties, and of the Publick; as Influenc'd by Those Parties, in this Conjuncture, offered to English Men. (London, 1692).
State Tracts: A Collection of Several Treatises Relating to the Government (London, 1689).
State Tracts: Being a Further Collection of Several Choice Treatises Relating to the Government (London, 1692).
Stillingfleet, Edward. *The Mischief of Separation. A Sermon Preached at Guild-Hall Chappel, May ii MDCLXXX* (London, 1680).
——. *The Unreasonableness of Separation: Or, An Impartial Account of the History, Nature, and Pleas of the Present Separation from the Communion of the Church of England* (London, 1681).
Tindal, Matthew. *An Essay Concerning Obedience to the Supreme Powers, and the Duty of Subjects in all Revolutions. With Some Considerations Touching the Present Juncture of Affairs* (London, 1694).
Tyrrell, James. *Bibliotheca Politica: Or an Enquiry into the Ancient Constitution of the English Government; Both in Respect to the Just Extent of Regal Power, and the Rights and Liberties of the Subject. Wherein all the Chief Arguments, as well Against, as For the Late Revolution, are Impartially Represented, and Considered in Thirteen Dialogues* (London, 1694).
——. *Bibliotheca Politica: The First Complete Edition Containing the Fourteenth Dialogue of 1702*. 2 vols. Classics of Legal History in the Modern Era (New York: Garland Publishers, 1979).
——. *A Brief Disquisition of the Law of Nature, According to the Principles and Method laid down in the Reverend Dr Cumberland's (now Lord Bishop of Peterborough's) Latin Treatise on that Subject* (London, 1692; 2nd edn, London, 1701; reprint, Littleton, Colo.: Fred B. Rothman and Company, 1987).
——. *A Brief Enquiry into the Ancient Constitution and Government of England, As well in Respect of the Administration as Succession Thereof* (London, 1695).
——. *The General History of England, Both Ecclesiastical and Civil; From the Earliest Accounts of Time, To the Reign of His Present Majesty, King William III*. 3 vols (London, 1704).
——. *Patriarcha non Monarcha. The Patriarch Unmonarch'd: Being Observations on a Late Treatise and Divers other Miscellanies, Published under the Name of Sir Robert Filmer Baronet. In Which the Falseness of those Opinions that would Make Monarchy Jure Divino are Laid open: And the True Principles of Government and Property (especially in our Kingdom) Asserted* (London, 1681).
Vox Populi, Vox Dei: Or, Englands General Lamentation for the Dissolution of the Parliament (London, 1681).
Whitby, Daniel. *An Historical Account of Some Things Relating to the Nature of the English Government, and the Conceptions Which Our Forefathers Had of It. With Some Inferences Thence Made for the Satisfaction of Those Who Scruple the Oath of Allegiance to King William and Queen Mary* (London, 1689).

[Wildman, John]. *A Letter to a Friend, Advising him in this Extraordinary Juncture how to Free the Nation For Ever* (London, 1689).

Secondary Published Sources

Ackerman, Bruce. *We the People: Foundations* (Cambridge, Mass.: Harvard University Press, 1991).

Anderson, Christopher. '"Safe Enough in His Honesty and Prudence": The Ordinary Conduct of Government in the Thought of John Locke'. *History of Political Thought*, 13, 4 (1992) 605–30.

Ashcraft, Richard. *Revolutionary Politics and Locke's 'Two Treatises of Government'* (Princeton: Princeton University Press, 1986).

———.'Revolutionary Politics and Locke's *Two Treatises of Government*'. *Political Theory*, 8 (1980) 429–86.

Ashcraft, Richard, and M. M. Goldsmith. 'Locke, Revolution Principles, and the Formation of Whig Ideology'. *Historical Journal*, 26, 4 (1983) 773–800.

Becker, Ron. 'The Ideological Commitment of Locke: Freemen and Servants in the *Two Treatises of Government*'. *History of Political Thought*, 13, 4 (1992) 631–56.

Beddard, Robert, ed. *The Revolutions of 1688: The Andrew Browning Lectures* (Oxford: Oxford University Press, 1991).

———. *A Kingdom without a King: The Journal of the Provisional Government in the Revolution of 1688* (Oxford: Phaidon Press, 1988).

Behrens, B. 'The Whig Theory of the Constitution in the Reign of Charles II'. *Cambridge Historical Journal*, 7, 1 (1941) 42–71.

Bennett, G. V. *White Kennett, 1660–1728, Bishop of Peterborough: A Study in the Political and Ecclesiastical History of the Early Eighteenth Century* (London: SPCK, 1957).

Bourne, H. R. F. *The Life of John Locke*. 2 vols (London: King, 1876; reprint, Darmstadt: Scientia Verlag Allen, 1969).

Bradford, A. T. 'Stuart Absolutism and the "Utility" of Tacitus'. *Huntington Library Quarterly*, 46 (1983) 127–55.

Brennan, Teresa and Carole Pateman. '"Mere Auxiliaries to the Commonwealth": Women and the Origins of Liberalism'. *Political Studies*, 27 (1979) 183–200.

Brewer, John. *The Sinews of Power: War, Money and the English State, 1688–1783* (Cambridge, Mass.: Harvard University Press, 1988).

Brooks, Christopher and Kevin Sharpe. 'Debate: History, English Law and the Renaissance'. *Past and Present*, 72 (1976) 133–42.

Buckle, Stephen. *Natural Law and the Theory of Property, Grotius to Hume* (Oxford: Oxford University Press, 1991).

Burgess, Glenn. *Absolute Monarchy and the Stuart Constitution* (New Haven: Yale University Press, 1996).

———. *The Politics of the Ancient Constitution: An Introduction to English Political Thought, 1603–1642* (University Park, PA: Pennsylvania State University Press, 1993).

Burns, J. H. with Mark Goldie, eds. *The Cambridge History of Political Thought, 1400–1800* (Cambridge: Cambridge University Press, 1991).

Butler, Melissa A. 'Early Liberal Roots of Feminism: John Locke and the Attack on Patriarchy'. *Feminist Interpretations and Political Theory*. Carole Pateman and Mary Shanley, eds (University Park, PA: Pennsylvania State University Press, 1991).

Butterfield, Sir Herbert. *Magna Carta in the Historiography of the Sixteenth and Seventeenth Centuries* (Reading: University of Reading Press, 1969).

——. *The Whig Interpretation of History* (London: G. Bell, 1931; New York: W. W. Norton, 1965).

Cherry, George L. 'The Role of the Convention Parliament (1688–1689) in Parliamentary Supremacy' *Journal of the History of Ideas*, 17 (1956) 390–406.

——. *The Convention Parliament of 1689: A Biographical Study of its Members* (New York: Bookman Associates, 1966).

Clark, J. C. D. *English Society 1660–1832: Religion, Ideology and Politics during the Ancien Regime* (Cambridge: Cambridge University Press, 2000).

Clark, L. M. G. 'Women and John Locke: Or, Who Owns the Apples in the Garden of Eden?' *Canadian Journal of Philosophy*, 7, 4 (1977) 699–724.

Claydon, Tony. *William III and the Godly Revolution* (Cambridge: Cambridge University Press, 1996).

——. 'William III's *Declaration of Reasons* and the Glorious Revolution'. *Historical Journal*, 39, 1 (1996) 87–108.

Condren, Conal. *George Lawson's 'Politica' and the English Revolution* (Cambridge: Cambridge University Press, 1989).

——. *The Language of Politics in Seventeenth-Century England* (London: Macmillan, 1994).

——. *The Status and Appraisal of Classic Texts: An Essay on Political Theory, its Inheritance, and on the History of Ideas* (Princeton: Princeton University Press, 1985).

Conniff, James. 'Reason and History in Early Whig Thought: The Case of Algernon Sidney'. *Journal of the History of Ideas*, 43 (1992) 397–416.

Coupe, Laurence. *Myth* (New York: Routledge, 1997).

Cranston, Maurice. *John Locke: A Biography* (Oxford: Oxford University Press, 1985).

Cruickshanks, Eveline, John Ferris, and David Hayton. 'The House of Commons Vote on the Transfer of the Crown, 5 February 1689'. *Bulletin of the Institute of Historical Research*, 52, 125 (1979) 37–47.

Cruickshanks, Eveline, David Hayton, and Clive Jones. 'Divisions in the House of Lords on the Transfer of the Crown and Other Issues, 1689–94: Ten New Lists'. *Bulletin of the Institute of Historical Research*, 53, 127 (1980) 56–87.

Daly, James. *Sir Robert Filmer and English Political Thought* (Toronto: University of Toronto Press, 1979).

Davies, R. G. and J. H. Denton, eds. *The English Parliament in the Middle Ages* (Philadelphia: University of Pennsylvania Press, 1981).

De Beer, E. S. 'The Great Seal of James II: A Reply to Sir Hilary Jenkinson'. *The Antiquaries Journal*, 42, (1962) 81–90.

de Krey, Gary S. 'The London Whigs and the Exclusion Crisis Reconsidered'. *The First Modern Society: Essays in Honor of Lawrence Stone*. A. L. Beier, David Cannadine, and James M. Rosenheim, eds (Cambridge: Cambridge University Press, 1988), pp. 457–82.

Dickinson, H. T. *Liberty and Property: Political Ideology in Eighteenth-Century Britain* (New York: Holmes & Meier, 1977).

Douglas, D. C. *English Scholars 1660–1730* (London: Eyre & Spottiswoode, 1951).

Dunn, John. *The Political Thought of John Locke: an Historical Account of the Argument of the 'Two Treatises of Government'* (Cambridge: Cambridge University Press, 1969).

——. 'The Politics of Locke in England and America in the Eighteenth Century'. *John Locke, Problems and Perspectives*. John W. Yolton, ed. (Cambridge: Cambridge University Press, 1969), pp. 45–80.

Earl, D. W. L. 'Procrustean Feudalism: An Interpretative Dilemma in English Historical Narration, 1700–25'. *Historical Journal*, 19, 1 (1976) 33–51.

Eliade, Mircea. *Myth and Reality* (New York: Harper & Row, 1963).

Elton, G. R. '"The Body of the Whole Realm": Parliament and Representation in Medieval and Tudor England'. *Studies in Tudor and Stuart Politics and Government: Papers and Reviews 1946–72*. vol. 2 (Cambridge: Cambridge University Press, 1974), pp. 19–61.

Farr, James, and Clayton Roberts. 'John Locke on the Glorious Revolution: A Rediscovered Document'. *Historical Journal*, 28, 2 (1985) 385–98.

Ferguson, Arthur B. *Clio Unbound: Perception of the Social and Cultural Past in Renaissance England* (Durham: Duke University Press, 1979).

Flood, Christopher G. *Political Myth, A Theoretical Introduction* (New York: Garland Publishers, 1996).

Franklin, Julian H., ed. and trans. *Constitutionalism and Resistance in the Sixteenth Century: Three Treatises by Hotman, Beza, and Mornay* (New York: Pegasus, 1969).

——. *Jean Bodin and the Sixteenth-Century Revolution in the Methodology of Law and History* (New York: Columbia University Press, 1963).

——. *John Locke and the Theory of Sovereignty* (Cambridge: Cambridge University Press, 1978).

——. 'Locke on the Dissolution of Society'. *Politics, Ideology and the Law in Early Modern Europe: Essays in Honor of J. H. M. Salmon*. Adriana E. Bakos, ed. (Rochester: University of Rochester Press, 1994), pp. 175–184.

Furley, O. W. 'The Whig Exclusionists: Pamphlet Literature in the Exclusion Campaign, 1679–81'. *Cambridge Historical Journal*, 13, 1 (1957) 19–36.

Fussner, F. Smith. *The Historical Revolution: English Historical Writing and Thought 1580–1640* (London: Routledge & Kegan Paul, 1962).

Gallie, W. B. *Philosophy and the Historical Understanding*. 2nd edn (New York: Schocken Books, 1968).

Gierke, Otto von. *Natural Law and the Theory of Society 1500 to 1800*. Ernest Baker, trans. and Introduction (Cambridge: Cambridge University Press, 1934).

Glat, Mark. 'John Locke's Historical Sense'. *Review of Politics*, 43, 1 (1981) 3–21.

Goldie, Mark. 'Charles Blount's Intention in Writing "King William and Queen Mary Conquerors" (1693)'. *Notes and Queries*, n.s. 25, 6 (1978) 527–32.
——. 'Danby, the Bishops and the Whigs'. *The Politics of Religion in Restoration England*. Tim Harris, Paul Seaward and Mark Goldie, eds (Oxford: Basil Blackwell, 1990) 75–105.
——. 'Edmund Bohun and *Jus Gentium* in the Revolution Debate, 1689–1693'. *Historical Journal*, 20, 3 (1977) 569–86.
——. 'James II and the Dissenters' Revenge: the Commission of Enquiry of 1688'. *Historical Research*, 66 (1993) 53–88.
——. 'John Locke and Anglican Royalism'. *Political Studies*, 31 (1983) 61–85.
——. 'John Locke's Circle and James II'. *Historical Journal*, 35, 3 (1992) 557–86.
——. 'The Political Thought of the Anglican Revolution'. *The Revolutions of 1688: The Andrew Browning Lectures*. Robert Beddard, ed. (Oxford: Oxford University Press, 1991).
——.'Restoration Political Thought'. *The Reigns of Charles II and James VII & II*. Lionel K. J. Glassey, ed. (New York: St. Martin's Press – now Palgrave Macmillan, 1997), pp. 12–35.
——. 'The Revolution of 1689 and the Structure of Political Argument: An Essay and an Annotated Bibliography of Pamphlets on the Allegiance Controversy'. *Bulletin of Research in the Humanities*, 83, 4 (1980) 473–564.
——. 'The Roots of True Whiggism'. *History of Political Thought*, 1, 2 (1980) 195–236.
Gough, J. W. 'James Tyrrell, Whig Historian and Friend of John Locke'. *Historical Journal*, 19, 3 (1976) 581–610.
——. *The Social Contract: A Critical Study of its Development*. 2nd edn (Oxford: Oxford University Press, 1957).
Grant, Ruth W. *John Locke's Liberalism* (Chicago: University of Chicago Press, 1987).
Greaves, Richard L. *Secrets of the Kingdom: British Radicals from the Popish Plot to the Revolution of 1688* (Stanford: Stanford University Press, 1992).
Greenberg, Janelle. 'The Confessor's Laws and the Radical Face of the Ancient Constitution'. *English Historical Review*, (1989) 611–37.
Hannay, R. K. 'On "Parliament" and "General Council"'. *Scottish Historical Review*, 18, 71 (1921) 157–70.
Harris, Ian. *The Mind of John Locke: A Study of Political Theory in its Intellectual Setting* (Cambridge: Cambridge University Press, 1994).
Harris, Tim. *London Crowds in the Reign of Charles II: Propaganda and Politics from the Restoration until the Exclusion Crisis* (Cambridge: Cambridge University Press, 1987).
——. 'The People, the Law, and the Constitution in Scotland and England: A Comparative Approach to the Glorious Revolution'. *Journal of British Studies*, 38 (1999) 28–58.
——. *Politics Under the Later Stuarts: Party Conflict in a Divided Society 1660–1715* (London: Longman, 1993).
Harris, Tim, Paul Seaward and Mark Goldie, eds. *The Politics of Religion in Restoration England* (Oxford: Basil Blackwell, 1990).

Harrison, John, and Peter Laslett. *The Library of John Locke*. 2nd edn (Oxford: Clarendon Press, 1971).
Helmholz, R. H. 'Continental Law and Common Law: Historical Strangers or Companions?' *Law in History: Histories of Law and Society*. vol. 2. David Sugarman, ed. (New York: New York University Press, 1996), pp. 19–40.
Herzog, Don. *Happy Slaves: A Critique of Consent Theory*. (Chicago: University of Chicago Press, 1989).
Hicks, Philip. *Neoclassical History and English Culture: From Clarendon to Hume* (New York: St. Martin's Press – now Palgrave Macmillan, 1996).
Hill, Christopher. 'The Norman Yoke'. *Puritanism and Revolution: Studies in Interpretation of the English Revolution of the Seventeenth Century* (London: Secker & Warburg, 1958; New York: reprint edn Schocken Books, 1964), pp. 50–122.
———. 'Parliament and People in Seventeenth-Century England'. *Past and Present*, 92 (1981) 100–24.
Hirst, Derek. *The Representatives of the People? Voters and Voting in England under the Early Stuarts*. (Cambridge: Cambridge University Press, 1975).
Hoak, Dale and Mordechai Feingold, eds. *The World of William and Mary: Anglo-Dutch Perspectives on the Revolution of 1688–89* (Stanford: Stanford University Press, 1996).
Holmes, Peter. *Resistance and Compromise: The Political Thought of the Elizabethan Catholics* (Cambridge: Cambridge University Press, 1982).
Hont, Istvan and Michael Ignatieff. 'Needs and Justice in the *Wealth of Nations*; An Introductory Essay'. *Wealth and Virtue: The Shaping of Political Economy in the Scottish Enlightenment*. Istvan Hont and Michael Ignatieff, eds (Cambridge: Cambridge University Press, 1983), pp. 1–44.
Hopfl, Harro and Martyn P. Thompson, 'The History of Contract as a Motif in Political Thought'. *American Historical Review*, 84, 4 (1979) 919–44.
Horne, Thomas A. *Property Rights and Poverty: Political Argument in Britain, 1605–1834* (Chapel Hill: University of North Carolina Press, 1990).
Horwitz, Henry. 'Parliament and the Glorious Revolution'. *Bulletin of the Institute of Historical Research*, 47 (1974) 36–52.
———. *Parliament, Policy and Politics in the Reign of William III* (Newark: University of Delaware Press, 1977).
Israel, Jonathan I., ed. *The Anglo-Dutch Moment: Essays on the Glorious Revolution and Its World Impact* (Cambridge: Cambridge University Press, 1991).
Jameson, J. Franklin. 'The Early Political Uses of the Word Convention'. *American Historical Review*, 3 (1897–98) 477–87.
Jenkinson, Hilary. 'What Happened to the Great Seal of James II?'. *Antiquaries Journal*, 23 (1943) 1–13.
Jones, David Lewis. *A Parliamentary History of the Glorious Revolution* (London: Her Majesty's Stationery Office, 1988).
Jones, J. R. *Country and Court, England 1658–1714* (Cambridge, Mass.: Harvard University Press, 1978).
———. *The First Whigs: The Politics of the Exclusion Crisis, 1678–1683* (Oxford: Oxford University Press, 1961).
———. 'James II's Whig Collaborators'. *Historical Journal*, 3 (1960) 65–73.

——. ed. *The Restored Monarchy 1660–1688* (Totowa, NJ: Rowan & Littlefield, 1979).
——. *The Revolution of 1688 in England* (New York: W. W. Norton, 1972).
Jones, W. J. *Politics and the Bench: The Judges and the Origins of the English Civil War* (London: George Allen & Unwin, 1971).
Kelley, Donald R. *The Beginning of Ideology: Consciousness and Society in the French Reformation* (Cambridge: Cambridge University Press, 1983).
——. '*De Origine Feudorum*: The Beginnings of an Historical Problem'. *Speculum*, 39, 2 (1964) 207–28.
——. '*Tacitus Noster*: The *Germania* in the Renaissance and Reformation'. *Tacitus and the Tacitean Tradition*. T. J. Luce and A. J. Woodman, eds (Princeton: Princeton University Press, 1993).
——. 'History, English Law and the Renaissance'. *Past and Present*, 65 (1974) 24–51.
——.'History, English Law and the Renaissance: a Rejoinder'. *Past and Present*, 72 (1976) 143–6.
Kenyon, J. P. 'The Revolution of 1688: Resistance and Contract'. *Historical Perspectives: Studies in English Thought and Society in Honour of J. H. Plumb*. Neil McKendrick, ed. (London: Europa, 1974) pp. 43–70.
——. *Revolution Principles: The Politics of Party 1689–1720*, reprint edn (Cambridge: Cambridge University Press, 1977, reprint 1990).
——. ed. *The Stuart Constitution 1603–1688: Documents and Commentary* (Cambridge: Cambridge University Press, 1966).
Kidd, Colin. *Subverting Scotland's Past: Scottish Whig Historians and the Creation of an Anglo-British Identity, 1689–c.1830* (Cambridge: Cambridge University Press, 1993).
Kliger, Samuel. *The Goths in England, A Study in Seventeenth and Eighteenth Century Thought* (Cambridge, Mass.: Harvard University Press, 1952).
Knights, Mark. 'A City Revolution: The Remodelling of the London Livery Companies in the 1680s'. *English Historical Review*, 112 (1997) 1141–78.
——. *Politics and Opinion in Crisis, 1678–1681* (Cambridge: Cambridge University Press, 1994).
Kramer, Matthew H. *John Locke and the Origins of Private Property: Philosophical Explorations of Individualism, Community, and Equality* (Cambridge: Cambridge University Press, 1997).
Landon, Michael. *The Triumph of the Lawyers: Their Role in English Politics, 1678–1688* (University, AL: University of Alabama Press, 1970).
Laslett, Peter. 'Sir Robert Filmer: The Man versus the Whig Myth'. *William and Mary Quarterly*, 5, 4 (1948) 523–46.
Levack, Brian P. *The Civil Lawyers in England 1603–1641: a Political Study* (Oxford: Clarendon Press, 1973).
Levine, Joseph M. *Humanism and History: Origins of Modern English Historiography* (Ithaca: Cornell University Press, 1987).
Mackie, J. D. *A History of Scotland*. rev. edn, Bruce Lenman and Geoffrey Parker, eds (London: Penguin Books, 1978).
Macpherson, C. B. *The Political Theory of Possessive Individualism: Hobbes to Locke* (Oxford: Oxford University Press, 1962).

McKenna, J. W. 'The Myth of Parliamentary Sovereignty in Late-Medieval England'. *English Historical Review*, 44, 372 (1979) 481–506.

McKisack, May. *The Fourteenth Century, 1307–1399* (Oxford: Clarendon Press, 1959).

McNally, David. 'Locke, Levellers and Liberty: Property and Democracy in the Thought of the First Whigs'. *History of Political Thought*, 10, 1 (1989) 17–40.

Marshall, John. *John Locke: Resistance, Religion and Responsibility* (Cambridge: Cambridge University Press, 1994).

——. 'John Locke and Latitudinarianism'. *Philosophy, Science and Religion in England 1640–1700*. Richard Kroll, Richard Ashcraft and Perez Zagorin, eds (Cambridge: Cambridge University Press, 1992).

Mellor, Ronald, ed. *Tacitus, The Classical Heritage* (New York: Garland Publishers, 1995).

Miller, John. 'The Glorious Revolution: "Contract" and "Abdication" Reconsidered'. *Historical Journal*, 25, 3 (1982) 541–55.

——. *Popery and Politics in England 1660–1688* (Cambridge: Cambridge University Press, 1973).

Milton, Philip. 'John Locke and the Rye House Plot'. *Historical Journal*, 43, 3 (2000) 647–68.

Mitchison, Rosalind. *A History of Scotland* (New York: Methuen, 1982).

Morgan, Edmund S. *Inventing the People: The Rise of Popular Sovereignty in England and America* (New York: W. W. Norton, 1988).

Nenner, Howard. *By Colour of Law: Legal Culture and Constitutional Politics in England, 1660–1688* (Chicago: University of Chicago Press, 1977).

Okin, Susan Moller. *Women in Western Political Thought* (Princeton: Princeton University Press, 1979).

Oliver, H. J. *Sir Robert Howard, 1626–1698: a Critical Biography* (Durham: Duke University Press, 1963).

Parry, Geraint. *John Locke*. (London: George Allen & Unwin, 1978).

Pateman, Carole. *The Sexual Contract: Aspects of Patriarchal Liberalism* (Stanford: Stanford University Press, 1988).

Pateman, Carole and Mary L. Shanley, eds. *Feminist Interpretations and Political Theory* (University Park, PA: Pennsylvania State University Press, 1991).

Patterson, Annabel. *Early Modern Liberalism* (Cambridge: Cambridge University Press, 1997).

Phillipson, Nicholas, and Quentin Skinner, eds. *Political Discourse in Early Modern Britain* (Cambridge: Cambridge University Press, 1993).

Pincus, Steven. '"To Protect English Liberties": the English Nationalist Revolution of 1688–1689'. *Protestantism and National Identity: Britain and Ireland, c.1650–c.1850*. Tony Claydon and Ian McBride, eds (Cambridge: Cambridge University Press, 1998), pp. 75–104.

Pitkin, Hanna Fenichel. *The Concept of Representation* (Berkeley: University of California Press, 1969).

Pocock, J. G. A. *The Ancient Constitution and the Feudal Law: A Study of English Historical Thought in the Seventeenth Century, A Reissue with a Retrospect* (Cambridge: Cambridge University Press, 1987).

——.'The Fourth English Civil War: Dissolution, Desertion and Alternative Histories in the Glorious Revolution'. *Government and Opposition*, 23, 2 (1988) 151–66.

——. *The Machiavellian Moment: Florentine Political Thought and the Atlantic Republican Tradition* (Princeton: Princeton University Press, 1975).

——. *Politics, Language and Time: Essays on Political Thought and History*, 2nd edn (Chicago: University of Chicago Press, 1989).

——. 'The Significance of 1688: Some Reflections on Whig History'. *The Revolutions of 1688: The Andrew Browning Lectures*. Robert Beddard, ed. (Oxford: Oxford University Press, 1991).

——.'The Varieties of Whiggism from Exclusion to Reform: A History of Ideology and Discourse'. *Virtue, Commerce and History. Essays on Political Thought and History, Chiefly in the Eighteenth Century* (Cambridge: Cambridge University Press, 1985).

Prest, Wilfrid R. *The Rise of the Barristers: a Social History of the English Bar 1590–1640* (Oxford: Clarendon Press, 1991).

Rahe, J. L. 'John Locke's Philosophical Partisanship'. *Political Science Reviewer*, 20 (1991) 1–44.

Rait, Robert Sangster. *The Parliaments of Scotland* (Glasgow: Maclehose, 1924).

Richards, Judith, Lotte Mulligan, and John K. Graham. '"Property" and "People": Political Usages of Locke and Some Contemporaries'. *Journal of the History of Ideas*, 42 (1981) 29–51.

Robbins, Caroline. *The Eighteenth-Century Commonwealthsman: Studies in the Transmission, Development, and Circumstance of English Liberal Thought from the Restoration of Charles II until the War with the Thirteen Colonies* (Cambridge, Mass.: Harvard University Press, 1959).

Rorty, Richard, J. B. Schneewind, and Quentin Skinner, eds. *Philosophy in History* (Cambridge: Cambridge University Press, 1984).

Rostenberg, Leona. 'Richard and Anne Baldwin, Whig Patriot Publishers'. *Papers of the Bibliographical Society of America*, 47 (1953): 1–42.

Rudolph, Julia. 'Rape and Resistance: Women and Consent in Seventeenth-Century English Legal and Political Thought'. *Journal of British Studies*, 39, 2 (2000) 157–84.

Salmon, J. H. M. *The French Religious Wars in English Political Thought* (Oxford: Oxford University Press, 1959).

Schlatter, R. B. *Private Property: The History of an Idea* (New Brunswick: Rutgers University Press, 1951).

Schochet, Gordon J. *Patriarchalism in Political Thought: The Authoritarian Family and Political Speculation and Attitudes Especially in Seventeenth-Century England* (New York: Basic Books, 1975).

——. 'Radical Politics and Ashcraft's Treatise on Locke'. *Journal of the History of Ideas*, 50 (1989) 491–510.

——. 'The Significant Sounds of Silence: the Absence of Women from the Political Thought of Sir Robert Filmer and John Locke (or, "Why can't a woman be more like a man?")'. *Women Writers and the Early Modern British Political Tradition*. Hilda L. Smith, ed. (Cambridge: Cambridge University Press, 1998), pp. 220–42.

——. 'Sir Robert Filmer: Some New Bibliographical Discoveries'. *The Library*, 5th series, 26 (1971) 135–60.
——. 'Why Should History Matter? Political Theory and the History of Discourse'. *The Varieties of British Political Thought, 1500–1800*. J. G. A. Pocock, with the assistance of Gordon J. Schochet and Lois G. Schwoerer, eds (Cambridge: Cambridge University Press, 1993), pp. 321–57.
Schwoerer, Lois G. *The Declaration of Rights, 1689* (Baltimore: Johns Hopkins University Press, 1981).
——. 'Locke, Lockean Ideas, and the Glorious Revolution'. *Journal of the History of Ideas*, 51, 4 (1990) pp. 531–48.
——. 'Press and Parliament in the Revolution of 1689'. *Historical Journal* 20, 3 (1977), 545–67.
——.'Propaganda in the Revolution of 1688–9'. *American Historical Review*, 82 (1977) 843–74.
——. ed. *The Revolution of 1688–1689: Changing Perspectives* (Cambridge: Cambridge University Press, 1992).
——.'The Right to Resist: Whig Resistance Theory, 1688 to 1694'. *Political Discourse in Early Modern Britain*. Nicholas Phillipson and Quentin Skinner, eds (Cambridge: Cambridge University Press, 1993) pp. 232–52.
Scott, Jonathan. *Algernon Sidney and the English Republic, 1623–1677* (Cambridge: Cambridge University Press, 1988).
——. *Algernon Sidney and the Restoration Crisis, 1677–1683* (Cambridge: Cambridge University Press, 1991).
Seaberg, R. B. 'The Norman Conquest and the Common Law: The Levellers and the Argument from Continuity'. *Historical Journal*, 24, 4 (1981) 791–806.
Seaward, Paul. *The Restoration, 1660–1688* (Basingstoke: Macmillan – now Palgrave Macmillan, 1991).
Shanley, Mary L. 'Marriage Contract and Social Contract in Seventeenth-Century English Political Thought'. *Western Political Quarterly*, 32 (1979) 79–91.
Shapiro, Barbara. 'The Concept "Fact": Legal Origins and Cultural Diffusion'. *Albion*, 26, 1 (1994) 1–26.
——. *A Culture of Fact: England 1550–1720* (Ithaca: Cornell University Press, 2000).
Skinner, Quentin. *The Foundations of Modern Political Thought*. 2 vols (Cambridge: Cambridge University Press, 1978).
——. 'History and Ideology in the English Revolution'. *Historical Journal*, 8, 2 (1965) 151–78.
Slaughter, Thomas. '"Abdicate" and "Contract" in the Glorious Revolution'. *Historical Journal*, 24, 2 (1981) 323–37.
——. '"Abdicate" and "Contract" Restored'. *Historical Journal*, 28, 2 (1985) 399–403.
Smith, Hilda L. *Reason's Disciples: Seventeenth-Century English Feminists* (Urbana: University of Illinois Press, 1982).
——. ed. *Women Writers and the Early Modern British Political Tradition* (Cambridge: Cambridge University Press, 1998).
Smith, R. J. *The Gothic Bequest: Medieval Institutions in British Thought 1688–1863* (Cambridge: Cambridge University Press, 1987).

Sommerville, Johann P. *Politics and Ideology in England 1603–1640* (London: Longman, 1986).
Sommerville, Margaret R. *Sex and Subjection: Attitudes to Women in Early-Modern Society* (London: Arnold, 1995).
Speck, W. A. *Reluctant Revolutionaries: Englishmen and the Revolution of 1688* (Oxford: Oxford University Press, 1989).
Stephen, Leslie, ed. *Dictionary of National Biography* (London: Smith, Elder, 1885–1904).
Stevens, Jacqueline. 'The Reasonableness of John Locke's Majority: Property Rights, Consent, and Resistance in the *Second Treatise*'. *Political Theory*, 24, 3 (1996) 423–63.
Szechi, Daniel. 'Mythhistory versus History: The Fading of the Revolution of 1688'. *Historical Journal*, 33, 1 (1990) 143–153.
Tarlton, Charles D. 'A Rope of Sand: Interpreting Locke's *First Treatise of Government*'. *Historical Journal*, 21, 1 (1978) 43–73.
——. '"The Rulers Now on Earth": Locke's *Two Treatises* and the Revolution of 1688'. *Historical Journal*, 28, 2 (1985) 279–98.
Thompson, Martyn P. 'History of Fundamental Law in Political Thought from the French Wars of Religion to the American Revolution'. *American Historical Review*, 91, 5 (1986) 1103–28.
——. 'The Reception of Locke's *Two Treatises of Government* 1690–1705'. *Political Studies*, 24, 2 (1976) 184–91.
——. 'Significant Silences in Locke's *Two Treatises of Government*: Constitutional History, Contract and Law'. *Historical Journal*, 31, 2 (1987) 275–94.
Tierney, Brian. *Religion, Law and the Growth of Constitutional Thought, 1150–1650* (Cambridge: Cambridge University Press, 1982).
Tuana, Nancy. *Women and the History of Philosophy* (New York: Paragon House, 1992).
Tuck, Richard. *Natural Rights Theories: Their Origin and Development* (Cambridge: Cambridge University Press, 1979).
——. 'A New Date for Filmer's *Patriarcha*'. *Historical Journal*, 29 (1986) 183–6.
Tully, James. *An Approach to Political Philosophy: Locke in Contexts* (Cambridge: Cambridge University Press, 1993).
——. *A Discourse on Property: John Locke and his Adversaries* (Cambridge: Cambridge University Press, 1980).
——. ed. *Meaning and Context: Quentin Skinner and his Critics* (Princeton: Princeton University Press, 1988).
Weil, Rachel J. *Political Passions: Gender, the Family and Political Argument in England 1680–1714* (Manchester: Manchester University Press, 1999).
Western, J. R. *Monarchy and Revolution: The English State in the 1680s* (Totowa, NJ: Rowan & Littlefield, 1972).
Weston, Corinne Comstock. 'Concepts of Estates in Stuart Political Thought'. *Representative Institutions in Theory and Practice: Historical Papers Read at Bryn Mawr College, April 1968*. Studies Presented to the International Commission for the History of Representative and Parliamentary Institutions, no. 39 (Brussels: Les Editions de la Librairie Encyclopédique, 1970).

Weston, Corinne Comstock and Janelle Greenberg. *Subjects and Sovereigns: The Grand Controversy over Legal Sovereignty in Stuart England* (Cambridge: Cambridge University Press, 1981).

Willman, Robert. 'The Origins of "Whig" and "Tory" in English Political Language'. *Historical Journal*, 17, 2 (1974) 247–64.

Wood, Gordon S. *The Creation of the American Republic, 1776–1787* (New York: W. W. Norton, 1972).

Ellen Meiksins Wood, 'Locke Against Democracy: Consent, Representation and Suffrage in the *Two Treatises*'. *History of Political Thought*, 13, 4 (1992) 657–89.

——. 'Radicalism, Capitalism and Historical Contexts: Not Only a Reply to Richard Ashcraft on John Locke'. *History of Political Thought*, 15, 3 (1994) 323–72.

Wood, Neal. *John Locke and Agrarian Capitalism*. (Berkeley: University of California Press, 1984).

Woolf, Daniel R. *The Idea of History in Early Stuart England: Erudition, Ideology, and 'The Light of Truth' from the Accession of James I to the Civil War* (Toronto: University of Toronto Press, 1990).

Wootton, David, ed. *Divine Right and Democracy: An Anthology of Political Writing in Stuart England* (New York: Penguin Books, 1986)

——. 'John Locke: Socinian or Natural Law Theorist?'. *Religion, Secularization and Political Thought*. James Crimmins, ed. (London: Routledge, 1989), pp. 39–67.

——. 'John Locke and Richard Ashcraft's *Revolutionary Politics*'. *Political Studies*, 40 (1992) 79–98.

——. 'Leveller Democracy and the Puritan Revolution'. *Cambridge History of Political Thought*. J. H. Burns with Mark Goldie, eds (Cambridge: Cambridge University Press, 1991), pp. 412–42.

Zook, Melinda S. *Radical Whigs and Conspiratorial Politics in Late Stuart England* (University Park, PA: Pennsylvania State University Press, 1999).

Index

abdication, 7, 10–11, 95, 98–100, 108, 121, 129, 165
abdication and vacancy resolution, 1, 11, 69, 85, 94, 98, 102, 103–5, 108, 117, 121, 124–5, 141, 148, 150
abjuration, 67, 107
absolutism, 3, 4, 31–2, 34–5, 37, 73
ancient constitution
  immemoriality, 57, 62, 72–4, 80, 83–8, 109–10, 141–2, 156
  merged with contract, 12, 20, 57, 64–5, 69, 72, 79, 81, 87–8, 109, 124, 126, 127–8 137–8, 156
  and Revolution Principles, 1–2, 11, 18, 62–3, 104, 117–18, 120, 141, 164
  and Whig history, 63, 69, 71–4, 76, 79, 82–3, 110–11, 152
ancient council, 20, 69, 72, 76–7, 80–4, 137, 143
Anglicanism, 4, 24, 32
Anne, Princess, 105
Aristotle, 37, 55, 57
Arnisaeus, Henning, 30
Astell, Mary, 41
Atkyns, Sir Robert, 102
Atwood, William, 10, 78, 109, 149, 154, 164
  The Fundamental Constitution of the English Government, 150–2
  Jani Anglorum Facies Nova, 63
  and Locke, 150–2
  and Tyrrell, 20, 65, 78, 151–2
  and Whig history, 20, 65, 78

Baudouin, François, 165
Barclay, William, 116, 129
Bellarmine, Cardinal Robert, 29
Besold, Christopher, 132

Beza, Theodore, 29
Bilson, Thomas, 116
Birch, John, 108
Blackstone, Sir William, 2
Blount, Charles, 108
Bodin, Jean, 29, 90, 165
Boscawen, Hugh, 101
Boyle, Robert, 16
Bracton, 108
Brady, Robert, 16, 20, 63, 73–9, 84, 164
  A Full and Clear Answer to a Book Written by William Petit, 63
  and historical method, 75–6, 89–91
  An Introduction to the Old English History, 64–5
  and Tory politics, 65, 90–1
  and Tyrrell, 20, 65–6, 73–9, 88–9
Britons, 71, 86
Buchanan, George, 29, 129
Burke, Edmund, 2, 10
Burnet, Bishop Gilbert, 1–2, 14, 120

Catholicism
  fear of (anti-popery), 4, 22–3, 29–30
  and James II, 4–6, 21, 23, 111
  and succession, 5, 23
Charles I, 25, 68
Charles II, 4, 23, 58, 70, 96, 111, 154
civil law, 66–7
Civil Wars, English, 10, 28, 29, 30, 33, 48, 55, 68, 132, 143, 144, 146, 154
Claridge, Richard, 115
Coke, Sir Edward, 88
Comber, Thomas, 120–3
common law
  and conceptions of truth, 16
  and jury trial, 15–16
common-law mind, 57, 62–3, 72, 83–4, 85–8, 102

Commonwealth, 10, 29, 33, 64, 104–5, 132, 154
conquest
 just war theory of, 120–3, 153
 Norman, 73–4, 78–9, 90, 91, 110, 130, 135, 137
 Saxon, 71, 79
 and William III, 6, 7, 130–1
consent
 and children, 41
 express, 53, 54, 112, 162
 and property, 46, 47–8, 50–3, 59, 76, 80, 110
 and servants, 41, 46, 59, 113
 tacit, 53, 112, 162
 and women, 41, 43, 46, 113
constituent power, 10, 12, 120, 132, 135, 154, 155, 157, 159, 163
contract
 and conquest, 122
 historical, 20, 57, 70, 76, 79, 81, 99, 102, 109–10, 114, 115
 marriage, 42–4
 merged with ancient constitution, 12, 20, 57, 64–5, 69, 72, 79, 81, 87–8, 109, 124, 126, 127–8, 137–8, 156
 original, 20, 36–8, 41, 52, 64, 69, 70, 72, 76, 79, 81, 84, 99, 102, 104, 105, 109–14, 126–7, 159
 rectoral, 112–15, 116, 118–19, 159
 social, 19–20, 36–8, 42, 46, 48, 52, 110, 112–15, 124, 127, 150–1, 159
 and Whig defense of resistance, 12, 19–21, 41, 54, 57, 64–5, 68, 70, 85, 93–4, 99, 104–5, 114–15, 121, 124–6, 130–2, 147, 154, 157
Convention
 debates in 1688–9, 8, 94–5, 97–105, 106, 108, 124–6
 example of 1660, 96, 144
 and great council, 137–8, 141, 143
 history of, 96, 143–7
 and Locke, 163–6
 and Parliament, 61, 96–7, 143–7

 and popular sovereignty, 61, 100–1, 138–9, 144–5, 147, 155, 163–4
 Scottish, 143–4
 and Tyrrell, 61, 85, 126, 128, 137–9, 141–2, 144, 157
 and Whig theory, 8, 9, 85, 120, 122, 149, 150, 153, 154–5
Cornbury, Edward Hyde, Viscount of, 102
coronation oath, 79, 102, 109, 111, 128
Cumberland, Bishop Richard, 48, 49, 51

Danby, Thomas Osborne, Earl of, 22, 23, 105
Declaration of Indulgence, 4–5, 27, 111
Declaration of Rights, 105
de facto theory, 79, 122, 153
deposition, 95, 99, 114, 116, 129, 134, 154
Digges, Dudley, 60, 139
dissolution of government, 2–3, 7, 9–11, 55, 85, 100–1, 103, 116–23, 130–2, 137–42, 148–58
divine right of kings, 19, 30–2, 37, 91, 113
Dolben, Gilbert, 98
Dolben, William, 98
Dugdale, Sir William, 75

Edward II, 134, 144
Edward the Confessor
 Confessor's law, 79, 109–10
Exclusion Crisis, 21–5, 39, 57, 63

Falkner, William, 116
family
 and origins of state, 38, 112–13, 127
 and political authority, 34, 44, 45, 127
 and resistance, 35, 40, 55, 115
Fanshaw, Charles, Viscount, 102
feudal interpretation of history, 74–5, 90–1
feudal law and tenures, 47, 74, 75–8, 79

feudal terminology, 75–6
Filmer, Sir Robert, 17, 22, 29, 41, 48
  The Anarchy of a Limited or Mixed Monarchy, 30
  and divine right, 19, 31
  The Free-holders Grand Inquest, 30, 63
  and Locke, 28, 30, 32
  Observations Concerning the Originall of Government, 48–9
  Patriarcha: The Naturall Power of Kinges Defended, 28, 30, 34, 63
  and patriarchalism, 31–2, 34
  and Tory propaganda, 28–9, 32–3, 48
  and Tyrrell, 28, 32–9, 49, 50–1, 55, 56, 57–8, 68, 160
Finch, Sir Heneage, 100, 101
Fitzharris, Edward, 100, 101
forfeiture, 53–4, 135–6
franchise, 53, 59–60, 146–7, 163
fundamental law, 9, 55–6, 58, 65, 69, 109, 127–8

Gale, Roger, 108
Georgeson, Sir P., 114, 115
Gothic constitution and liberty, 71–2, 74, 75, 79, 84, 86, 91, 102, 110
Grotius, Hugo, 30, 35, 46, 48, 50, 81, 108, 115–16, 121, 123, 129, 160

Hale, Sir Matthew, 57
Halifax, George Savile, Marquis of, 97–8
Hampden, John, 98, 100
Hampden, Richard, 98
Hearne, Thomas, 107, 174 n5
Henry III, 82, 84
Henry IV, 83, 104, 144
Henry VI, 83
Henry VII, 95, 96
Heylin, Peter, 25
historiography
  and Brady, 63, 65, 73–5, 90–1
  and feudalism, 74–5, 77, 78
  Renaissance methodology, 89–90

Revisionist, 3, 13
  and Whigs, 13, 17, 63, 65, 69, 74–5, 78–9, 83, 86, 88–92, 137, 164–5
Holt, John, 103
Hooke, Robert, 16
Hooker, Richard, 102
Hotman, François, 71–2, 165
Howard, Robert, 98–100, 101, 104
Howe, John, 98
Humfrey, John, 163
Hunton, Philip, 29, 30, 55–6, 62, 70–1, 160

Immemoriality, 57, 62, 72, 73, 80, 83–8, 109–10, 135
Indians, American, 38, 49

James VI and I, 25, 102, 128, 143
James II (Duke of York), 1, 2, 4–9, 23, 27, 58, 68, 85, 91, 93, 94–5, 96, 97, 98–9, 100, 102, 104, 108–9, 111, 120–2, 123, 124, 125, 126, 128, 134, 136, 150, 165
John, King, 82, 134
jus gentium, 121–2

Kennet, White, 111–12, 115–16
Kingston, Richard, 149–50, 154–5

Lambarde, William, 75, 78, 79
Lawson, George, 10, 29, 112, 118–19, 123, 132, 137, 138, 144, 149, 152, 153, 155, 157, 201 n27, 202 n33
Lee, Thomas, 104
Levellers, 48–9, 53, 64, 163
Liberalism, 12, 149, 159, 166–7
Locke, John, 14, 16, 37, 38
  on dissolution, 9–10, 55, 131, 157–9, 164
  An Essay Concerning Human Understanding, 26
  on English history, 164–5
  and Filmer, 28, 30, 32, 34, 160
  and Lawson, 10, 132, 149, 153, 157
  and Levellers, 53, 163

and *Patriarcha non Monarcha*, 28, 160
political activity, 27, 163, 165
on property, 48, 50–1, 53, 162–3
radicalism, 21, 27, 158–61, 163–4, 166
relationship with Tyrrell, 17, 24–8, 107, 160–1, 165
on religion, 28, 159
reputation, 158–9
on resistance, 9–10, 54–5, 153, 157–8, 165–6
Two Treatises of Government, 17, 21, 27, 28, 54, 68, 123, 131, 149, 153, 160–4
and Whigs, 9–10, 12, 17, 94, 111, 112, 114, 123, 127, 148–9, 152–3, 156–67
on women, 34–5, 40–1, 45, 161–2

Magna Carta, 2, 78, 79, 109, 111, 128, 134
Mapletoft, John, 25
marriage contract, 42–4
Mary (of Orange) II, 3, 5, 9, 95, 96, 97, 98, 105, 106–7, 108, 109, 120, 122, 153
Masham, Lady Damaris, 25
Maxwell, John, 60
Maynard, John, 99, 101, 103, 165
mixed government, 10, 70, 109, 117–18, 152–3, 155
monarchomach theory, 29–30, 127
Monmouth's Rebellion, 3, 4, 100

natural law, 19, 26–7, 31, 35–7, 45–7, 49, 103, 111–17, 159, 160, 162
nonjurors, 67, 68, 107, 121, 122

obedience
  to government authority, 30, 52, 54, 125
  passive, 32
  of wives and children, 35, 40, 43, 55
original Convention, 18, 39, 61, 85, 94, 101, 123, 137–8, 141
original people, 18, 19–20, 38, 39, 46, 52, 57–9, 61, 91, 113, 118, 134–8, 140–1, 151

Parliament
  and debate about antiquity, 20, 63, 72–84, 88, 90–1, 137
  and elections, 22–3, 96–7, 147
  and representation, 59–61, 80–4, 91, 133, 139–40, 145–6
Parker, Henry, 139
Parr, Richard, 25
Parsons, Robert, 29
Ponet, John, 29
parliamentary sovereignty, 10–11, 105, 117–18, 132, 137–8, 140–1, 151–2, 153, 155
patriarchalism, 31–2, 39
Pembroke, Thomas Herbert, Earl of, 96
Petition of Right, 128
Petyt, William, 102, 164
  The Antient Right of the Commons of England Asserted, 63, 75
  and Brady, 20, 63, 65, 75
  and Tyrrell, 66, 73, 75, 76, 78, 107
politique theory, 29, 30
Pollexfen, Henry, 101, 104, 107
popular sovereignty, 10, 12, 16, 20–1, 56, 58–61, 77–8, 81, 99–101, 116–17, 119–20, 132–8, 144–7, 149, 153, 158, 166–7
Powle, Henry, 97–8
property, theory of, 46–54, 162
  and consent, 46, 47–8, 50–3, 110
  and Levellers, 48–9
  and Locke, 48, 50–1, 53, 162–3
  and political representation, 39, 46, 48, 74, 76–8, 146, 162–3
  and Tyrrell, 46, 47–54, 76–8, 83, 135–6
provisional government, 6–7, 95, 97
Prynne, William, 29, 30, 75
Pufendorf, Samuel, 30, 35, 37, 42–4, 46, 48, 49–50, 126–7, 129, 132–3, 150–1, 160

real majesty, 10, 119, 132, 135–6, 137, 144, 154, 155–7
resistance *see* contract, Locke, tyranny, Tyrrell

resistance *in extremis*, 1, 35, 115–16, 122, 130
Revolution principles, 1–2, 11, 14, 93–4, 105–6, 108, 142, 167
Richard I, 134
Richard II, 96, 99, 108, 134
Russell, Lord John, 100, 104
Rye House Plot, 27, 100

Sacheverell, Rev. Dr Henry 94
Sancroft, Archbishop, 67
Sawyer, Sir Robert, 60, 100–1, 107, 125, 130, 139–40, 147, 163
Saxon government, 70–3, 79–80, 84, 88, 91, 102, 110, 134–5
Scotland
  Convention of 1688–9, 144
  and history of Convention, 143–4
Selden, John, 16, 57, 79, 102
Seymour, Edward, 102
servants, 41, 46, 59
Shaftesbury, Anthony Ashley, Earl of, 23, 24, 25, 27, 100
Sidney, Algernon, 100
social contract *see* contract
Somers, John, 103
sovereignty, 8–12, 23, 106–7, 116–22, 132, 137–8
  absolute, 4, 31–2, 34–5, 73
  Restoration legislation concerning, 9, 70
  see also parliamentary sovereignty, popular sovereignty
Spelman, Sir Henry, 75, 76, 78, 80, 90, 102
Spelman, John, 60
standing army, 56, 129
state of nature, 36–7, 41–3, 70, 84, 103, 111–12, 127, 130–1, 153
Stillingfleet, Edward, 24–5, 160
succession, 5, 23, 57–9, 91, 95, 98, 101, 104–5, 106–7, 120, 122, 136, 140, 152
Sydenham, Thomas, 25

Tacitus, 71–2, 75
Temple, Sir Richard, 8, 11, 98, 109
Thorogood, Captain, 59–60, 163
Tindal, Matthew, 113, 149–50, 152–4, 157
Treby, George, 101, 103, 107
trial of the Seven Bishops, 4–5, 6, 100, 101, 104
tyranny
  and dissolution, 9–10, 54–5, 103, 116–17, 121, 130, 150, 152–5, 157
  and James II, 2, 7, 9, 85, 99, 103, 109, 121, 125, 128–9, 150
  and resistance, 1–2, 9–10, 54–5, 65, 70, 85, 99, 103, 105, 108–9, 114, 115–16, 125, 128–30, 152–4, 157
Tyrrell, James
  and Atwood, 20, 65, 78, 151–2
  Bibliotheca Politica, Ch. 3, Ch. 5
  and Brady, 20, 65–6, 73–9, 88–9
  A Brief Disquisition of the Law of Nature, 176 n27, 186 n12, 206 n40
  A Brief Enquiry into the Ancient Constitution and Government of England, 66
  and Convention, 61, 85, 126, 128, 137–9, 141–2, 144, 157
  and Cumberland, 48, 49, 51
  on dissolution, 18, 66, 68, 85, 120, 123, 130–2, 137–42, 148–50, 152, 157
  education, 25, 107–8
  and English history, Ch. 3, Ch. 5, *passim*, 164–5
  and Filmer, 28, 32–9, 49, 50–1, 55, 56, 57–8, 68, 160
  The General History of England, 66, 86, 164–5
  and Hunton, 55–6, 62
  and Lawson, 118, 132, 137, 138, 152, 157
  Patriarcha non Monarcha, Ch. 2, 68
  and Petyt, 66, 73, 75, 76, 78, 107
  political activity, 24, 27–8

on property, 46, 47–54, 76–8, 83, 135–6
and Pufendorf, 35, 42–4, 48, 49–50, 126–7, 129, 132–3
relationship with Locke, 17, 24–8, 107, 160–1, 165
on religion, 24, 28, 32–3
on resistance, 17–18, 22, 35, 41, 54–7, 62, 68–9, 85, 88, 123, 126, 128–34, 142, 148, 152, 160
and Revolution principles, 15–18, 22, 58, 66–9, 85, 87–8, 90, 92–4, 104, 114, 123, 126, 131–2, 137–9, 141–2, 147–50, 157, 167
Tyrrell family, 25, 108
and Ussher, 25
on women, 34–5, 39–45

Ussher, Archbishop James, 25

Vane, Henry, 144

Whig interpretation of history, 13, 17, 62–3, 69, 86, 91–2 *see also* historiography

Whitby, Daniel, 109
Wildman, John, 163
William I, the Conqueror, 73, 74, 76, 77, 78–9, 110
William III (of Orange), 3, 5–9, 68, 93, 95–8, 105, 106–8, 109, 120–3, 138, 153, 165
Declaration of Reasons, 6, 7, 8, 95
Williams, William, 101
women
biology of, 43, 45, 161
and consent, 41, 43
and contract, 39, 41–5, 112–13
freedom of, 39–40, 43
and Locke, 34–5, 40–1, 45, 161–2
and patriarchalism, 34–5, 39
physical punishment of, 40
and property, 45
and self preservation, 35, 39, 43
sexuality of, 42, 45
subjection of, 39–45, 113, 161–2
and Tyrrell, 34–5, 39–45